Social Justice are

Equal Rights Are

Also Entitlements)

Bill Clay

POWER
of
PRINCIPLED
POLITICS

POWER
of
PRINCIPLED
POLITICS

**A Liberal Reflects on His 32 Years in
Congress, interacting with 6 Presidents, and
8 Speakers of the House of Representatives**

William L. Clay, Sr,
U.S. Congress, Retired

**An "outsider" who gained "insider" status
without losing credentials as a "reformer"*

with a Foreword by
Congresswoman Maxine Waters

Clay, William L.
     Power of Principled Politics: A Liberal Reflects on His 32 Years in Congress, interacting with 6 Presidents, and 8 Speakers of the House of Representatives
2011 / by William L. Clay
                    ISBN 0-944514-42-1
                    $32.95

1. Afro-Americans in politics—History. 2. United States politics and government. 3. United States. Congress—History.

CECIL WILLIAMS PHOTOGRAPHY/PUBLISHING
1865 LAKE DRIVE
ORANGEBURG, SOUTH CAROLINA 29115

To my wife Carol
For her love and friendship

And

To my children, Vicki, Lacy, Michelle,
For patience, understanding and support

They were all there to celebrate the successes,
agonize in the setbacks, bounce back up and
continue on the path towards our goal

Books by
William L. Clay

To Kill or Not to Kill
Thoughts on Capital Punishment

Just Permanent Interests
History of Blacks in U.S. Congress

Political Voice at the Grass Roots
Clay's Involvement in St. Louis Politics

Jefferson Bank Confrontation
Struggle for Economic Justice in St. Louis

CONTENTS

The William L. Clay Scholarship Fund

The Clay Scholarship Fund incorporated in Missouri February 1983, is a not-for-profit 501 C (3) tax-exempt organization authorized by the Internal Revenue Service.

The Fund awards scholarships to assist talented, disadvantaged youth who because of inadequate financial resources would not be able to fulfill their quest of a college education.

Since its inception, more than two-hundred (200) Clay Scholars have graduated from 52 major colleges and universities. Many have pursued post-graduate courses or are gainfully employed in their fields of professional training.

The cost of educating Clay Scholars during our 25 year history exceeds $5.6 million. This figure represents the removal of a roadblock that once stood between Clay Scholars and a college degree. This is a significant investment in the future.

The Fund's Board of Directors is very proud of this accomplishment. It has been possible to educate so many students because most monies collected go to the scholars. We have no major operating expenses: no paid employees, no office rent or utilities, and printing is done in-house. Volunteers solicit city, state, bi-state and other agencies for employee payroll deductions.

The Board of Directors and the scholarship recipients appreciate the efforts of hundreds of individuals whose contributions keep this valuable project functioning, and thank you for your generosity.

CONTRIBUTIONS MAY BE SENT TO:

W.L. Clay Scholarship Fund   or   **W.L. Clay Scholarship Fund**
P.O. Box 4693   **14917 Claude Lane**
St. Louis, Mo. 63108   **Silver Spring, Md. 20905**

FOREWORD

"Advancing the cause of the underrepresented was valida-
tion of lifelong ambitions I dreamed of while growing up in St. Louis'
notorious ghettoes."

These words were spoken by the author of this book, former United States Congressman from Missouri William L. Clay, Sr. – or as I refer to him, my friend Bill. When he asked me to pen the foreword to his fifth published book, I was honored and humbled to do so because I acutely relate to that quote. I was also born in St. Louis, one of thirteen children to a mother on welfare living in public housing. Like Bill, I too know what it is like to grow up and see social justice denied and economic opportunity stifled for too many. This upbringing shaped my worldview and made me determined, like Bill, to be a reliable and relentless voice for the voiceless.

Indeed, after working as a volunteer and teacher with Head Start, a community organization, and an Assemblywoman in the California Legislature, I learned to hone that voice even further when I arrived in Congress in 1991. Of course Bill had already been there for over 20 years at that point, but he remained a consistent and fierce advocate for women, communities of color, the poor, working people, children, students, veterans, and our men and women in uniform.

I believe Bill Clay has been a constant voice for equality and justice because his life before Congress was one of service, sacrifice, struggle, and social change. After growing up under difficult circumstances in St. Louis, he graduated from St. Louis University and then served in the United States Army. Bill entered political life as a St. Louis Alderman, which had him on the ground throughout the city, listening to the concerns and aspirations of his constituents. In 1963, he and 18 other civil rights leaders were jailed after they were accused of violating a court order for protesting at Jefferson

Bank, which wouldn't hire African Americans in white collar jobs. Bill and his allies, steadfast in their efforts, were effective: the bank and other local companies hired hundreds of blacks in white collar and sales positions. The confrontation, as Bill's book about the incident calls it, was a watershed moment in the civil rights struggle in St. Louis.

The focus of this fascinating, informative and entertaining book is the years that followed—Bill's service in Congress for more than three decades. During this time, he interacted with legends, inspirations, and criminals. The intrigue, process and politics that happen at ends of Pennsylvania Avenue from Capitol Hill to the White House, are brought to life with real insight as a civil rights and social justice champion for the least of these.

That description, an outsider's insider, is held up by the hundreds of pieces of legislation Congressman Clay had a hand in writing, passing or supporting, including the Family and Medical Leave Act; COBRA; pension reform, including for women workers; and critically important public policy to support elementary, secondary, and higher education. He maintained important connections with his constituents and the American public even as he rose to become a committee chairman and the leader of the Missouri Congressional delegation.

Bill is an articulate, well-read, and respected gentlemen for whom I have the utmost admiration. But if there is one word I would use to describe him, it would be 'leader.' He was a leader as a young activist with a mission, a placard, and even willingness to go to jail, while fighting for civil rights in St. Louis; he was a leader in uniform during a time of global uncertainty; and in Congress he was a leader with a pen and a podium, working to make life better for his constituents in Missouri and people nationwide.

As an original founder of the Congressional Black caucus, Bill was—and remains—an advocate for and steward of the "permanent interest" of African Americans all over this country. The William L. Clay Scholarship and Research Fund, which helps talented, financially disadvantaged youth attend college, is just one example of his enduring commitment to our community.

From President Nixon to President Clinton, from Watergate to Iran-Contra and Kent State, from resignations and impeachments to elections and transitions, Bill saw it all while serving in Congress from 1969 to 2001. The stories within these pages will shock you, make you laugh, make you shake your head in wonderment, and make you reflect on where our country was, where it is today, and where it is headed in the future.

In this time of economic, political, and social uncertainty, America needs more progressive, dare I say liberals, who are not afraid to advocate for an agenda that puts all Americans on a path to prosperity. We are lucky to have people like Congressman Bill Clay help show us the way. I thank him for his service to our country, and I commit to him and all of you that the work goes on.

—U.S. Congresswoman Maxine Waters
35th District, California

AUTHOR'S NOTES

Seeds of discontent aroused and angered by harsh policies of racial discrimination and segregation permeated every black community during the 1960s. Loud voices of indignant protest demanded radical, immediate change in policies and practices that denied them decent housing, good schools, adequate health care, and equal employment opportunity. Wherever significant numbers lived, thousands participated in non-violent, passive resistant demonstrations challenging four centuries of societal accepted white racist behavior. Traditionally regarded as humble, happy-go-lucky people, some not associated with the civil rights movement, in anger and frustration turned to burning and looting major cities. But, the confrontation between the 'Establishment' and insurgent non-violent 'freedom fighters,' constituted the most serious effort in American history to secure rights for black citizens.

Determination to eliminate legal constrictions and entrenched customs that prohibited the exercise of citizen rights, was not limited to one sector, section or segment of black society. Unemployed and underemployed, college trained and unskilled custodian, lawyers working as U.S. Postal Clerks, doctors denied staff positions at white hospitals, realized the commonality of the problem was rank discrimination and rigid segregation.

In addition to economic justice and social equality the group also included the quest for political independence. To gain unconditional freedom, black leadership became more militant in its demands and presented a pattern of provocative engagements that America was unprepared to address.

Identifying the common enemy made it more difficult for City Fathers to divide the black community as in past efforts. "Free-

Now" became the rallying cry that fueled the resolve of insurgents manning the highly organized non-violent sit-ins, wave-ins, kneel-ins, picket lines, and boycotts.

Leaders of the protest movement were aware that within the confines of intercity ghettoes there existed latent political power. Younger, less cautious leaders learned from protest activity that efficient organization, adequate political education, and proper discipline effectuated major change in the way groups viewed conditions affecting their lives. The community came to realize that one critical flaw needing immediate remedy was the lack of black elected officials.

The political battle cry quickly changed to "we can speak for ourselves" better than anyone else. The new civil rights mantra preached that through political empowerment and its aggressive execution, liberation would bring racial equality much faster if blacks controlled the reins of power in areas where they resided.

In the mix of black confrontation and white confusion, some white Americans found their status of privilege and preference crumbling under the weight of street demonstrations on one hand, and enactment of new laws that prohibited racial discrimination on the other.

This book recounts my 32 years in the U. S. House of Representatives beginning in 1969, the year Richard Milhous Nixon was elected, and ending in 2001 when William Jefferson Clinton left the White House. Spanning the administrations of six presidents, sixteen Congresses, and eight House Speakers, I document important events of those exciting, intriguing, confrontational years of changing times and evolving politics.

Exchanges with fellow politicians, expressed in straightforward, blunt, sometimes harsh language explain how contentious issues are resolved. I present candid, insightful looks into the political process in a snapshot, and a composite rendition of interfacing with individuals who possessed differing constituent interests.

I recount struggles, victories, losses, in revealing the racial and class divide at play in the world of real politics. The book covers these issues and others in minute detail.

Serving in Congress through some of the nation's most turbulent years is a history worth recording.

I was present to witness a government near anarchy, losing control of its rudders and drifting in uncharted waters of permissive, illicit behavior. It was a chilling experience that resulted in a series of scandals involving high level officials who considered themselves above and outside the law.

I was there to witness the Watergate burglary cover-up; a vice-president forced to resign in disgrace, failed assassination attempts on two sitting presidents and another on a candidate for the presidency.

I was there as a victim, along with others to see overzealous government agents manufacture crimes against innocent, outspoken critics of despotic policies, while those making war in the name of blind patriotism were given free range to undermine democratic practices and constitutional rights.

Criminal charges and countercharges were rampant: the conviction and imprisonment of more than twenty attorneys appointed by Nixon or associated with his campaign who were involved with the seven Watergate burglars; conviction of seven Members of Congress in the ABSCAM FBI sting; impeachment proceedings against two Presidents; the forced resignation of three Speakers of the House; the trading of illegal arms by top Reagan officials in the Iran-Contra debacle; and President Bush's pardoning of convicted felons in the Contra scandal.

I joined the group that lobbied the successful Senate rejection of two reactionary Nixon appointees to the Supreme Court, and the defeat of another three Reagan nominees to the Federal Bench who were inclined to reverse legal gains of women and minorities.

Resilient and Resolute Form of Government

In the last three decades of the 20th century, honest, compassionate, effective government at all levels, rarely existed. There was no end to the shameful behavior of officials based on intolerance, excessive greed and profiteering: the Savings and Loan debacle, the racist tinged anti-busing controversy, defiance of Court edicts, perjury before Congressional hearings by tobacco executives, presidents and top appointees criminally breaking laws that prohibited assassinations of foreign heads-of- states, the overt rape or our environment and natural resources in direct exchange for campaign contributions from special interest lobbyists. Scandals by scoundrels at all levels and in all areas of government were treated by elected officials, politicians, the media, the public as ordinary operational necessities.

I reviewed the six years that President Nixon flagrantly and criminally manipulated specific laws to deny Americans their individual rights; four years of President Carter stubbornly refusing to change inept polices to counter high inflation, high interest rates, high cost of gasoline, and high unemployment; twelve years of Presidents Reagan and Bush attacking the civil rights of minorities and privacy rights of women; eight years of divisive, partisan bickering over taxes, apologies for racist government abuses and budget reductions during President Clinton's administration.

Despite the acrimony, bitterness, hostility, scandal and scornful deeds caused by these shameful events, the country miraculously survived, even if it did not atone for its mistakes, or eliminate divisive policies based on hate and ignorance.

Crises Continue

As serious domestic problems went unattended, the public tended to favor armed conflict over peaceful negotiation in settling foreign disputes. Condoning aggressive militaristic actions resulted in highly questionable unjustified excursions into Vietnam, Cambodia, Laos, Panama, Grenada, and the Persian Gulf which needlessly sacrificed young lives and squandered resources that could have eased the suffering of vulnerable citizens.

The period saw Americans taken hostage in Iran, our embassies destroyed in several countries, and the unceremoniously retreat of our armed forces from Vietnam, Somalia and Lebanon.

Each crisis reminded me why I chose politics as a career. In a sense, my involvement in challenging the core of widespread injustice permeating society, presented an opportunity for me personally to become more vigilant, more tolerant, more reform minded.

Advancing the cause of the underrepresented was validation of lifelong ambitions I dreamed of while growing up in St. Louis' notorious ghettoes.

Before embarking on a political career, I developed a moral compass that envisioned a system where race, color and national origin would not guarantee failure, nor provide an impediment to success. When elected to Congress, I pledged to devote my efforts to secure justice, equity, and equality to all through the legislative process.

Despite ideals contradicting prevailing political practices, I was on the right path. I knew something was drastically wrong when a government did not protect its citizens from intolerant, inhumane conditions caused by racial bigotry, corporate greed, and general unconcern. Something was amiss when the richest nation on earth refused to house its homeless, clothe its naked, treat its sick, and feed its hungry. A nation left to drift unchallenged, in these denials, despite its glorious Bill of Rights, renders itself undeserving to model as the moral leader of the world. I knew a majority finding peace and comfort by ignoring the pervasive and callous insensitivities of political, business and religious institutions, made mockery of the endearing principles of our Founders.

It was indelibly burned in my moral psyche that the hallmark of a civilized, decent government is the extent to which it honors and promotes individual dignity. Conversely, the trademark of a decadent society rests in its capacity to ignore the plight of its underprivileged.

In pursuing career goals, I encountered rough and tumble confrontation with six presidents because I insisted on representing a national constituency whose interests were traditionally ignored, neglected, and often abused by the powers that set policy and or my list of priorities did not coincide with their publicly stated values. My mission was to confront conventionally accepted ideas and to defy malicious proposals offered by cynical people in positions of influence. I did not pause to ponder personal consequences when fighting established unjust customs. Historically, those engaging in unorthodox action when necessary made America a better, stronger nation.

Considered an "outsider" by many for my unwavering stance in protecting the interests of the 'have-nots,' I managed to attain the status of an institutional "insider" without losing my credentials as a reformer. In stark disagreement with political powerhouses over legislative priorities, I maintained my idealistic concept that an indisputable purpose of government was to protect those who could not protect themselves.

Seniority provided the protective armor that prevented my efforts from being minimized or ignored. I served on multiple committees: thirty-two years on Education and Labor, twenty-two years on Post Office and Civil Service, 10 years on House Administration. I chaired the full committee of the Post Office, chaired two subcommittees dealing with worker's rights: Labor Management having jurisdiction over approximately 60% of all labor legislation, and the Pension Task Force with responsibility for enforcement of the Employment Retirement Income Security Act (ERISA). Other chairmanships included the Ad Hoc Committee on Overseas Schools, the Non-appropriated Fund Organizations (PXs and Commissaries), and the members Postal Franking Committee.

During the process, two hundred ninety-five (295) bills bearing my imprimatur became law, among them landmark legislation: the Family and Medical Leave Act, Hatch Act Reform, 5 Year Vesting in Pensions, Sixty day plant closing notification, Women's Pension Equity Act, Revision of ERISA, reauthorization of the Higher Education Act, and the Elementary and Secondary Education Act.

My proudest moments were joining with others to pass legislation: working with Congresswoman Pat Schroeder of Colorado who spear-headed the fight to pass the Family and Medical Leave Act; with Congressman Bill Ford of Michigan, to reform the Hatch Act, sitting next to Frank Thompson of New Jersey as our committee hammered out provisions of the Employment Retirement Income Security Act (ERISA), John Dent of Pennsylvania allowing me, a newcomer, to offer language extending minimum wage coverage to domestic workers, working with Louis Stokes in providing money for higher education, especially for black colleges.

I am grateful to chairman Carl Perkins of Kentucky and Augustus Hawkins of California who supported my taking the lead to enact legislation which reduced vesting in pensions from 10 years to 5 years, and to protect survivorship rights of workers through the passage of the Retirement Equity Act. It was under their chairmanships that I negotiated the provisions of the Consolidated Omnibus Reconciliation Act of 1986 (COBRA) which provided for continued coverage of survivors in employer provided group health plans.

My Agenda for Progress

Despite well-financed efforts by reactionary forces to repeal, nullify or stymie the advancement of socially redeeming initiatives in the areas of race and sex, our progress during this period was phenomenal.

In the book, I reflect on the major role played in effectuating much of the change that improved the quality of life for ordinary citizens. While pursuing an agenda that respected and appreciated the vital needs of the nation, I found it in the national interest to address the critical problems hampering the growth and prosperity of those in poverty because they lacked sufficient education or a job paying a livable wage. Implementing new ideas and promoting new legislative initiatives to deal with the concerns of the unrepresented and under-represented, was critically important to me.

My career efforts were devoted to an advocacy for better housing, better jobs, better health care, betters schools and better teaching methods for all students without blaming our educators for the deficiencies or attempting to destroy the public school system.

Archimedes, an early Greek philosopher, wrote, "Give me a place to stand and I will change the world." The voters of Missouri provided me with a noble arena in which "to stand"–the chamber of the U.S. House of Representatives. From that vantage point, if I did not change the world, I am satisfied that in a very practical, positive and tangible way my actions favorably impacted issues that did.

1

"The problem is not gaining power but using it. In our opinion, Bill Clay has demonstrated that he knows how to use power for the good of the community."[1]

— Editorial Endorsement *St. Louis Argus,*
31 May 1968

The description distinguished between the process of being elected and the subsequent role of public service. In earlier times, 'black power' was a convenient cliché often shouted by politicians and others to evade responding to legitimate questions concerning their activities and purposes. Without understanding how to use the awesome, often destructive, imposing force of real power inherent in elective office, I realized it would remain a nice, provocative slogan.

Hard Fought Battle for Congress

To highlight the perverse racist practice of gerrymandering, my father once told me that in a twenty year period, he lived in three different congressional districts without moving. The sinister act of denying elected office to blacks was as lethal in the North and West as physical and coercive intimidation were in the South.

Conversations about biases and bigotry, coupled with personal injustices I experienced, shaped major positions in my life and formed seeds of activism that led me to seek election to congress.

Following defeat of Representative George White (R-N.C.) in 1901, black people were without a single spokesman in the U.S. Congress. State legislatures and city councils also excluded black elected officials. Millions of black citizens helplessly watched their constitutional rights systematically eroded and legal protections methodically repealed. No person of color served in any state legislature until New York, California and Missouri elected their first blacks in 1916, 1918 and 1920, respectively. Massachusetts did not elect its first black to the state legislature until 1946 and Illinois in 1956. The same was true for municipalities. The cities of New York, St. Louis and Los Angeles elected their first blacks to city councils in 1941, 1943 and 1963, respectively.

In 1928, Oscar De Priest of Illinois was elected to the U.S. Congress. The Chicagoan become the first African American elected to that body in the 20th century.

The political situation facing blacks was dismal and disgraceful. East, West, North and South no opportunity existed for them to hold elective office. The prevailing mood of racial and ethnic preferences, in varying degrees and in some form throughout the country, rendered their elections impossible.

In the North and West, the inability of blacks to influence the size, shape and population of boundaries for city councils, state legislatures was the culprit in denying elective representation. In the polarized voting districts of these areas because blacks seldom constituted a majority, gerrymandering was the preferred instrument for diminishing the impact of their votes.

Missouri, a former slave state that abided by strict rules and customs separating the races, differed in one major respect from other southern states. Its politics was more similar to that in northern cities like Chicago and New York where no laws as poll taxes, all-white primaries, or literacy tests prevented blacks from registering to vote. There were no widespread threats of intimidation, overt or covert, to prevent the free exercise of the ballot.

Blacks in St. Louis, for more than 40 years, waged numerous and spirited campaigns for representation in the U.S. Congress, legislative districts and school boards. Each failed. The most serious challenge to Missouri's all-white congressional delegation came in 1928, when Joseph L. McLemore lost the Democratic primary by 7,000 votes. Rebuffed repeatedly in efforts to reap economic stability and social justice through the political process, black leaders Wayman Smith II, Margaret Bush Wilson, Robert Witherspoon, Josiah Thomas, Sydney Redmond and others continued to campaign unsuccessfully for congress.

Democrats Opposed Creation
Black Majority District

In 1967, the Missouri Senate drew new congressional districts including one fifty percent (50%) black which gave minority voters for the first time a realistic opportunity for election.

Fifty-seven (57) white Republicans, nine (9) white Democrats from the rural area, and thirteen (13) black Democrats in the Missouri House of Representatives, abandoned racial hang-ups to protect their self interests, and to preserve the economical and political integrity of their regions. Political analysts considered it miraculous that a rebellious coalition of inner-city blacks, rural white Democrats and suburban Republicans reached common ground to create congressional districts that withstood tremendous pressures from an overwhelmingly controlled Democratic legislature, dictated to by Warren Hearnes, an autocratic Democratic governor.

The common thread cementing the resolve of The Unconventional Coalition was stronger than appeal to party, or to race or to traditional prejudices. The underlining motivation was understandable: rural Democrats seeking a voice to protect their agricultural economy in a Southeastern part of the state; urban Republicans intent on saving a congressional district in suburban St. Louis County to represent upper middle income white constituents; and race-conscious blacks supporting a majority-black district mostly within the city limits of St. Louis.

A stunned Democratic leadership filed a lawsuit to overturn the legislative verdict: arrogantly asking the Federal Court, under provisions of the Voting Rights Act, to support a plan dispersing the black population into three districts. However, the U.S. Supreme Court on 4 March 1968 ruled the district drawn by the legislature did in fact protect the rights of minorities under the Voting Rights Act and mandated use of the new boundaries for the next election.

A Preemptive Campaign Strike

Two days after the Court decision, I heard on my car radio that the incumbent of twenty two years, allegedly disgusted by the racial composition of the new district, decided not to seek reelection. Immediately, I parked near a public telephone booth, placed a call to my wife who agreed that I would be a good congressman. Then, I contacted my close political ally, committeeman Leroy Tyus whom I had associated with on a daily basis. He committed support and advised me to reach out to Frank Mitchell, publisher of the *St. Louis Argus* and Larry Callanan, head of the Pipefitter's Union. I went to see Mitchell whose office was only a few blocks away. We discussed the kind of representative that should replace the incumbent, Frank Karsten. Wisely, I postponed calling my employer, Callanan until I consolidated support in my base.

I was employed by Callanan's union, the pipefitters, to develop and oversee a program integrating black journeymen and apprentices into membership. We established a crisis hiring program that mandated fifty-percent (50%) of all new hires must be black. It was the first real breakthrough for hiring blacks in the construction industry.

In a matter of hours, meeting with several dozen influential members of the black media, the clergy, elected officials and key supporters, among them Gwen Giles, Doris Moore, Walter Lay, Reverend Willie Ellis and Frank Payne, an intensive campaign was planned and put into motion with 'all deliberate speed.'

I owned a printing press and by nightfall, scores of supporters were on the streets distributing thousands of brochures declaring "Bill Clay is ready-are you?" It was a preemptive strike clearly establishing me as the leading candidate.

We counted on early public endorsements to offset attacks surely to follow from critics of my leadership style. In 72 hours, allies locked up support from the most important community sources, jettisoning my candidacy into a lead others would find hard to overtake.

Prominent black leaders: Joseph Clark, a city alderman; NAACP president Ernest Calloway, a teamster union official; two state legislators Ray Howard and Fred Williams announced intention of filing for the position. James Troupe, committeeman, state representative, an official of the Steelworkers Union who led the fight to draw the majority black district, had filed prior to the court opinion.

My background, experience and commitment to racial justice, equaled, if not excelled that of the other potential candidates. My record positioned me in good stead to win the primary. I was involved in the civil rights movement, first as founder and president of an active NAACP Youth Council chapter, and then as an activist in the Committee Of Racial Equality (CORE). Involvement in protesting segregated restaurant policies and challenging endemic employment discrimination resulted in my being arrested several times. Once, I was sentenced to 270 days of which I served 118 days before an outraged citizenry forced City Fathers to arrange for my release.

I served 5 years on the Board of Aldermen, compiling a remarkable record of passing legislation to advance the civil rights of blacks and the civil liberties of the entire community. I wrote and sponsored the City's first Fair Employment Law and passed legislation to prohibit the police from releasing arrest records of persons not convicted of the crimes charged.

In 1964, I resigned after being elected Democratic ward committeeman, a non-paying, but politically powerful position that controlled patronage and endorsed candidates for public offices.

After several weeks of intensive campaigning, I emerged the clear choice of most seasoned black community leaders and young activists. Four of the seven (7) black ward committeemen endorsed me. In addition, I had the unconditional support of the white committeeman of the 22nd ward which was majority black, and the tacit support of the white Regular Democrat Organizations in the 2nd and 3rd wards both racially mixed. My friend and employer Callanan, initially announced neutrality but later recanted.

A number of black ministers rallied around my campaign and neighborhood groups provided hundreds of volunteers to canvass the precincts on my behalf.

Forty two (42) candidates running to unseat incumbents in

ward committee races, and state legislature contests gave me their endorsements. Two smaller labor unions, Local 5 of the Seafarers International and Local 160 of the Leather and Luggage Workers issued press releases on my behalf.

The *St. Louis American* Newspaper favored Calloway. But, the lion's share of support from the remaining black newspapers went to me. Four of the six black weeklies editorially endorsed my candidacy: *Argus, Defender, Crusader, and People's Guide*. The oldest of the city's black journals, the *Argus* wrote:

> *"The St. Louis Argus* recommends William 'Bill' Clay for Congress because his portfolio contains outstanding credentials... [He] is a civil rights and political activist. He organized and led the fight for racial justice in this city when others thought there was no hope." [2]

The depth and width of those supporting my candidacy constituted an impressive, dedicated group of black opinion makers.

Editorial Comment A Mixed Bag

The *St. Louis Post Dispatch* reached a different, more novel conclusion about who should be the next congressman. After acknowledging I was the front runner among black voters, it embraced the idea that blacks not only had a right to congressional representation, but also the right to choose their own leaders, the newspaper editorialized with a tad of doubt: "Everyone of the black committeemen is supporting the younger Bill Clay. Although our own choice would be Mr. Calloway, we respect the right of the black community to choose for itself."[3]

The mixed message from the city's most read daily was countered by the People's Guide that wrote, "Bill Clay is the man to elect. He has demonstrated in every conceivable way the capabilities we need in a Congressman."[4]

Whites Lined-Up Behind One Candidate

The campaign degenerated into the City's usual racially polarized campaign when four politically well-known white contenders
withdrew from the race the same day, and endorsed Milton Carpenter a former City Comptroller and former State Treasurer. The ploy,
orchestrated by top Democratic Party officials, assured he would be
the favorite white candidate in a primary contest with the possibility
of four black challengers. It was apparent that the Democratic Party
was not only opposed to creating a majority black district, but was
also determined that a black would not represent them in Congress.

Radio and television stations, business journals, white week-
ly newspapers, and labor unions consolidated efforts behind Milton
Carpenter. *The Globe Democrat's* news and editorials were especially critical of my candidacy and extremely biased in its coverage.

Carpenter carried heavy political baggage in the black community. He was part-owner of the Howard Johnson Restaurant located in the center of a black community that did not allow blacks
to enter the premises. It was the restaurant where Attorney Ray
Howard and I were arrested eight years prior for challenging its discriminatory policy.

The owners who went to court seeking an injunction to stop
CORE from peacefully demonstrating, resisted serving blacks until
the very end. Allegedly, the Carpenters sold their interest rather
than feed black patrons. The incident convinced blacks that Carpenter's representation would not be sympathetic to our cause.

Consolidation of white support for Carpenter generated a
similar effort to maximize black voter power by supporting a single
black candidate. Committeeman Frederick Weathers, dean of black
elected officials and Calloway's chief backer, held a series of meetings in his home attempting to reach a consensus candidate.

Subsequently, Alderman Clark withdrew, refusing to endorse
any candidate. Howard and Williams decided against filing. Representative Troupe withdrew, throwing his support to me, but too late
to remove his name from the voting machine.

After it became apparent that I was the only black capable

of rallying sufficient support to win the primary election, and that Calloway's campaign threatened that possibility, Weathers, unsuccessful in persuading him "to get out," withdrew his endorsement and supported me.

Unique Type of Campaigning

Our campaign committee added an unusual and innovative element to my bid for Congress. Normally, the residents in economically depressed inner-city areas are not included in the actual electoral process. They are considered important only on election day when special teams are hired to get them to the polls.

Believing a large voter turnout increased my chances of winning the primary, we determined their active involvement critical, and devised a plan to give them a key role in getting out a big vote.

They were organized into "sign and T-shirt brigades" responsible for operating the silk screens produced by my campaign committee members that stenciled the picture of a ballot and a torch of freedom beside the name of 'Bill Clay for Congress' onto the shirts. Thousands of white T-shirts were purchased at $5.00 per dozen and the neighborhood volunteers prepared them each day, allowing to dry at night.

Designated block leaders organized teams that distributed T-shirts to children between the ages of 4 and 12, and placed window signs in the homes of their parents.

Adults volunteering to canvass precincts, abandoned the traditional role of spectators and became participating partners in the political process, convincing their neighbors the importance voting played in their lives.

Calloway Stays in the Race

Despite dismal prospects of winning, Calloway remained in the race and intensified his campaign. His committee headed by Senator T.D. McNeal as chairman and Dr. Jerome Williams as treasurer issued a harsh statement declaring Calloway "The man the money-grubbing Uncle Toms feared. The man the political Uncle

Toms must destroy because he walks alone in freedom and respect with no white politician's collar around his neck." McNeal and Williams were respected leaders but their statement on this subject had no appreciable impact on black voters.

Calloway adopted a slogan from the Bible "young men for war, old men for counsel" that appeared in all his literature. He asserted that because of my youth, I was unprepared to assume the great responsibility of sitting in the world's highest legislative body.

I turned the tables on his biblical injection into the debate, kidnapped his slogan, wrapped it around my shoulders and exploited the connotation to the fullest. In every public appearance, including debates we had, I credited the statement to Calloway and then reminded voters of my youth, citing my opponent as 23 years my senior. I boasted that at age 38, if elected, I would be one of the youngest in the Congress and with a potential to accrue the all-important seniority to gain power and return benefits to the district.

Flipping the message, I acknowledged that indeed there was a war going on in the nation's Capital and it was imperative that the voters send a "young, experienced warrior" to do battle with modern-day Philistines who were waging a sinful battle of neglect against the poor and minorities in America's slums. I declared it necessary to combat those who allowed poverty and racism to flourish while sheltering the rich in their denying essentials of life to the needy.

Then, I would state emphatically that elder statesmen like Calloway should remain home to provide young energetic men like me the "counsel" and advice required to address gross inequities existing in our society.

Contest Between Two Unions

Two powerful labor leaders, Larry Callanan of the pipefitters and Harold Gibbons of the teamsters took opposing sides in the race. Callanan headed the smallest, but politically the richest union in Missouri and surrounding states. Generous contributions from its well endowed political fund gave him national prominence. Gibbons presided over the state's largest union. The two labor Goliaths, personal friends of long-standing, often clashed in political contests to determine who was kingpin. Callanan resented the generous media treatment accorded Gibbons whom they often described as a "white hat" to highlight the distinction between him and Callanan, a "black hat."

The Globe Democrat reported that Callanan in a telephone conversation asked Gibbons to pressure Calloway into withdrawing so the black community could unite behind my candidacy. Reportedly, Gibbons told him "the head of a small union like the pipefitters" should spend time increasing membership instead of dabbling in serious politics." Allegedly, Gibbons stated that Calloway would win hands down because the Teamsters would rally their 43,000 members, including 7,000 blacks behind his campaign. The Pipefitters had only 1,000 members, including 39 blacks. The taunting remark and the front page story of the *Globe Democrat* article written by Jack Flach titled "Teamsters, Steamfitters to Fight In 1st District Democratic Race," caused Callanan to abandon his position of neutrality.

The newspaper hit the streets about 10 o'clock at night. By midnight, Callanan was on the telephone berating its publisher, assailing Gibbons, and arranging a meeting at the union hall to discuss the matter.

The next morning, he was in rare form. Cursing, shouting, pacing the floor, in one of his famous tirades. In a loud voice, hands gesticulating, he summoned into the office, his check writer for the political campaign fund, and in an even louder voice, said, "Write Clay a check for what he needs now and for whatever he needs on a daily basis."

At that very moment the race for congress between Clay, Calloway and Carpenter became moot. Unfortunately, my two opponents did not know that the only thing left was counting the votes on election night and a celebration in the inner-city. Calloway, Gibbons of the Teamsters; editor Duncan Bauman, Governor Hearnes, reporters and subscribers to the *Globe Democrat;* suburban newspapers, pro-Carpenter labor leaders, and candidate Carpenter-were doomed to futility in continuing to advocate my defeat.

The most uninformed and misinformed of the Clay/Callanan coup d'etat were the so-called expert political gurus. They continued to predict my loss until the votes were counted on election night, showing Carpenter with 16,927, Calloway 6,405, Leahey 1.526, Relles 1,258, and Troupe whose name remained on the voting machine 3,186. I was victorious with 23,758 votes.

Two Blacks Compete For One Seat
(A Win-Win For Black Voters)

My opponent in the general election was Curtis Crawford, a black who had no trouble winning the Republican nomination. He was a well liked lawyer who at one time was the Assistant Circuit Attorney for the city of St. Louis. He was a former Democrat who switched parties to make the race, believing that a white candidate would be nominated by Democrats and he would be the overwhelming favorite of black voters in the general election.

Debate in the community was spirited and intense. Churches and colleges invited us as guest speakers. We made the rounds to the schools, block units and senior citizen homes. Conversations in the bars, pool rooms and PTA's buzzed with speculation and jubilation. The election had historic implications for them. The victor would be the first of our race elected from Missouri, a former slave-state, and from any southern state to the U.S. Congress in the 20th century. He would be only the 2nd black elected West of the Mississippi River (Augustus Hawkins of California preceding me by 6 years).

Nothing in recent political history had inspired, interested or excited the black community as this election. The thought of a black man standing on the floor of Congress articulating the ills of mal-treated ghetto residents in the Saint Louis metropolitan area, and in a position to effectuate change for improvement, gave new meaning to political involvement. It generated an exhilarating sense of pride among those cognizant of its significance.

Most Caucasians in the congressional district viewed me as racist-an angry black radical. I managed to live-up in part to their preconceived, erroneous notion. Angry, yes! Racist, No! At their rallies, I would preface my remarks with "There are two kinds of black politicians who speak to white groups. One tells you what you want to hear-to grovel for your vote. I am here to tell you what will benefit you by hearing it whether I get your vote or not."

I continued to promote the agenda advanced in the primary: racial equality, workers rights, opposition to the war and a place at the table for minority views. I pledged to protect equal rights, preserve Social Security and Medicare, increase funding for student loans, support job creation and job training programs. I tried, apparently unsuccessfully, to make white groups realize that government assistance was as critical to their standard of living as it was to black citizens.

In the general election, I received 79,295 votes to Republican Crawford's 44,316. Half of his votes (21,011) came from the heavily Democratic white precincts of St. Ferdinand and Washington Townships -areas that had traditionally voted overwhelmingly Democrat for decades.

I was victorious in the primary and general elections because, unlike too many politicians, I was not still addicted to the old fashion belief that the average voter was not interested in basic change. I beat the opposition because my troops were actively advocating change in how elected officials respond to constituent needs. We had the most disciplined, best trained campaign workers, and I like to think, immodestly of course, by far the most attractive candidate.

Notes

1/Editorial endorsement, *St. Louis Argus,* 31 May 1968.
2/Ibid.
3/"In the First District," *St. Louis Post Dispatch,* 24 July 1968, page 2E.
4/*People's Guide* (St. Louis Publication), 30 July 1968, pg. 1..
5/*Washington Post,* Racism, Poverty, blamed for Riots. March 1, 1968, page 1.

2

The first black elected to Congress from Missouri is not verification of the state's unlimited opportunity for black citizens. Rather, it is an indictment of the state's 150 years of denying equal opportunity."[1]

— William L. Clay, Sr.
Election Night, November 1968

Family and I Depart for U.S. Capitol

Carol, Vicki, Lacy and Michelle joined me on a flight to Washington, D.C., the seat of world power, for the swearing-in ceremony. The Trans World Airline (TWA) captain announced soon after take-off that a newly elected Congressman was aboard, and the flight attendant presented us with a bottle of champagne. Passengers gathered to offer congratulations.

Before I boarded the plane, I read what a local reporter wrote in that day's edition: "Friend and foe agree that Clay has leadership ability, political acumen, energy, articulateness and a rapport with the people who inhabit the corners of the ghetto." The flattering description would become the centerpiece of my congressional endeavor, especially as it related to the poor who were forced to dwell in impoverished conditions.

The article's content renewed my resolve to seize the moment in confronting racial injustice, in fighting for economic equity, in raising issues about war and poverty that had been ignored too long and debated too little. I looked forward to engaging in debate about the terrible effects of endemic poverty. I was on cloud nine, contemplating the addition of my voice to others in giving leadership substance to concerns affecting a segment of society miserably shortchanged in the past.

Atmosphere for Social and Economic Change

January 3, 1969, I joined a large class of like-minded freshmen who won election to the 91st Congress by campaigning against the Vietnam War. I was in a position, alongside them, to play a role in creating legislation focused more acutely on addressing social and economic inequities at home. The group destined to be heard on important national questions was already renowned personalities in their local communities - among them: Mario Biaggi, New York City's most decorated police officer; Shirley Chisholm, nationally known advocate for children's education; Edward I. Koch, district leader New York City borough; Allard K. Lowenstein, organizer of the national movement against the Vietnam War; Abner J. Mikva, brilliant attorney from Chicago; and Louis Stokes of Cleveland, criminal lawyer who won the landmark Supreme Court Case of Terry v. Ohio, regulating police search and seizure.

Making Black History

The election of Shirley Chisholm (D-N.Y.), Louis Stokes (D-Oh.) and me was unprecedented. Joining six black incumbents was an historic occasion: nine blacks seated simultaneously, the first in history; three elected to the same Congress, another first. One hundred eight (108) white women had served in Congress but Shirley Chisholm was the first African American so honored. Scores of whites had been elected from Missouri and Ohio but Stokes and I were the first of African American descent.

Thousands of constituents, arriving by chartered planes, buses, trains and private autos, came to witness the taking of the oath and to participate in the festivities. Hundreds of Saint Louisans, Clevelanders, and Brooklynites braved extremely cold weather to watch the installation of three black congresspersons. The degree of enthusiasm and jubilation was heartwarming.

Rules of the House of Representatives allowed children fourteen and under to sit in the chamber during proceedings. My three children accompanied me to the House floor. Watching expressions on their little faces was an unforgettable experience. When I stood to recite the oath of office, so did they. The four of us raised our right hands and repeated after Speaker John McCormack, swearing "to uphold the Constitution and to obey the laws of the land." Another first, four Clays theoretically became members of Congress at the same time.

I glanced at my parents sitting next to my wife in the gallery, and my eyes swelled with tears of joy and pride. What I saw in the faces of the ones I love the most was a once in a lifetime and it taught me the true meaning of family value.

Afraid to fly, mom and dad traveled from St. Louis on a train for nearly 2 days, with a long layover in Chicago. Neither my wife nor I, in our wildest dreams, ever contemplated that someday I would sit in the most powerful, most influential legislative body in the world. A poor boy who at one time had little hope of escaping the devastating ravishes of St. Louis' notorious slums, was now in a position to improve the conditions of those similarly victimized by neglectful and insensitive government policies. Rising from such incredible beginnings to overcome tremendous obstacles, proved the American dream held out some hope for other black citizens.

An Awesome Responsibility

Becoming a member of the United States Congress is a humbling, awesome experience. The grave responsibility placed on the shoulders of one entering that exclusive body, especially for the first time, is mindboggling. Standing in the decorous stately chamber, observing the ornate surroundings and absorbing the amazing American history concealed in its rafters, stirred every emotion in my being.

FOOTNOTE
Election to the U.S. Congress is a singular honor conferred only on few citizens. The rare privilege was bestowed on me 16 times or 32 years. Only two other Missourians served longer: Clarence A. Cannon for 41 years 2 months

(March 4, 1923 to May 12, 1964) and Richard Bolling for 34 years, 8 days (January 3, 1949 to January 3, 1983). Thomas H. Benton followed closely behind me with 31 years, 6 months.

Only 11,708 individuals were elected to the Congress from 1789 until 2004, (9,833 serving only in the House and 1,240 in the Senate), with 635 dividing their careers between the House and the Senate.

At the time of my retirement in 2001, two hundred-thirteen (213) members had served 30 years or more in the House. I was in a select group of 60 who served 32 years or more.

Awakening to New Realities

The days and months following my induction were filled with exciting experiences. No, to say exciting misrepresents reality. Each day was exhilarating, stimulating, incredible, and positively wonderful!

I looked forward to the first meeting of the House as merely a formality, but was quickly awakened to the high level intrigue of life on Capitol Hill. My first impression was enhanced by the political maneuvering necessary to get the House properly organized and to agree on parliamentary rules. The fight to select a Speaker and other officers gave insight into behind-the-scene conferences vitally important in successfully securing party leadership positions.

Serious activity, however, did not diminish the fun atmosphere of parties and receptions. The St. Louis Club, an organization with 150 members who formerly lived in my district, now working in D.C., celebrated my arrival with a festive gathering. My political campaign committee and several local businesses sponsored other galas. Lobbyists, well-wishers and veteran congressmen joined the festivities. A grand reception in my honor, promoted by an unexpected, gracious and powerful political icon attracted the biggest, most prestigious names in Washington. Despite a majority of labor unions in St. Louis supporting my opponent, my victory was hailed as another success for organized labor.

George Meany, President of AFL-CIO and former member of the Plumbers and Pipefitters, sponsored an affair in my behalf, and stood at the door, introducing me to several hundred of Washington's politically powerful. He emphasized that I would be his personal representative on the Education and Labor Committee. Among the attendees were House Speaker John McCormick, Majority Leader Carl Albert, Whip Hale Boggs, Senators Ted Kennedy and Sturart Symington, House members Thomas P. "Tip" O'Neill, Jr., John Brademas, John Dingell, Claude Pepper, Lee Hamilton, John Conyers, Morris Udall, Emanuel Cellar, Richard Bolling, Leonora K. Sullivan, and others.

George Meany: A Man of His Word

Initial committee assignments are critical in determining future power and influencing colleagues. Seniority usually determines the selection of committee Chairmen. House rules dictate that when changing committees, members start at the bottom of the seniority list regardless of total years so the initial assignment is important..

Rep. Wilbur Mills, Chairman of the Committee on Committees had the power to make committee assignments. He apparently was not impressed as Meany by my sterling labor credentials. Three days after Meany's endorsement, the media reported that other members beat me out for a coveted seat on the labor committee. I was placed on two rather insignificant committees.

Disappointed, I telephoned Meany to express thanks for his unsuccessful effort. His reaction taught me an important lesson about Washington politics: don't antagonize powerful interests unless necessary, and then only when your actions are supported by equally influential interests. Meany practically came through the telephone. Shouting expletives and stuttering in a fit of anger, he said, "You are no longer the issue. My honor is at stake. That Bimbo (Rep. Wilbur Mills) from hick town USA is not going to put me in short pants."

Knowing the committee assignments had been printed and publicly distributed, I was puzzled as to what changes might occur at this late date. But my curiosity was short-lived. Two days later, Mills reconvened the committee, secured my assignment to the Labor Committee, and granted me seniority over those his committee had previously assigned. Apparently, Meany exerted his powerful influence on Party leaders to convince Mills that he misinterpreted my unique qualifications in the field of labor.

Public Housing–A Great Buy

Carol started the treacherous search for a reasonably priced home in a good neighborhood, befitting the scant salary of a Congressman. As a Missouri real estate broker, I thought I knew something about housing and housing markets. Our home in St. Louis, on a private street, brick and stone, 4 bedrooms, full basement was purchased for $14,000.

Moving up in prestige, if not in earned income (congressional salary $28,500), I decided to splurge. Proudly, I informed Carol that we should seek a house in the $30,000 range. The cost of housing in D.C. was extremely inflated and because of inferior public schools, it was necessary to factor-in another $4,000 per child for private schooling.

After a week of serious scouting with several real estate agents, Carol came home elated to inform me that she found the perfect place within our budget. She said, "It's located in a public housing project."

Needless to say, we recognized the artificially inflated cost of housing in the District of Columbia, and went to settlement on a house in Montgomery County, a Washington, D.C. suburb. It was one of the richest counties in the country with a school system that ranked nationally in the top five. The subdivision encompassed about 100 units, each sitting on 1/4 acre with open space, many trees and a small stream engulfing the area. It was a wonderful house that became a grand home-9 rooms, 4 bedrooms, 3 baths, finished basement.

The Westover Elementary Public School was located within the subdivision where our youngest, 10 year old Michele walked the one block. Our other children, Vicki, the oldest at 14 and Lacy 12, were bused two miles to White Oak Middle School.

We were the first black family in the subdivision. The neighbors were friendly, save one. We learned six months after moving in that our next door neighbor had gone door to door soliciting signatures calling for a meeting at the school to discuss strategies preventing integration of the neighborhood. We also learned that another neighbor circulated a counter-petition aimed at ousting our next door neighbor. The night of the meeting was hilarious. Only eight people attended, but the petition to oust had more signatures than the one to prevent our moving in.

Our move into the neighborhood was without incident and Carol immediately transferred the children to neighborhood public schools in Montgomery County for the remaining two months so they would make friends before the summer recess.

Adjusting to a new city was not easy for the children. Vicki, missing her St. Louis friends, attempted to keep in touch by telephone. She ran up a large long distance telephone bill and succeeded in hiding it for two months. Finally, we discovered the misdeed, lectured her and established a monthly allowance for long distance calls for each of the three children.

Mail Box Bombing

A year later, while Carol and I were out of town, a powerful explosive was planted and detonated in our mail box. Parts of the large wooden receptacle were found in the back of the house more than 100 feet away. Immediately, we suspected a racial incident.

The U.S. Postal inspectors thoroughly investigated and reported back several weeks later, ruling out race as a motive. They found that on the same night another Congressman's mail box was destroyed. Representative Al Quie, a white Republican living 3 miles from us, was also the victim of a mail-box bombing containing the same explosive materials.

The conclusion was that both of us served on the Education and Labor Committee and probably irritated some "devout legislative terrorist" by our vote on a particular issue.

Reality of Congressional Work Schedule

Adjusting to the rigorous duties of a congressman was difficult. Most of my adult life, I worked in positions that required no regular hours, reported to no one for assignments, determined my own agenda and decided how much time would be devoted to each task. I was an insurance salesman, realtor, union organizer, educational coordinator for a labor union, consultant to a radio station, and owner of several small businesses.

In Washington, I arrived at my Capitol Hill office at 8:30 a.m. and rarely left before 7:30 or 8:00 p.m. The average day was crowded with hurried conferences, committee hearings, Democratic caucuses, staff meetings on legislative issues, and greeting constituents.

The first weeks, I joined staff in compiling a mailing list because my predecessor had refused to share his. He donated his files, including pending cases that needed further attention, to a college. The records were considered a contribution to a non-profit organization and resulted in a substantial tax write-off for the retiring Congressman.

I worked 12 hour days, spending four days in D.C., attending committee hearings, floor debate, and voting. I spent the other three days traveling back to St. Louis to perform constituent services.

It was a tough grind that left scant time to spend with my wife and children and time only to pay short visits to my parents while in St. Louis. The life of a congressman is not the bed of roses often portrayed by the media.

A Hectic Beginning

The first 150 days were incredibly exciting. I journeyed back to my district eight times, opening two offices-one in the new Federal Building and the other in midtown; traveled more than 35,000 miles, including trips to honor singer James Brown in New York, spoke in Detroit for the Scottish Rites Masons, lectured at Texas Southern Law School in Houston, participated in a Dr. King memorial in Memphis, attended hearings on equal employment in Los Angeles, inspected Gary Job Corps Center in Texas, and visited former President Lyndon B. Johnson at his ranch in Texas.

It was a whirlwind tour. The first month, I met with James W. Symington, Bill D. Burlison (each elected from Missouri the same day as I) and other newly elected Democrats. We joined Majority Leader Carl Albert at a meeting with President Johnson in his remaining day in the White House.

I appeared on five television programs at home and was interviewed by numerous newspaper reporters in D.C.; was featured in an article of *Ebony Magazine*; spoke at Carr Elementary School in my old neighborhood; and gave the commencement address at Vashon High School in my district.

In February, I introduced my first bill. It called for an increase in the minimum wage to $2 per hour, and to extend protection of the Fair Labor Standard Act to all federal, state and local government employees not covered. I also had the thrill of presiding over a session of the Congress when Speaker McCormack handed me the gavel during debate on the relevancy of the House Un-American Activities Committee.

Congressional Fender Bender

Three months after I was in office, I went to the Capitol Hill garage and found a large dent in the side of my automobile. I noticed a note under the windshield wiper which stated "I hit your car. Please call me." It was signed by an individual claiming to be a member of Congress.

I rushed back to my office, called the operator and asked for the Congressman. She informed me there was no such person. The next day, a call came from the same fellow asking why I never called about the accident. I was furious because I thought he was rubbing it in.

But it turned out that he, David Obey, had been elected in a special election to replace Melvin Laird of Wisconsin who was named Secretary of Defense by President Nixon. Obey had not been sworn-in, assigned an office or a telephone when I tried to reach him.

Obey paid for the repair and subsequently became a respected friend.

St. Louis Argus Award

In May, along with Joseph L. McLemore of New York, I was presented the *St. Louis Argus*' Outstanding Achievement Award at its 14th annual Distinguished Public Service Award Banquet. Mc-Lemore was the unsuccessful candidate for Congress from Missouri in 1928. In his unsuccessful bid for the seat, the Democratic Party nominated him. He was the first person of color nominated for Congress by a major political party since Reconstruction.

My First Congressional Travel Overseas

Also in May, Rep. John Dent, Chairman of a labor subcommittee and a veteran member from Pennsylvania asked Stokes and me to join a fact-finding trip to England to study coal mine conditions. Our committee had jurisdiction over the proposed Coal Mine Safety Act. Miners were being killed by unsafe conditions and dying from unnecessary high levels of dust which caused the crippling "Black Lung" disease. Thousands were physically incapacitated at young ages, victims of a hazard that could be eliminated by reduction of dust levels in the mines. We spent two days in Wales, England inspecting coal mines, interviewing employees and government officials to determine how they instituted safety work rules that reduced levels of toxic coal dust.

On the return trip, the committee spent one night in London. While there, a call came early the next morning from the well known columnist and muckraker, Drew Pearson. He expressed outrage that Stokes and I had taken what he described as an "all-expense paid junket on the taxpayers" so early in our careers. I informed Pearson that if my constituents knew I turned down such a trip, they probably would launch a recall campaign. He was not amused. He wrote in his nationally syndicated column, "The Congressmen could merely have sent a messenger to the Bureau of Mines in downtown Washington to pick up detailed reports on what England and Wales are doing about coal dust."

Pearson died several months after the article without seeing the utilization of the information we attained in England, coupled with our subsequent inspections of coal mines in Pennsylvania and West Virginia and comprehensive hearings which enabled us to establish legislation addressing this serious problem.

Our colleagues and constituents were made aware of hazardous conditions coal miners faced, and we passed the landmark Black Lung Benefits Act of 1969-providing monetary benefits to workers disabled by black lung disease.

We developed a second bill (the Federal Mine Safety and Health Act) that mandated the reduction of dangerous and explosive levels of coal dust in the mines. It insured safer working conditions for mine workers. But opposition from coal mine owners and their surrogates in the media to that provision delayed its passage for eight years. Those impeding, stalling, delaying its passage were never attacked by yellow journalists of national repute.

James Brown and B'Nai Brith

In early June, I traveled to New York to present James Brown, the "King of Soul" the Humanitarian Award for 1969 from the Music & Performing Arts Lodge of B'nai B'rith. He was honored for his daring exploits during the 1968 riots in Washington, D.C. following Dr. Martin Luther King's assassination. The famous entertainer walked the streets of the city attempting to quiet the melee. He went on television and radio during the riots appealing for calm.

The prestigious event was held at the New York Hilton Hotel. Composer Burt Bacharach and lyricist Hal David received the organization's Creative Award. I presented Brown with a portfolio of letters of commendation written by members of Congress.

More than a thousand donors showed up for the festivities and while enjoying cocktails in an outer room, Dr. George Wiley, founder of the National Welfare Rights Organization and about 500 uninvited members of the organization invaded the main dining room. They occupied the tables, ate the bread, butter, salad, drank the juices and remained seated asking to be served the main course.

Dr. Wiley explained that his followers were hungry and could not afford $250 a plate for the meal. The publicity stunt paid dividends. After 45 minutes of negotiations, B'nai Brith, with minimum fanfare and no police interference, agreed to make a substantial contribution to a feeding program administered by the Welfare Rights Organization.

Plates, silverware, salads and bread were replaced as the affair proceeded without further incident.

Quakers Protest War in Vietnam

In the spring of 1969, the war in Vietnam was still a nagging issue that the Congress refused to address. Capitol Hill police were arresting members of the American Friends (Quakers) who were holding peaceful, quiet demonstrations on the steps of the Capitol. The protestors were neatly dressed in black, orderly behaved and not obstructing public access to the legislative chamber. Their only crime was reading the names of the more than thirty-eight thousand (38,000) American servicemen already killed in Vietnam.

After many were arrested in violation of their right of free speech and assembly, I joined colleagues–George Brown of California, Abner Mikva of Illinois, Ed Koch and Shirley Chisholm of New York–in defending their 1st Amendment rights. We assembled on the steps of the Capitol to express solidarity with them in protest against the war. When they were arrested, we continued to read the names of the troops who had fallen in battle. We were immune from arrest for a misdemeanor while the House of Representatives was in session.

Our challenge to the frivolous charges and the illegal arrests brought an abrupt end to the heavy-handed policy of the Capitol Hill police. However, the incident sparked a furious debate on the House floor, unfortunately, not about the war but about Congresspersons demonstrating on the steps of the Capitol. Accusing us of aiding and abetting the enemy-whatever the hell that meant, was a diversion by House leaders, Democrats and Republicans, to avoid debating the wisdom of the shameful war in Vietnam.

There was no defense for the horrors of war being conducted against the Vietcong. More tonnage of bombs was dropped on Indochina in Nixon's 3 years than President Johnson's 5 years. More than one ton of bombs per minute, every second of Nixon's years in office fell on Vietnam.

More than 50,000 American mothers received telegrams from two Commanders-in-Chief Johnson and Nixon telling them, "I regret to inform you...." I agonized with the survivors, understood their grief, but did not understand Congress' conspiracy of silence.

Speech at the Capitol Hill Press Club

I enjoyed an unusual honor for a freshman Congressman, an invitation to speak before the Capitol Hill Press Club. My remarks attacking the Nixon Administration's contempt for the poor were publicized extensively. In response to those who advised that black people did not support Nixon and should not criticize him, I stated, "I happen to believe that the President has a responsibility to rise above partisan political considerations-he is obliged by the office to serve all the people. He is still my president. Remaining silent while observing injustices - I would do no service to the office, my conscience, or my constituents."

A Speech I Remembered

Early in the Nixon Administration, I delivered a speech at the Cow Palace in San Francisco that I will never forget. I arrived late the evening prior and was driven to the St. Francis Hotel. The next morning after breakfast, I was chauffeured to the auditorium for the 8:15 keynote address.

We entered the convention hall through a rear door and proceeded to the stage area. I stood behind the curtain as the president of the National School Board Association introduced me. Strolling to the microphone amidst loud applause, glancing at the huge audience, I was stunned. Twenty thousand (20,000) delegates were waiting to hear a speaker who usually spoke to several hundreds.

Instead of opening my speech folder to utter remarks about a subject they knew better than I, my instinct convinced me to launch into an attack on the draconian policies of Nixon, Agnew and the conservative "bandits" as I described those who were recommending reduction of federal funding for educational programs.

I spoke of Nixon's exaltations about improving the quality of education for deprived, denied children in ghetto and barrios. Then, I enunciated specific times in the past that he supported use of government resources to deny the quality of life for them. I cited his opposition to "forced busing on the one hand and his support of "forced housing patterns" on the other. My remarks were interrupted numerous times by applause and at the end, I received a standing ovation.

First Year Ends on a Sour Note

During the first year in the Capitol, there was the good, the bad, and the unfortunate. Former President Dwight D. Eisenhower died, hundreds of Vietnamese civilians were massacred at Mylai by U.S. Troops, and Charles Manson killed five people in Los Angeles. On a more pleasant note, Apollo 11 successfully landed on the moon and Astronaut Neil Armstrong proclaimed, "One small step for man, one giant step for mankind."

But on December 11, 1969, the House took a giant step backward, when it voted against a five-year extension of the Voting Rights Act of 1965. Instead, a substitute recommended by Attorney General John Mitchell was accepted that nullified the provisions directly responsible for the election to public office of more than 400 blacks in southern states where there had been none since Reconstruction.

Notes

1/William L. Clay, Sr. rally election night, St. Louis, Missouri, November 1968.

3

"President Richard M. Nixon is not a man of principle but a man in need of principle."[1]

– Congressman Louis Stokes

Richard Nixon was known for his intense, sometimes questionable, unethical campaign tactics. But what happens while scrambling for leverage at the bottom of the heap does not explain or excuse what occurs after arriving at the top. Persons who ignore all ethical rules in getting elected usually continue to disgrace their trust of office once assuming the responsibility to lead.

In every field of human endeavor and personal relations are those who abuse the power conferred on them, who toil constantly to deny rights and privileges meant to be extended for the totality of mankind. President Nixon although adept at concealing his duplicitous behavior involving matters of race, was guilty in many instances of insidious racial practices.

Richard M. Nixon's Presidency—A National Disgrace

During the closing days of the 1968 presidential election, American voters were in a state of apprehension, confusion, suspicion, disbelief and uncertainty about our government's commitment to protect them from looming dangers, both real and imagined. Fantasies spanned the ideological and philosophical spectrum: (1) substantial numbers believed the world's military superpowers were on a collision course toward nuclear war, (2) right-wing extremists chafed at Cuba's President Fidel Castro spreading anti-American propaganda throughout the Caribbean and South America, (3) church leaders recoiled at Soviet Premier Nikita Khrushchev expanding anti-god Communist influence in undeveloped nations, (4) self-proclaimed ideological patriots bristled at China's Chairman Mao Tse-Tung's threats of another invasion of Taiwan, and (5) war hawks cringed at North Vietnam's Ho Chi Minh making mockery of United States' invincible military might.

America's image of the world's most dominant power, tarnished in the ideological Cold War everywhere except Western Europe, faced a challenge of racial unrest at home that it was unprepared to address.

The once impregnable status of unlimited preferential privilege enjoyed by white males was crumbling from the force of massive civil rights demonstrations and legal assaults on denial of civil liberties. Blacks demanded an immediate end to the inequities of racial discrimination and legal segregation; college students questioned the legitimacy of government conscripting them to fight an undeclared war; women sought equality of opportunity through political empowerment and passage of the Equal Rights Amendment to the Constitution; and seniors pressured Congress to preserve Social Security and extend other benefits to the elderly.

Nixon to the Rescue

Desperate for victory in Vietnam, eager for return to a racially separatist society, and disgust with street demonstrations, conservative voters united in hope of electing a Messiah with magical powers to halt intrusions on their sanguine way of life. They envisioned a 'strong-man' politician capable of returning the country to the status quo that existed prior to the marches, the sit-ins, the picket lines, the anti-war street demonstrations.

In the midst of deep division and conflagration Richard M. Nixon rose from the catacombs of the political graveyard after being defeated by John F. Kennedy in the 1960 presidential election and losing his bid for governor of California two years later.

The disastrous Barry Goldwater campaign for President in 1964 established the battle plan for Nixon's political reincarnation.

LBJ's trouncing of Goldwater which also carried to defeat scores of Republican incumbents in the House and Senate, left the Republican Party in shambles. Goldwater's extremism alienated the left and the center of his party, leaving Nixon as the logical person to bring the dissidents together because he had friends on the left, respect on the right, and enthusiastic support in the center.

Resilient, more determined, after Barry Goldwater's humiliating defeat by Lyndon Johnson, Nixon abandoned his self-imposed political exile. He re-entered the skirmish, and became the GOP's 1968 standard bearer.

He conducted a vigorous campaign based on appeal to core principles of conservatism. In glowing generalities, he waged a war of words against the dangers of a permissive society, demanded a return to law and order, pleaded for domestic tranquility, and promised victory with honor in Asia. This mantra became the resonating formula that reenergized the Party and defeated Hubert H. Humphrey, the Democratic candidate.

Democrats lost five seats in the Senate and four in the House, but even so, Republicans were unable to capture control of either body. Democrats retained a majority of 57 to 43 in the Senate and of 243 to 192 in the House.

The Nixon Years: A Struggle
Between Liberal-Conservative Policies

I was there to witness Nixon's assault on progressive, established measures and to combat his attempts at curbing the movement toward a more tolerant, compassionate society.

Shamefully, public pronouncements of administration spokespersons were riveted with animosity toward the poor, and its policy decisions were antagonistic toward people of color. One of Nixon's first official dictums was ordering Secretary of Health, Education and Welfare (HEW) Robert Finch to stop enforcing Title VI of the Civil Rights Act, which required termination of federal contracts to school districts that opposed desegregation of its facilities.

To fully understand the extent of damage the new administration inflicted on civil rights and government's obligation to the economically deprived, it is necessary to review major events which preceded Nixon's arrival. President Harry S. Truman seriously challenged America's racist "apartheid" policies, and proceeded to use the influence of office in rectifying past injustices. Presidents Eisenhower, Kennedy and Johnson continued the effort to eliminate racial disparities, pursuing policies to abate poverty and inequity. They established an Office of Equal Opportunity designed to eradicate discrimination in housing, education and employment. They expanded Medicare, Medicaid, programs for Senior Citizens, and established Federal Aid to Education.

Nixon responded to these legislative and executive actions in the customary public statements of insensitive, reactionary theorists. He decried poverty and racism in the traditional, meaningless jargon of conservative ideologues who portrayed both societal afflictions as unfortunate predicaments and shameful blotches on America's conscience. But his rejoinder invariably lapsed into a long dissertation about the victim's lack of personal discipline, failure to appreciate hard work, and lack of respect for law and order.

Nixon's standard trademark rebuttals included: The poor are poor because they wanted to be poor. Blacks suffer disproportionately because most lack initiative and drive. Attacking the victims of government neglect and legal protection instead of the perpetrators responsible for their conditions was a convenient tactic that allowed him to avoid discussing solutions.

Nixon's Declaration of War

Winning the election by the slimmest margin in recent history, Nixon governed as given a mandate to radically restructure the functions of government. In shattering the hopes of millions depending on a sympathetic government to assist them in times of economic crisis, he declared war on the War on Poverty Program—the one viable program established during the Johnson's Administration that was making an improved impact on their lives.

Nixon eliminated decades-old social programs in his haste to dismantle the War on Poverty, and reversed much of the legal effects of 'Brown v. Board of Education which outlawed discrimination in public schools. His aggressive budgetary assault on anti-poverty, anti-racial programs gave encouragement to those who believed allegations of neo-conservatives that monies spent on welfare and food stamps were wasted tax funds.

Nixon's top appointees seemed obsessed with abolishing what they considered expensive ventures into social experimentation by socialist engineers: low-income housing, school lunches, child nutrition programs, CETA, the Job Corps, and college loans. The administration brigade of budget ax-wielders consolidated executive power and nullified the intent of the programs by placing agency management in the hands of those committed to "annihilating" the Office of Economic Opportunity (OEO), Model Cities, and Legal Services.

The public attitude of Nixon operatives toward the War on Poverty was brutally frank. Patrick Buchanan, special White House assistant, suggested the transfer of anti-poverty grants from economically depressed black and Latino ghettoes to more affluent Jewish and Italian neighborhoods. The War on Poverty never really got off the ground because it was undermined by Nixon and his cohorts after the 1968 election. The program was "sabotaged by Nixon, Howard Phillips, and others who were commissioned to wage war"[2] on it.

Revenue Sharing

Adopting Nixon's "Block Grants" was a clever policy initiative designed to mask subliminal intent to nullify effects of programs enacted to combat economic and racial discrimination. Despite the publicly announced purpose to give fifty states more flexibility in tailoring programs to fit specific needs, and address unique situations, the underlying reason was much more politically sinister: to eliminate federal categorical grants that originally targeted monies to specific areas for protecting the poor, sick, aged and minorities.

When congress passed the 'block grant' measure which I opposed, Republican supporters blitzed the airwaves with propaganda about local officials "knowing better" how to serve local needs than bureaucrats in Washington, D.C. And they surely began to serve local needs—their own. More parks, street lights, police equipment, and recreational facilities were provided to upper income neighborhoods at the expense of blighted and poor ones.

Under lenient block grant rules, states quickly diverted resources from programs for the poor to higher income, influential individuals and neighborhoods. Lacking political clout and government oversight, the interests of minorities, the elderly and the handicapped were compromised or ignored altogether. The "no strings attached" federal monies were transferred to other state priorities unrelated to their original intent.

Closing of Job Corps Centers

Nixon instructed Secretary of Labor George Shultz to eliminate 59 Job Corps centers. The presidential order proposed scaling down the number of student trainees from 17,000 to 4.500. The centers represented the only viable government sponsored training system for disadvantaged youth.

The program cost $8,000 per student, per year with a recorded 30% dropped-out rate. But every job corps enrollee was already a drop-out. Amazingly, 70% of the former drop-outs who completed the program, graduated and became productive income-earning, taxpaying citizens. This return made the investment one of our government's most successful.

The facility in my district that enrolled 600 women was closed. It had trained them in clerical work, retail selling, graphic arts and cosmetology. After 16 months of rigorous training, a majority of the young adults were placed in meaningful jobs.

Rep. Carl Perkins (D-Kent), chairman of the House Education Committee, appointed me to a special committee to investigate ramifications of the closures. Texas congressman Jake Pickle invited the committee to tour the Gary Job Corps Center, a flagship training facility, located in his district.

Republicans and Democrats visited the facility and other sites, examined their programs, and structured legislation that saved 60% of the centers the administration slated for closure. It became apparent that the centers revealed that with minimal federal dollars, individuals receiving training in job skills could become productive, tax paying members of the community.

Later, I secured funds for opening a new site in my district.

Nixon Pushed Repressive Crime Bill

During the election campaign, there was a prevalent and pervasive rumor that the President and his cohorts had a secret plan to build concentration camps to incarcerate radical black dissidents. By the middle of Nixon's first year in office, the rumor grew legs. Attorney General John Mitchell drafted and introduced in Congress the District of Columbia Court Reform and Criminal Procedure Act, declaring the measure to be "a model" for other cities suffering a crime epidemic. The bill called for imposition of life imprisonment for a third felony conviction; stated there was no justifiable or excusable reason for forcibly resisting arrest, even if the arrest was unlawful; provided that juveniles 16 or older would be tried as adults if charged with murder, forcible rape, first-degree burglary, armed robbery, or assault with the intent to commit any of those offenses.

The most obnoxious and controversial features were: (1) authorization of pretrial detention for up to 60 days for a person charged with a dangerous crime, and (2) a no-knock provision that allowed police officers to enter private premises without notice or search warrant if the officer had probable cause to believe that notice was likely to result in the destruction of criminal evidence or to pose a danger to the life and safety of the police or another person.

The administration bill passed both houses of Congress by wide margins. On July 29, 1970, President Nixon signed into law the District of Columbia Court Reform Act. However, there was no attempt to extend the same stringent provisions nationwide. Limiting the racially motivated, politically inspired crime reduction measures to a city of 75% Black population tended to give credence to the fear expressed about concentration camps for incarcerating African Americans.

Retreat of Civil Rights Enforcement

Clifford Alexander, Jr., chairman of the Equal Employment Opportunity Commission (EEOC) charged the U.S. Civil Service Commission with gross discriminatory practices within its own agency. In addition, he produced evidence of rampant acts of discrimination throughout the entire system.

During Senate hearings, Republican Leaders Strom Thurmond and Everett Dirksen accused him of harassing private **businesses** and threatened to get him fired. The next day, Nixon announced that he was replacing Alexander.

Five House members, including me, took issue, sending the President a letter, stating, "We view with grave concern the current attacks on the EEOC in its efforts to seek compliance with the duly constituted law enacted by Congress in the Civil Rights Act of 1964."[3]

We cited approval of Defense Department contracts to Southern textile mills that practiced racial discrimination, and the Transportation Department' not requiring proof of non-discrimination before awarding highway contracts. Neither caused concern among administration leaders.

We were more disturbed when Alexander's successor, appointed by Nixon proposed to hold hearings on charges of discrimination in closed session. We objected, stating that such procedure of the public's business would allow Dirksen, Thurmond and others to, "effectively manipulate the machinery established to prevent compliance with the law in the darkness of night."[4]

Divisive Vietnam War

The issue of dividing Vietnam between the North and South was the most divisive incident for Americans since the Civil War fought to prevent a similar division of the United States. The controversy also divided Congress between those for and against (hawks and doves); between super patriots who wanted to stop the spread of communism from the North and opponents who refused to fight for a corrupt government in the South; between young men expected to fight, and old men deciding when and where they would meet the enemy. It divided American men into two classes: those who would use their power, influence and education to dodge the military and those not educated nor clever enough or politically connected enough to evade the mighty draft were called up for duty and sent off to fight.

For the black community, it was all of theses and the added one of its effect on the moral struggle for equality. Blacks were divided as sharply, acutely and vehemently as the rest of society.

Dr. Martin Luther King, Jr.'s announcement of opposition to the war and a commitment of his resources to end it, caused serious disruption among acknowledged leaders in the fight for equal rights. Roy Wilkins of the NAACP, Whitney Young of the Urban League and James Farmer of CORE described his position an attack on President Johnson and a diversion of energy and resources away from the struggle for civil rights. Younger leaders, including myself, saw no disrespect for the heroic efforts extended by LBJ to win our freedom. I recognized, understood and appreciated that Lyndon Baines Johnson established the mold for measuring all past and future Presidents on the question of racial fairness and the sharing of responsibility and power. With the exception of President Truman, none measured up to LBJ in this regard. President Johnson appointed the first black in history as Solicitor General (Thurgood Marshall"; the first black to sit on the U.S. Supreme Court (Thurgood Marshall); two blacks, Spottswood W. Robinson and Wade H. McCree Jr., to the Court of Appeals, the first black cabinet member (Robert Weaver) as Secretary of Housing and Urban Development, the first black to the Federal Reserve System (Andrew Brimmer); the first black female Ambassador (Patricia Harris); the first black director of the Export-Import Bank (Hobart Taylor Jr.); the first black female judge (Constance Baker Motley); the first black member of the Atomic Energy Commission (Samuel Nabritt); and the first black director of the U.S. Information Agency (Carl Rowan).

As a somewhat history buff, I was well aware of President Johnson's contribution to our struggle but like others who felt a grave obligation to oppose a war 7,000 miles of questionable value, I stated my opposition against a war not the sterling civil rights record of the icon that established it.

Agitation for War Moratorium

Legislators attempting to force a full and open debate of the United States' continuing to pursue its misguided policy in Vietnam, were repelled by leaders of both parties and the President. Failure to secure time to discuss the issue in regular session of the House resulted in our scheduling an all-night 'talkfest' that coincided with the observance of a National Moratorium Day against the war.

Twenty members reserved thirty minutes each under the Special Order Rule which permitted such action after the conclusion of the House's regular business. At approximately 8:30 p.m. the marathon discussion began. At 1:50 a.m., ten minutes before my turn to speak, a supporter of the war came to the floor and requested a quorum call. Impossible to assemble 218 members at that time of morning, the session was forced to a premature closing.

The next day, I was recognized by the Speaker and given an opportunity to vent displeasure with the panic-struck pro-war member who felt Congress had no right to question a policy which had taken 45,000 American lives, drained the country's financial resources, and generated massive and disruptive street protests.

Expressing dissatisfaction with the country's lack of action, I stated in part:

> *"Eight hundred and fifty-nine of my fellow Missourians have fallen in Vietnam and still our Government cannot tell us why...I am here today because I have hope that this Government of the people–will eventually respond to the will of the people."* [5]

Response to Nixon's 1970 State of Union

In his 1970 State of the Union, Nixon accused Democrats of wanting to spend the country into an inflationary spiral with added social programs. A week later, he vetoed a $1.3 billion health, education and welfare funding bill. Thirty-five southern Democrats abandoning the Party's convention platform supporting the provision, joined Republicans in sustaining the veto. Liberal and moderate Democrats were furious.

In a dramatic rebuttal to Nixon's State of the Union address, we organized a nationally televised response to the President's inaccurate statement for vetoing the measure. The national networks granted us one hour to respond. Instead of selecting one person to deliver the "True State of the Union," we divided the time into 4 segments and presented 15 minutes in four separate regions. Unlike traditional responses, (12) Senators and (11) House members journeyed to five states, responding in a coordinated fashion. Thousands gathered in auditoriums to hear us expose the President's partisan, erroneous charges.

Accompanied by Senator William Hart of Michigan and Rep. Bill Green (D-Pa.), I went to Detroit. We met in downtown Detroit and delivered our message to a nationally televised audience and to a capacity crowd at the spacious Cobo Hall.

Nixon charged in his veto message that appropriating funds for health programs was inflationary. My retort, "Nixon can live with a budget that appropriates $400 per person for defense, but not a bill that appropriates $13 per person for health."[6]

Supreme Court Nominations Rejected

A full blown, major confrontation between the President and the Congress was his nomination of a reactionary southern judge to the Supreme Court.

Attempting to fill the seat vacated when President Johnson's appointee, Abe Fortas, laboring under a cloud of alleged criminal misconduct, resigned, Nixon nominated Clement F. Haynsworth of South Carolina as the replacement, claiming it necessary to restore sectional and ideological balance to the Court. He believed it important to place a southern conservative on the bench because under Chief Justice Earl Warren, 'the Court' had gone too far in reflecting liberal bias.

Liberals, moderates, minorities, academics, union leaders accused the President of using the appointment to reward the deep south for supporting his election, and organized to stop the enhancement of his "southern strategy." The American Trial Lawyers Association feared that Haynsworth would "undermine confidence in the Court." Labor leaders cited his numerous conflicts of interests in rulings. The Leadership Conference said that he "paid lip service to desegregation." The Executive Director of the NAACP claimed Haynsworth would grant Negroes their rights with "an eye dropper."

Eight black members of the House issued a statement opposing the nomination. Five of us, Chisholm, Conyers, Diggs, Stokes and I testified before Senator Philip A. Hart (D-Mich.) chairman of the Senate Judiciary Committee, accusing him of "infidelity to the principles of racial equality." Conyers served as the spokesperson for the group. Nix, Powell and Hawkins, not in attendance, also opposed the nomination. Haynsworth was rejected by a vote of 55 to 45.

Carswell Nominated and Rejected
for Supreme Court

Nixon's second nomination for the judicial seat was G. Harrold Carswell, another southern bred conservative politician. He was appointed in 1953 as the U.S. Attorney for the Northern District of Florida by Eisenhower. Five years later, at age 38, Eisenhower appointed him a federal judge, the youngest in the nation.

It was expected that Carswell would have no difficulty in being confirmed. But Nixon's aspiration to elevate southern extremists was tested again. Carswell's high-speed express train toward confirmation was derailed when the contents of a speech delivered to the Mercer University law school 22 years prior surfaced. While campaigning for the state legislature in Georgia, he bragged of his cultural upbringing and declared his life-long commitment to upholding intolerant principles of racism.

In a campaign speech before an American Legion chapter at Gordon, Georgia on August 2, 1948, Carswell said:

I am southern by ancestry, birth, training, inclination, belief and practice. And I believe that segregation of the races is proper and the only practical and correct way of life in our states. I have always so believed and I shall always so act.

I shall be the last to submit to any attempt on the part of anyone to break down and to weaken this firmly established policy of our people. I yield to no man, as a fellow candidate or as a fellow citizen, in the firm, vigorous belief in the principles of white supremacy, and I shall always be so governed.[7]

During the same speech, he denounced the Fair Employment Practices Commission as a sham and referred to the Civil Rights Program as the Civil Wrongs Program. He said that pursuing a course of racial equality was an attempt to "corral the bloc voting of Harlem."[8]

His opponent, Alexander Stephen Boone, also an avowed racist and great advocate of white supremacy, easily won the election.

In a written statement, I noted, "there is no place for a racist in the highest judicial office. In the letter's closing, I wrote, "The Senate must determine, not whether Carswell has the 'right' to serve, but whether he has earned the 'privilege'."[9]

Based on the nominees 1948 inflammatory statements, and his more recent activities of extra-judicial conduct in advising sheriffs to evade the law, aiding and abetting in a scheme to elude the legal integration of a city-owned golf club, and an obvious lack of judicial qualifications, the Senate rejected Carswell 51 to 45.

President Nixon Denies Having
A Southern Strategy

Although President Nixon constantly denied that he was developing a 'southern strategy,' deeds by him and his chief administrative officers flew in the face of evidence to the contrary. Most of his policy initiatives were designed to garner white voters in the South by questioning the legitimacy of black quests for racial justice.

Numerous southern construction companies were illegally awarded government contracts without signing compliance papers on equal employment requirement; southern school districts were allowed inordinate amounts of time to delay desegregating as mandated by court order; openly and admitted bigoted attorneys were appointed to the U.S. District and Appellate Courts; two were even nominated but defeated for the U.S. Supreme Court; appointed officials to the Department of Housing and Urban Development (HUD) who ignored open housing violations.

Nixon was silent as Republican House Minority Leader Gerald Ford unabashedly supported passage of an amendment to the Health, Education and Welfare appropriations bill that would legalize "freedom of choice" school desegregation plans which had already been declared unconstitutional by the courts.

In the area of voting rights, Nixon opposed extension of the 1965 Voting Rights Act and his Attorney General John Mitchell laid out recommendations to dilute the act. The President reiterated his position that there was no justification for regional voting rights legislation. He supported Mitchell's call for placing registrars equally throughout the nation, even in areas where there was no intimidation of Negroes attempting to register. The effort to weaken the effectiveness of the Act was viewed as honoring a commitment to southern supporters.

Despite denying a 'southern strategy,' it was a fact of life in the Nixon administration.

Boycott Nixon's State of Union Address

In 1971, the consensus of the CBC was a 'deep and dangerous alienation' of the country's 25 million blacks existed and the need to take the matter up with President Nixon was urgent. For months, he refused to meet with the CBC.

Seated on the House floor two days before Nixon was to deliver his State of the Union address, Stokes told me we must do something dramatic and suggested CBC members boycott his address.

The 12 black members, in a bold move of unity, agreed. The media and elected officials, Republican and Democrats, feigned indignation at the disrespect shown for the Office of the President. Unfortunately, most of them were not equally aggrieved by the occupant of the 'Oval Office' in his callous and contemptuous disrespect of the rights of the minority citizens.

Nixon's Minority Appointees
(A Sparkle of Light)

In stark contradiction to Nixon's hard-line, extremely conservative opposition to specific civil rights initiatives and general attempts to reverse well established gains of minorities, his record of appointing credible, non-judicial blacks was praiseworthy.

Although none was named in his first term to the cabinet, distinguished blacks were appointed to sub-cabinet and other important positions. In the first 18 months, he placed 65 blacks in policy-making positions. The highest ranking were James Farmer, assistant secretary of Health, Education, and Welfare; Arthur Fletcher, assistant secretary of Labor; Samuel Jackson, assistant secretary of HUD; Abraham Venerable, assistant secretary of Commerce; and William Brown III, chairman of the Equal Employment Opportunities Commission.

Most appointees were individuals of integrity, experience, and ability who served the nation well, and at the same time strived to insure that members of their race received government benefits comparable to others.

Appointees John Wilks, deputy assistant secretary of labor; John Blake, director of manpower; Curtis Crawford, U.S. Parole Commission, Robert Brown, Special Assistant to the President; General Daniel "Chappie" James, liaison to the Defense Department; C. Payne Lucas, of the Peace Corps sometimes publicly disagreed with Administration policy of matters affecting minorities. Their advice sometimes in private, often not so private, frequently went un-heeded.

Arthur Fletcher was typical of the character and quality of appointees. The title "father of affirmative action" was conferred on him by Democrats and Republicans for implementation of the 'Philadelphia Plan' which forced the racially discriminatory construction unions to set goals for hiring minorities and to make "good faith effort" to meet those commitments or face sanctions.

The Philadelphia Plan

Inclusion of blacks in construction jobs on projects funded with federal dollars was immensely successful due to the personal ability and insistence of Fletcher. After a series of disruptive protests at job sites in Pittsburgh, Chicago, and other cities between blacks seeking jobs in the construction industry and members of the rigidly segregated AFL-CIO Building Trades Union, Secretary of Labor George Schultz proposed the 1969 Philadelphia Plan. The far-reaching proposal required equal job opportunities for minorities on federally assisted construction projects.

Fletcher who drafted the plan was assigned the responsibility of enforcing it. He was the driving force behind its implementation and doggedly pursued its objectives until labor unions admitted minorities into membership.

African Americans Absent in Nixon's 2nd Term

Before the general election in November 1972, Nixon invited his highest black appointees to a meeting and requested they submit preferences of positions in the next administration. Some chose the cabinet. A few wanted to head independent agencies. Others expressed interests in ambassadorships to African and Caribbean nations.

In the 1968 campaign, political analyst credited Nixon's close victory to his last minute promise of a secret plan to end the war. Four years later and tens of thousands human fatalities, the secret was still secret. Again in the 1972 balloting, he proclaimed that peace was imminent and he won in a landslide over George McGovern-victorious in 49 of the fifty states.

But failure to win substantial black voter support (only 15%), caused a reevaluation of the strategy to showcase blacks in high positions.

Those blacks hoping to become ambassadors, agency heads, or cabinet members were more than disappointed. In the 2nd Administration, they were fired from their present positions.

Busing: The Nixon Manifesto–
Separate But Unequal

The method by which Nixon and other politicians aroused public anger over busing was fraught with coded messages fomenting bigotry. Inflammatory phrases as "busing for racial balance" and "forced integration" to describe the transportation of black children to desegregate all-white schools and equalize the distribution of tax resources, was a ploy to generate support for candidates seeking to preserve separation of the races.

Nixon's attitude in this regard was cynical and callous. He stated that busing was a "classic case of the remedy for one evil creating another evil."[10] Concurrent with his attack on busing, the President unsuccessfully attempted to extend tax-exempt status to "segregated academies" in violation of government policy and Constitutional law. More than 500,000 students had enrolled in these illegal schools to avoid attending desegregated public schools.

In March 22, 1971, I delivered extensive remarks on the House floor denouncing the fraud:

President Nixon disgracefully called for a return to public education as it existed prior to May 17, 1954. Appealing to the base instincts in American people, he added fuel to the flames of racial hate which now engulf our country. He started his defense of a separate but equal society on a false premise that U.S. District Courts have been ordering "massive busing" for the purpose of racial balance. What might I ask constitutes "massive busing? Is it real or illusory?

The real issue...is that of race. The so-called evils only become emotional monsters when that big yellow bus filled with little white kids terminates at the little red school house which happens to have black and brown students enrolled. There is no such animal in the educational system as "neighborhood school." Anyone who alludes to it is injecting a dimension into the debate which smacks of racism. The fact is that more than 60% of all American children attending school today are arriving there by bus.[11]

Nixon's Civil Rights Stance Attacked

The disagreement between administration spokesmen and

black leaders over civil rights continued to make front page news. In March 1970, twenty-one leaders lambasted the Nixon Administration for a "calculated...systemic effort" to overturn the civil rights gains of the 1950's and 1960's. In October 1970, the U.S. Civil Rights Commission stated:

> ...total civil rights policy has not been developed (by the Nixon Administration), nor have overall national civil rights goals been established to govern components by the Federal civil rights efforts.[12]

A year later, the Commission criticized what it described as "...inertia on the part of the federal bureaucracy, in some cases a blind, unthinking, fidelity to the status quo, in others a calculated determination to do nothing to advance the cause of civil rights."[13]

Rep. Hawkins spoke out, "Nixon completely overlooked and refused to even mention any of the more than sixty proposals presented to him by the Congressional Black Caucus. The entire message (State of Union) in our view, was received as evangelistic meandering with nothing encouraging or helpful for the situation of black people..."[14]

Nixon and Allegations of Racism

Columnist Milton Viorst of the now-defunct *Washington Evening Star* newspaper, wrote:

> "Is Nixon a racist? Before we can answer that question, we had better—as we often said when in college—define our terms.
>
> We know, of course, that he's no gallus-snapper of the old school of racist demagogues. We know, too, that he's probably no Archie Bunker, paranoid that some black is about to take his job, if not seduce his daughter."[15]

Despite any or all definitions of racist, a majority of black Americans believed—correctly or incorrectly—that Nixon's list of priorities threatened them as a class, and sensed that racism motivated most of his decisions. Black leaders, even those considered moderate, viewed the policies and programs promoted by Nixon and his Administration detrimental to the continued well-being of their people.

Nixon was adept at fanning the flames of a "white backlash" against the advancement of Negro rights. His carefully concealed anti-black rhetoric and bombast was an effective means of giving credibility and respectability to the latent racism pervasive in the country. Congressman Stokes (D-Ohio) expressed the sentiment of most black leaders in describing Nixon's administration "a nightmare for black Americans."

Nine days after assuming the presidency, the President postponed for 60 days the implementation of a directive issued by the Department of Health, Education and Welfare to cut off federal funds to five southern school districts that had failed to abolish practices of segregation. That was the first volley in a constant series of attempts to nullify court and congressional mandates against racial inequality.

Nixon used inflammatory phrases to describe black children bused to desegregate unconstitutionally segregated schools in 11 southern states. He advocated weakening guidelines to comply with the law although 90 percent of the white children were being bused to all-white public schools.

The philosophical basis used by the Administration to justify its failure to aggressively pursue equal rights for blacks was captured in a now famous memorandum from domestic advisor to the President. Daniel Patrick Moynihan, later the U.S. Senator from New York asserted that continued government aid to blacks would have the potential not only to enrage large number of whites, but also to stymie individual initiative of blacks. He emphasized that the progress of Negroes was more than they expected and much more than whites could humanly tolerate. In the memo, he counseled that "the time may [have] come when the issue of race could benefit from a period of 'benign neglect.'"[16]

The President provided the forum, the vehicle, and the cover of respectability for acts of racism by others. His intentions were legitimately questioned by decent citizens familiar with his past performances. His stand on busing was indicative of intellectual dishonesty. Concurrent with his attack on it, he attempted to extend tax-exempt status to "segregated academies" in violation of government policy and law.

In August 1972 the House of Representatives passed the Equal Educational Opportunities Act, a mischievously-named, anti-busing proposal recommended by the President. Rep. Louis Stokes (D-Ohio) issued a blistering attack on the measure as "fraudulent and bigoted" supported by segregationists and so-called liberals alike…"[17]

A coalition of 126 civil rights organizations asked President Nixon to cut off federal aid to communities that violated the Open Housing Act by barring housing needs to low-income families through illegal zoning practices. His response was that the government would not prosecute open-housing cases on economic grounds. He stated that to equate poor with black does a disservice to the truth. However, it was clear that the issues involved were separate. The Leadership Conference declared that the President had "diagnosed a cancer and prescribed aspirin as the remedy."[18]

The attacks launched by Nixon and his Administration on social programs were seldom expressed in anti-black rhetoric but the result was the same. They wanted it both ways: support for "economic discrimination" in suburban housing yet he issued a pious declaration decrying the conditions under which minorities were forced to live. He opposed forced busing on the one hand, but protected "forced" patterns of housing discrimination on the other.

President Nixon confided in John Ehrlichman that Johnson's Great Society programs were a waste of resources and that "America's blacks could only marginally benefit because blacks were genetically inferior to whites."[19] He also ordered the Internal Revenue Service to investigate big Jewish Democratic contributors. He said to Chief of Staff H.R. Haldeman, "Please get me the names of the Jews. You know, the big Jewish contributors to the Democrats. Could you please investigate some of the [expletives]"[20]

It is an interesting and unusual phenomenon that so many scribes, reporters, and historians (both black and white) raise the question of Nixon and racism. Author Charles V. Hamilton in The Black Experience in American Politics projects the question in a different venue:

Obviously, then, it is difficult to tell whether or not Nixon himself is racist or whether he supports racist, or whether his administration is an apologist for racist philosophy cloaked in frontier-style American fundamentalism (which was itself racist).[21]

Novelist Kenneth O'Reilly, author of Nixon's Piano, in questioning the President's racism, said:

"He did so [courted the white majority] not necessarily because he was racist himself per se (although there is some sad evidence of that), but because he saw political fortune in the simple fact that there were more white people than black."[22]

Earlier in this chapter, I quoted an article by Milton Voirst that asked if Richard M. Nixon was a racist. It ended by saying: "We may all be racists. But Richard Nixon has shown a willingness to use his power to be more racist than the rest of us."[23]

Watergate Brought Down President Nixon

In mid-1971, the *New York Times* began a series of articles based on what it called the Pentagon Papers. The papers released by Daniel Ellsberg, a government analyst, were top secret documents that revealed horrendous, possible impeachable activity engaged in by high level administration officials. According to Nixon, the leaked classified Vietnam War documents violated the law. But the Supreme Court ruled the newspaper's printing them was constitutionally protected speech under the First Amendment.

Ellsberg was indicted for theft of government property and the unauthorized possession of documents and writings related to national defense. Fearful that he had also given records to the Democratic candidate, George McGovern, President Nixon, through his White House operatives, authorized the creation of a thuggish group to thwart any use that might be embarrassing. The group, headed by a former CIA agent, surreptitiously burglarized the offices of the National Democratic Committee located in the Watergate apartments.

Search for Politically Damaging Documents

At first, White House Press Secretary Ron Ziegler described the break-in as a: "third-rate burglary attempt." But when it was revealed that five men accused of the break-in had close ties to high-ranking Nixon operatives, the suspense of the drama began to unfold. The cover-up and the unlawful activities of the Nixon Re-election Committee, conspiring with Cabinet members and the President were exposed for public consumption by two *Washington Post* investigative reporters, Carl Bernstein and Bob Woodward.

Three top Nixon aides were convicted: Attorney General John Mitchell, Chief of Staff H.R. Haldeman and domestic advisor John Ehrlichman. Federal Judge John Sirica sentenced them from Two-and-a half to eight years for involvement in the Watergate cover-up. Twenty others went to jail for their part in the conspiracy. The five White House "plumbers" as the burglars were called pleaded guilty to breaking into the Democratic national headquarters and went to prison.

Demand for Impeachment of the President

In an October 1974 letter to Speaker Carl Albert, I was one of the earliest members to insist on gathering information to decide if President Nixon should be impeached. I stated, "Many recent developments, including the resignation of Spiro T. Agnew and the maneuvering in his 'plea bargaining', raise grave questions concerning our system of government. If the House of Representatives is the most deliberative body in the world, and if indeed here "the people speak," then our obligation is to seek answers to these most pressing questions.

Therefore, Mr. Speaker, before the body considers the nomination of Rep. Gerald Ford for Vice-President, it is incumbent on us to deal with this more fundamental crisis.

At the root of the question is whether or not Mr. Nixon should be impeached... If confidence in government is to be restored, the House cannot acquiesce to the traditional game of politics, but must act with conscience and respond to the concerns of the people."

A month later, I joined three other members of the CBC, Parren Mitchell, Andrew Young, and Louis Stokes, in asking for preliminary proceedings leading to consideration of impeachment. Our demand was based on President Nixon's attempt to keep the infamous White House tapes secret from the U. S. Courts and Congress, the impropriety hanging over the purchase of his San Clemente home, the legality of the Howard Hughes contribution, the Soviet Wheat Deal, the ITT anti-trust situation and other alleged indiscretions.

Nixon never admitted wrong doing and never served time in jail. Under the threat of impeachment, however, he resigned. Accepting a pardon from President Ford, he stated that he was wrong in not acting more decisively and forthrightly in dealing with Watergate. His confession was ironic. His crime was that he acted too decisively and too forthrightly in conducting the Watergate criminal cover-up.

The 37th President of the United States, always complex and complicated, strived all his life for respect among his peers and yearned for respectability among the general public. He received the former, but somehow the latter eluded his grasp.

Other Illegal Activities of CIA

Watergate was not the only horrendous act involving the CIA on President Nixon's watch. The agencies 1970 covert mission in destabilizing the democratically elected government of Salvador Allende in Chile was another stain on the Agency's record.

Chief Executive Harold Geneen and Senior Vice President Edward Gerrity of International Telephone and Telegraph, fearing its conglomerate would be nationalized, in collaboration with CIA Director Richard Helms plotted to undermine the fiscal stability of Chile's economy and supported the military overthrow of the government. Nixon ordered a number of crippling economic sanctions against the country—all in the name of stopping the spread of communism in South America.

The CIA alleged that Allende committed suicide rather than be captured alive. But creditable evidence indicated he was murdered by the conspirators who replaced him with dictator Ugarte

Pinochet who murdered and tortured tens of thousands during his 17 year repressive rule.

Enemies of America

While the sordid mess was untangling, it was revealed that Nixon had compiled an enemies list composed of corporate heads, lawyers, former Cabinet members, elected officials, insurance executives, labor leaders, civil rights advocates, publishers, and editors. On the list were 10 members of the Senate and 18 of the House, including me.

Hundreds of individuals and groups were spied upon, their telephones illegally tapped, and homes and businesses electronically wired without court warrants. We were subjected to numerous kinds of harassment by government officials and agencies, including the Internal Revenue Service and Justice Department. Damaging, and often false information was released by government agents who alleged criminal conduct or unethical behavior where none existed.

The Lesson of Watergate Unheeded

Watergate in the final analysis was a crude conspiracy against the people of the United States who disagreed with those in political power. Its abuses of law and denial of liberties uncovered during the break in began long before the burglars were apprehended. The country's chief law enforcement agencies and their agents were breaking the law in numerous and arbitrary ways.

If we did not learn the lesson from this horrible experience, then all have been in vain. Obviously, it was a continuation of official government policies of abuse that had been silently condoned for years. Giving credence to the charge of conspiracies against political opponents was verified in a report of the Senate Intelligence Committee, headed by Senator Frank Church (D-Idaho). Its investigation into the activities of the FBI and CIA gave a sordid picture of the extent government officials would go to malign and destroy their opposition. FBI Director J. Edgar Hoover instituted campaigns to destroy the Socialist Workers Party, the Southern Christian Leadership Conference, the Student Nonviolent Coordination Committee

(SNCC), the Committee on Racial Equality (CORE), and individuals as Dr. Martin Luther King, Jr. and Malcolm X.

The well established paranoia of a federal agency and its schizophrenic director [Hoover] on the matter of African American and liberal leadership should have been sufficient cause for the Congress to ask whether Watergate was an isolated effort, or whether it was a pattern more pervasive in governmental life? Sadly, It did not.

NOTES

1/Congressman Louis Stokes, Chase-Park Plaza
Hotel, St. Louis, Mo. June 1970.
2/Carl T. Rowan: *Breaking Barriers,* Little, Brown and Company, Boston, 1991, page 354.
3/Rep. William L. Clay's Letter to President Nixon from five members of Congress, re: EEOC
4/Congressman William L. Clay, statement challenging chairman of EEOC, William Brown.
5/Congressman William L. Clay (D-Mo), Speech on Vietnam War, U.S. House of Representatives, Washington, D.C., 15 October 1969.
6/Congressman William L. Clay, Detroit Michigan,. Response to Nixon's State of the Union.
7/Harrold Carswell, "Excerpts from Carswell Talk," *N.Y. Times*, 21 January 1970, page 1.
8/Ibid., page 10
9/Congressman Clay, Letter to /Senate
10/President Nixon on Busing, source unknown.
11/Congresssman Clay, *Congressional Record,* U.S. House of Representatives, May 25, 1971, pp. H 4333-4367.
12/Report of the U.S. Civil Rights Commission, 1970.
13/Ibid.
14/Congressman Augustus Hawkins, CBC press release entitled, "From the Administration Which Gave Us Benign Neglect," March 1972.
15/Milton Viorst, *Washington Evening Star,* 7 September 1972.
16/Daniel Patrick Moynihan, *The Negro Almanac*: A Reference Work on the Afro-American, edited by Harry A. Ploski (New York: The Bellwether Company, 1976, page 61.
17/Louis Stokes, press release, 22 March 1972, Washington, D.C.
18/Lawrence F. O'Brien, chairman Democratic National Committee, 1 October 1971.
19/*The Free Press,* Nixon's Piano, Kenneth O'Reilly, 1995, New York, page 327.

20/ Barbara J. Saffir, Nixon Ordered Probe of the "Big Jewish Contributors," *Washington Post,* 11 December 1996, A-8.

21/Charles V. Hamilton, *The Black Experience in American Politics*, New York: Capricorn Books, G. Putnam' Sons, 1973, page 343.

22/*The Free Press,* Nixon's Piano, Kenneth O'Reilly, 1995, New York, page 279.

23/Milton Viorst, *Washington Evening Star,* 7 September 1972.

24/Congressman Clay, Letter to Speaker, Carl Albert, October 1974

4

The Congressional Black Caucus was founded in conscious deliberation and dedicated to eliminating the lingering barriers to equal justice and equal opportunity.[1]

—L. Douglas Wilder, Governor
Commonwealth of Virginia

Forming Congressional Black Caucus

The absence of black representation in the seats of government revealed a glaring fallacy in America's claim of representative democracy. But the 1968 national elections reflected a changing fortune in minority politics. The elections of Shirley Chisholm, Louis Stokes and me sent a clear message that black folk were serious about inclusion in institutions that wielded political power and dispensed economic benefits.

We joined six blacks from five other states (Conyers and Diggs of Michigan, Nix of Pennsylvania. Dawson of Illinois, Powell of New York, and Hawkins of California.) With the exception of Dawson, the other four were also the first of their race elected from their respective states. Nine African Americans from seven states, although an accomplishment worth celebrating, also highlighted the lack of minority elective opportunity in the other 43 states.

Before our arrival, Diggs, Conyers and Hawkins organized the Democratic Select Committee to address critical problems facing black Americans. Diggs, as titular head of the umbrella group, was a contact with the Democratic leadership in seeking legislative support of issues pertinent to the welfare of minorities.

Hearing on Black Panther Executions

The ad hoc committee's first nationally publicized activity took place When Alderman A.A. "Sammy" Rayner and other Chicago black elected officials requested our assistance to investigate police complicity in the killing of two black leaders. Rayner described the killing of Black Panthers Fred Hampton and Mark Clark as "assassinations."

Under the banner of the National Black Panther Party, Hampton and Clark implemented relief programs to feed the hungry, established after-school recreation activities, and provided shelter for the homeless. Their initiatives undercut Mayor Richard Daley's boastful propaganda of adequately providing for the city's needy.

Despite their humanitarian agenda and community acceptance, the Panthers were labeled radicals, accused of designs to overthrow the government, and targeted for harassment by the media and law enforcement agencies. Agents of the Justice Department tapped telephones of the Panther's headquarters, and bugged the homes of its leaders.

FBI Director J. Edgar Hoover called them the single "most dangerous enemy" to the internal security of the United States. It was a characterization he often used to label black leaders as Dr. Martin Luther King, Malcolm X and others. It was also a commonly used phrase of Adolph Eichmann, architect of the policy that sent Jews to the death camps.

At 4:44 A.M, December 4, 1969, fifteen Chicago policemen, on instructions from Cook County state attorney, Edward V. Hanrahan, in unmarked cars, armed with 38 caliber revolvers, .30 caliber carbines, 357 magnums,.45-caliber Thompson submachine guns, went to the Westside dwelling of Black Panther members. With a map of where the two Panthers slept, within a matter of minutes, they riddled with bullets the wooden framed four room residence, killing Clark and Hampton.

Hanrahan announced that they were killed in a shoot out with police and produced photographs of 18 weapons allegedly seized in the raid. Seven other people were asleep in the house, four of them critically wounded. The police admitted firing more than 300 rounds into the house.

Black Chicagoans were shocked and outraged by photographs appearing in the newspapers and on television, showing the extent to which the house was pierced with bullets. Thousands paid last respects to the remains of Clark and Hampton. Rev. Ralph Abernathy, Jesse Jackson and Dr. Spock spoke to more than 5,000 mourners at a memorial service.

On December 20, 1969, the Select Committee convened a hearing at A.R. Leaks Colonial House in Chicago, hearing testimony that described the illegal campaign of harassment conducted against the Panthers by the police, FBI and the media. The only logical conclusion was it was a well-planned massacre.

Physical evidence at the scene indicated that police broke in while the occupants were asleep and fired shots into their bodies while still in bed.

Four respected leaders testified: Ralph Metcalf, Gus Savage, Harold Washington and Bobby Rush. In later years, each was elected to congress. Rush, a close friend of Clark and Hampton, was an officer in the Panthers organization.

The ad hoc committee released a highly critical report on January 26, 1970 titled, "Investigation of Black Panther killing." Subsequently, the U.S. Justice Department launched its own investigation and a federal grand jury indicted Hanrahan and thirteen co defendants.

The presiding judge recommended for appointment to the bench by Mayor Richard Daley, showed bias toward federal prosecutors at every stage of the proceedings. Despite proof that only one shot was fired by occupants of the building and more that 300 by police, Mr. Hanrahan contended it was a shootout. Photos that he pointed to prove the shootout, turned out to be nail heads instead of bullet holes. He was acquitted of conspiracy and murder charges.

The black community, angry over the travesty of justice, retaliated by casting sixty percent of their ballots in the November 1972 election for the Republican candidate who challenged Hanrahan. The unprecedented switch of black voters caused a major political upset for the reputed politically invincible Mayor Daley. It was one of his most humiliating defeats in his long career. Bernard

Carey, the Republican, defeated Hanrahan for Cook County Prosecutor by 129,000 votes.

Thirteen years later, after a long and bitter civil suit, survivors of the massacre and families of the victims, were awarded $1.85 million as a judge ruled the government conspired to deny the Panthers their civil rights.

Jackson State College Massacre

In May 1970, several days following the U.S. invasion of Cambodia, and shortly after the killing of anti war protestors at Kent State College, students at the all black Jackson State College in Jackson, Mississippi staged a protest on campus. Protesting against cars driven through the campus by local white citizens using the college's main thoroughfare as a shortcut to and from work, they blocked their passage and threw some rocks.

Temperature was in excess of 100 degrees Fahrenheit the day of the confrontation, and the overcrowded classrooms and dormitories lacking air conditioning, presented an ideal occasion for such behavior. Although no injuries were reported after the rock throwing incident, local police apparently felt compelled to teach the 'uppity' students a lesson about proper respect for the safety of 'hard working' folk.

At midnight, heavily armed Jackson City police and Mississippi State Highway Patrolmen, converged on the campus, opening fire on unarmed students who were casually walking around the grounds. The 28 second barrage of gunfire, killed two students and wounded twelve others.

The women's dormitory, housing 1,050 female students was strafed with 400 bullets and shotgun pellets. Police claimed they spotted a sniper on one of the upper floors. No evidence of such was forthcoming. The federal investigation produced the usual response from the FBI in race-hate crimes that insufficient evidence existed to warrant an indictment.

But Russell Davis, the white mayor of Jackson, was not satisfied and initiated his own inquiry. Governor John Bell Williams, one of Mississippi's renowned proponents of white supremacy, ordered the state highway patrol not to cooperate. The city commissioner, Ed Gates, running for state attorney general, advised city police officers not to testify.

Undeterred, the mayor conducted a full-scale inquiry, subpoenaed evidence and interviewed eyewitnesses. The eye witnesses testified that: students running away from police when shot, no tear gas canisters tossed to disperse students, no verbal warning issued, no warning shots fired, and no order to fire given.

Despite the findings, no official action was taken against the police, and no one was charged with killing the two unarmed students. The public relations machine to justify the murdering of unarmed students went into overdrive. The federal judge, Harold Cox, parroted the sentiment of the white community. Prior to his appointment to the judiciary, he once said:

...students   participating in civil disorders "must expect to be injured or killed."[2]

FBI Director J. Edgar Hoover chimed in telling Vice President Agnew:

"sniper fire on the troops provoked state police to return fire at the dormitory. The police memos described the two murdered and twelve wounded students as "nigger gals" and "nigger males."[3]

Members of the Democratic Select Committee chartered a plane and conducted an inquiry on the campus. Several white colleagues of the House of Representatives joined Senators Birch Bayh of Indiana, Walter Mondale of Minnesota, and Ted Kennedy of Massachusetts at the inquiry. Testimony of eye witnesses taken in the school auditorium, gave riveting accounts of the tragic assault by the police force.

The purpose of the hearing was to draw national attention to the miscarriage of justice suffered on the campus. But, its maximum impact was blunted by Senator Edward Brooke of Massachusetts' decision not to fly with the Caucus to Jackson.

Instead, he (the only black U.S. Senator) arrived 24 hours earlier, met with segregationist governor Bell, and the two held a press conference in which the Governor stated: "In the interest of self-preservation...the officers did not instigate the problem, did not encourage it. The responsibility must rest with the protestors."[4]

Failing to contradict Bell's statement, Brooke gave tacit agreement to the governor's absurd misstatement and compromised the newsworthy edge of the committee's investigation.

Monumental Task Facing Black Congressmen

Clarence Mitchell of the NAACP was the only full-time paid black lobbyist in the Capitol at the time the CBC was formed. But there was a definite need for clear, clarion voices at the national level to speak in unison and with resolve on behalf of black causes.

Chisholm, Stokes and I declared we did not come to Congress with any specific plan for advancing black political empowerment, but with a general concept for moving toward the goal: to educate people of their entitled rights, to establish a vehicle for achieving them. To succeed, we recognized a necessity to increase the number of black members of Congress, to promote legislation assuring enforcement of old civil rights laws, and to enact new ones.

Cognizant of the need, we urged black members to reach decisions by consensus, establish a vehicle for speaking with one voice, and interacting with each other to arrive at unified positions.

According to Stokes it was only "logical" to create a formal group to elect officers and to build an organization capable of focusing on the long neglected priorities of black citizens. In conversation and consultation with Hawkins and Diggs, we agreed to establish the Congressional Black Caucus (CBC) to accomplish both goals.

Kongressional Koffee Klatch Memo

New Year's Eve 1971, I drafted a memo and circulated it to members of the Democratic Select Committee, stating: "Without adequate programming and planning, we (Select Democrat Committee) might well degenerate into a Kongressional Koffee Klatch Klub."[6]

The memo called for (1) formal election of Chairman, Vice chairman, Secretary and Treasurer, (2) establishment of an executive committee as the major policy making instrumentality, with authority to act in behalf of the group in cases of emergency, and (3) formation of subcommittees in specific areas of concern to black Americans.

The ranks of the CBC increased by three in January 1971. Bill Dawson of Illinois was replaced by Ralph Metcalfe. Another black from Illinois, George W. Collins was elected. Charles Rangel defeated incumbent Powell. Parren J. Mitchell of Baltimore, Maryland and Ronald V. Dellums of Oakland, California defeated white incumbents. A fourth addition came when Walter Fauntroy was elected in March to the newly created position as a nonvoting delegate for the District of Columbia. The thirteen black members of congress became the nuclei for the birth of the CBC.

No Permanent Friends, No Permanent Enemies, Just Permanent Interests

The memorandum I circulated advised:

"If we're going to be successful, it will be because we've completely revised our political philosophy–to be selfish and pragmatic, based on the premise that black people have no permanent friends, no permanent enemies, just permanent interests."[7]

The latter was adopted as the CBC motto.

Democrats and Liberals Uncomfortable

Black members forming the CBC were the most legitimate and best positioned to advance the political interests of blacks. However, forming the entity was not accepted with open arms by some allies in the struggle for equal rights.

Misunderstanding and misconception of the role the CBC would play, caused major speculation: civil rights leaders sensed the Caucus would usurp their traditional position of setting the agenda and dictating the course of action in racial confrontations; black elected officials accused the group of attempting to establish **a** national clearinghouse for local problem solving; union leaders feared a group not financially or politically obligated to organized labor was a threat to its ability to mobilize blacks for various political and economic purposes. Labor's fear was understandable since seven of the thirteen original CBC members won election by defeating AFL-CIO and Teamster endorsed candidates.

Some liberals understood the need for the CBC, and supported its formation. Others displayed irritation in subtle ways, expressing surprise that black leaders were showing ingratitude by attempting to influence how far, how fast blacks should progress without consulting them. They were perplexed, smarting at the audacity of "newcomers" to the struggle, identifying the enemy and planning the strategies for confrontation.

For years, white liberals and labor leaders planned, organized, and executed the limits of protest in the fight for racial justice. Their dedicated efforts were appreciated, not necessarily universally endorsed. The time had arrived for blacks to represent themselves at the negotiating table. It was not a question of ingratitude for the contributions of white allies, but time for blacks to exert the leadership. The responsibility and obligation was as Frederick Douglass described when saying:

> *...the man who has suffered the wrong is the man to demand the redress, the man struck is the man to cry out... he who has endured the cruel pain...is the man to advocate liberty. We must be our own representatives and advocates— not distinct from, but in connection with our white friends...[8]*

Replacement of Middle Men

It was obvious that black political independence could no longer depend on whites to negotiate their destiny or articulate their aspirations. The new militant mood demanded replacing the politics of accommodation and appeasement with one of more aggressive assault on all impediments to equality.

Despite attacks by the white media and white politicians, the CBC organized around the principle of protecting its own interests. There were other caucuses in the House: peanut, potato, cotton, Republican, Democrat, liberal, conservative, state caucuses, regional caucuses that existed to protect their interests.

The Black Caucus was necessary because sometimes basic rights of minorities conflicted with the interests of other caucuses. While our people were enduring a status of powerlessness, some liberals were busily establishing meaningful power blocs by befriending large segments of the black community and using that relationship as a leverage to gain control of certain institutions. They garnered substantial influence in politics and in the labor movement by effectively positioning themselves as buffers between blacks and the establishment. Using that wedge, they infiltrated key positions in political districts and labor organizations. The time was at hand to replace middle-men.

Power and Influence of the South

The establishment of a national support network was critical to achieving the CBC mission. Pressure had to be applied on members outside the deep-south with substantial numbers of registered black voters in their districts-to challenge civil rights abuses by southern chairmen. Those who refused had to be identified and exposed.

A major factor motivating creation of the CBC was lack of any representative political voice speaking for the millions of blacks living in the South and Southwest. Their well-being was grossly ignored by white members of congress who opposed every issue beneficial to them.

To correct the inequity, it was compulsory to dislodge segregationist politicians from the seats of power—namely, the chairmanship of key committees. Realizing the difficulty and the inadvisability of modifying seniority, it became the organization's mantra to make it uncomfortable and unwise for those elected from non-southern racially mixed districts to continue ignoring racist measures advocated by southern congressmen.

The year Chisholm, Stokes and I arrived in Congress, senate Democrats from the thirteen southern states represented twenty-five percent of the membership but wielded 66 1/3 percent of the power vested in committee chairmanships. They chaired ten of the fifteen Senate's full committees: John Sparkman of Alabama, Banking and Currency; Allen Ellender of Louisiana, Agriculture; Richard Russell of Georgia, Appropriations; John Stennis of Mississippi, Armed Services; Russell Long of Louisiana, Finance; J.W. Fulbright of Arkansas, Foreign Relations; B. Everett Jordan of North Carolina, Rules and Administration; John McClellan of Arkansas, Government Operations; James Eastland of Mississippi, Judiciary, and Ralph Yarborough of Texas, Labor and Public Works. With the exception of Yarborough, none supported legislation to enhance the lives of blacks who lived in their states.

In the House, representatives from southern states chaired thirteen of the twenty-one full committees and members from border states chaired another four. Representing less that 20 percent of total House members, they chaired sixty-one percent of the standing committees. The State of Texas, alone, had four persons serving as full committee chairmen; W.R. Poage, Agriculture; George H. Mahon, Appropriations; Wright Patman, Banking and Currency; and Olin E. Teague, Veterans Affairs. Wilbur Mills of Arkansas chaired the powerful Ways and Means Committee. South Carolina had two chairpersons: L. Mendel Rivers Armed Services and John L. McMillan District of Columbia. William Colmer of Mississippi chaired the Rules Committee and Carl D. Perkins of Kentucky presided over Education and Labor. With the exception of Perkins, this group of chairmen, in alliance with senators from their states, constituted the most powerful enemies of first-class citizenship for our people. They stood as a bulwark between widespread prevailing racist policies and the civil rights of black Americans.

These individuals wielding life and death power over legislation that would afford equal opportunities to blacks were elected from twelve states where blacks were denied the vote. Today, low voter turnout in Iraq and Afghanistan because of the threat of violence, is sufficient to cast doubt on the legitimacy of the elections. However, no such concerns were expressed in the case of millions of blacks not allowed to vote in their districts.

Power disproportionately held by southern representatives did not equate to tangible benefits to their districts. Their states had the poorest schools and the worst educational systems, lacked even minimal health facilities, and possessed more housing units without hot running water and indoor plumbing of any states.

The inhumane conditions existed while southern congressmen used their power to protect an agrarian aristocracy and business elite. A priority of the leadership was exploiting the labor of its uneducated, unskilled white populace, and scheming to keep its blacks economically and politically subservient. While blocking legislation designed to extend first class citizenship to blacks, they appeased other elements by protecting large cotton and peanut growers, and building military bases to provide jobs for their poorly educated, unskilled white constituents.

African Americans Ill-Represented

The overwhelming concentration of power in the hands of southerners constituted an impregnable barrier to the advancement of minority rights. The situation was more serious and more detrimental than merely voting against civil rights. The influential cabal assaulted every issue proposed to extend full citizenship rights to blacks. The chairmen were supported by ninety-five percent of the Congressmen from southern states. In each instance, the solid bloc of approximately one hundred-five House members and 19 Senators from the 13 states cast votes against economic justice, income enhancement, welfare benefits, and other legislation beneficial to blacks and poor whites.

Unified opposition against racial equality was reflected in the votes of nineteen (19) Senate amendments to the 1960 civil rights bill. The amendments were aimed at undermining the effectiveness of the bill. The southern bloc voted for all nineteen anti-civil rights amendments. Senators Byrd (Va.), Hill, Jordon, Robertson, Smothers, Stennis and Talmadge voted for eighteen of the nineteen killer amendments. Kefauver voted for fifteen of the amendments.

The vote on passage of the 1964 Civil Rights Bill was almost identical. The entire delegations of ten states voted against the bill. There were six southern votes for the bill: two from Kentucky and Oklahoma, one each from Tennessee and Texas.

In the House, the united resistance to civil rights was evinced in the 1957 vote to adopt a rule on a Civil Rights Bill. One hundred-nine of the 118 members from southern states opposed it. Entire delegations of nine states voted against the proposal: Alabama, Arkansas, Florida, Georgia, Louisiana, Mississippi, North Carolina, South Carolina and Virginia.

Five of 8 members from Kentucky and seven of 9 from Tennessee voted against the proposal. Four of the 6 member Oklahoma delegation and twenty of the 22 Texas delegation were against the civil rights bill. Two did not vote.[5]

The shame of a nation was manifested by total exclusion of black elected officials to Congress from 13 states where fifty-one percent of the black population or 12 million lived. The voice of black Americans was effectively stifled by practices (terror, intimidation, murder) that prevented them from registering and voting.

Series of Conferences and Hearings

Our enlarged legislative group conducted unofficial public hearings and raised issues concerning discrimination against blacks in the military, the media and other areas.

Between July 1971 and September 1972, we sponsored seven national conferences and conducted three public hearings aimed at formulating a priority agenda for black America.

Hearings on Racism and Repression in Military

Chaired by Reps. Shirley Chisholm and Ronald Dellums, the sessions were held in November 1971 on ten military bases throughout the country. The committee heard from experts in military law and administrative practices. At the conclusion, the CBC presented Pentagon officials its evidence of racial inequities in military justice, discharge policies, enlistment, promotion procedures and other areas.

Conference on the Status of Health

The conference held December 9 - 11, 1971 at Meharry

Medical School in Nashville, Tennessee was sponsored jointly by the National Medical Association, the National Dental Association, Meharry Medical School, Howard University and the CBC. Ralph Metcalf (D-Ill.) chaired the hearings.

More that 600 participants from thirty states gathered in developing a plan to narrow the gap in the delivery of health care between the middle class and the poor which had a disproportionate number of minorities.

Hearings on Communications

The School of Communications at Howard University and the CBC jointly sponsored two "Black Careers in Communications" conferences, held in 1971 and 1972. I co-chaired with Tony Brown, dean of Howard University's Communication School

Witnesses representing every aspect of the communications industry testified regarding the lack of blacks in mass media–in front of the camera, behind it, in the front office, on the staff as solicitors of advertisement, editors, studio managers and most important the lack of black owned licenses for radio and television stations.

At the conclusion, we released a seventy-six page report documenting the plight of blacks attempting to penetrate the mass communications media wall of resistance.

National Black Enterprise Conference

The conference was held January 27 through 29, 1972 on the campus of Morgan State College in Baltimore, Maryland. Chaired by Rep. Parren Mitchell (D-Md.), with the assistance of 500 black economists and business persons who developed a ten-year plan for black enterprise to remedy the traditional exclusion of minorities from business.

Hearings on Racism in the Media

On March 6 and 7, 1972, I chaired a hearing to consider

the issue of racism in the mass media. Twenty-three black media workers, representing a cross-section of the industry, told how the black community had been grossly excluded, distorted, mishandled, and exploited by the white-controlled news media. Witnesses cited the media's failure to employ blacks in decision-making capacities, discriminatory union practices, lack of minority programming, exclusion of blacks from the Federal Communications Commission (FCC), and mistreatment of members of the black press as 'second-class' reporters.

Blacks held only five of the 1,219 news executive positions in the country and not one black owned a television station. Out of a total of 7,000 radio stations, blacks owned nineteen. At the conclusion, among other resolutions, the CBC formed a watchdog committee to monitor fairness in the media, to challenge licenses, and to file lawsuits.

Conference on Education

In March 1972, the CBC under the direction of Augustus Hawkins (D-Cal.), joined Delta Sigma Theta Sorority, the Metropolitan Applied Research Center, the NAACP Legal Defense Fund, the National Council of Negro Women, the National Association for Equal Opportunity in Higher Education, the National Urban League, and the United Negro College Fund, to sponsor a conference on education to develop a policy on issues facing the nation.

The groundwork laid at the conference led to the creation of a permanent organization to act as the guardian over educational policies and programs, to research and measure the growing and changing needs of black students, and to influence decisions at policy-making pressure points.

The CBC also sponsored conferences on other subjects in other localities. It convened the Harvard Forum on Our National Priorities at Cambridge, Massachusetts; the Conference on Black Politics in Washington, D.C., the Southern Regional Forum in Birmingham, Alabama, and the Southwest Regional Forum on the campus of Texas Southern University in Houston, Texas.

Nixon Refuses to Meet With CBC

The collective voice of the CBC was heard around the world when Nixon refused to meet and discuss "the deep and dangerous alienation" of the country's twenty five million blacks.

His refusal was a slam-dunk public relations blunder, leading to months of sustained attacks on his insensitive, anti-black policies. The insult was publicized worldwide by international news agencies. BBC, Soviet TASS News, and Communist China's Radio Peking. Europe, Asia and Africa were satiated with reports of the president's affront. Media outlets around the world, even among U.S. allies, reported how to the country's highest black elected officials were snubbed.

Meanwhile, the CBC escalated the battle of words. In addressing the House, I said:

> *"The President has traveled more than 35,000 miles in foreign countries... entertained hundreds of foreign dignitaries...But has failed to give priority to such domestic concerns of poverty, housing and unemployment."*[9]

60 Recommendations to the President

Nixon capitulated to the CBC request for a meeting when Senator Edward Brooke arranged for the President and the CBC to come face-to-face at the White House on March 25, 1971.

During the interim, Carl Holman, national chairman of the Urban Coalition; attorney Frankie Freeman, national president of the Delta Sigma Theta Sorority; Ofield Dukes, a public relations specialist; and Edward Sylvester, chief staffer for Congressman Diggs, with the help of black academicians, economists, lawyers, and civil rights activists, organized a task force and prepared a document to present the President.

President Nixon was presented 60 recommendations, buttressed by research data for each. He accepted the "Black Paper" in the presence of his entire cabinet and camera crews from almost every nation.

At conclusion of the meeting, Chairman Diggs requested the President respond to the recommendations by May 17, 1971.

The date was chosen to commemorate the landmark 1954 Supreme Court Decision outlawing racial segregation in public schools.

On May 18, missing the target date by 24 hours, Nixon responded in writing to the recommendations. His voluminous reply took 2 months to prepare, consisted of 115 pages, and-according to his own admission-was compiled by more than 200 people.

CBC Members Appear on Meet the Press

When announced that three members of the Black Caucus would appear on "Meet The Press" the Sunday following the official reply, the President hurriedly assembled 36 black supporters at the White House. They were hosted in the Rose Garden the day before our appearance and encouraged to counter whatever they anticipated we might say in opposition to the President's response.

Diggs, Hawkins, and I appeared on "Meet The Press," responding to questions from host Lawrence Spivak, regular panel members; James Kilpatrick, Washington Star Syndicate; Gordon Graham of NBC News and Bill Monroe the moderator:

Diggs stated that the President's reply was "deeply disappointing."[10] Hawkins recalling the President wanted to be judged by his deeds not his words, declared, "I now understand, because his words have very little meaning, and the enumeration of his deeds in terms of the accomplishments.. .was certainly very faulted."[11]

Commenting on the President's inaccurate statement of nominating 115 judges, of which eleven were blacks, I responded:

...One judge appointed to the Virgin Islands which traditionally was reserved for blacks who served at the president's pleasure, and of the eight black judges in the District of Columbia, seven were term limited appointments.[12]

First CBC Dinner

The CBC's first fund raising dinner, held June 18, 1971 in the nation's capitol attracted the movers and shakers of black America. The gala established a new direction in black politics as an enthusiastic audience of two thousand seven hundred sixteen persons jam packed the ballroom of the Sheraton Park Hotel.

As Chairman of the dinner, I had the honor of introducing the key note speaker, Ossie Davis who was brilliant and eloquent. He grasped the mood of the crowd, reflecting the attitude of Caucus members and our supporters.

His subject was profound. His delivery superb. His rendition magnificent. In his characteristic deep, melodic voice, he electrified the crowd, stating:

> *[My] text is very simply: it's not the man, it's the plan...those of us still caught up in the dream that rhetoric will solve our problems, let me state it another way...it's not the rap, it's the map...(T)he burden of my appeal to the 13 Congressional Black Caucus members, give us a plan of action. A ten black commandments; a simple, moral, intelligent plan...[13]*

The speech captured the essence, the true meaning of the assembled group, finding the soul of a people who marched gallantly through the ravages of three centuries to bring the race to a point of seriously assaulting the system of American style apartheid.

CBC Reached Legislative Maturity

In making a difference, Congressman Julian Dixon (D-Ca.) said,

> *"The Caucus has been the cutting edge opposing administration policies of Nixon, Ford, Carter, and Reagan. On the floor of the Congress, in committee hearings, before the press and across America, we have spoken out against policies which undermine the enforcement of civil rights and civil liberties, respect for law and order, disregard for personal rights of privacy, and attempts to infringe on the rights of free speech."[14]*

The strength of the CBC was found in its ability to align with certain dynamics in black communities. The black church, the black media, black professionals, black activists looked to the CBC as the catalyst for organizing and unifying efforts in the struggle to attain equal opportunity and impartial justice. The masses of the black populace depended on it to discern the black interest and to articulate the black perspective.

By the Mid-1980s, the CBC influence and power in the House had increased to such an extent that the Democratic leadership had no alternative but accommodate its legislative agenda. Unlike the influence used by southern members, the Black Caucus insisted that the agenda include provisions for the betterment of all people.

In 1985, Bill Gray was elected Democratic Caucus chairman, the third ranking party position in the House. It was an indication that CBC members had reached the crest of power on the Hill and our group had become of political age. We were situated strategically on every important committee to defend against the usurpers of institutional power and to protect against administration ax-wielding intruders engaged in cutting funds for domestic programs. Indeed, the CBC had become the unshakable flagship in the continuing struggle for equal rights and social justice.

Voice for the Disadvantaged

It was the leadership of the Congressional Black Caucus that effectively deterred the efforts of five presidents during the 1970s and 1980s to reverse the social, political, and economic gains of minorities and the poor. It was the Congressional Black Caucus that challenged conservative ideologies and preserved vital domestic programs that affected the economically disadvantaged when everything else was being sacrificed in the name of increased military spending.

The Congressional Black Caucus, along with scores of black mayors, state representatives and city councilmen, was an integral part of the 1970s black political revolution: Gus Hawkins' telling President Nixon that "unless he faces up to the problems of black Americans, there will be chaos," articulated the angry mood of black Americans. Charles Diggs' acknowledging that blacks were increasing in numbers within the political system and enhancing strength" truly seeing the facts of life. Louis Stokes' suggesting a boycott of the president's State of the Union address indicated the depth of dissatisfaction with current government policy. Parren Mitchell's admonition that "the black community has [not] been hijacked into silence or lulled into apathy," gave notice of a people determined to be involved. Charles Rangel's warning, "Where there are causes that can benefit by coalition politics, we shall coalesce," forecast the Caucus's willingness to work with other groups to achieve our goals. My call in 1971 for black communities to "develop the same degree of political sophistication as others" was therefore not far-fetched. It did not appear to be the case then, but urging a new, tough approach to solving problems of racism and discrimination was a realistic goal that paid handsome political dividends.

NOTES

1/Foreword *"Just Permanent Interests,"* Amistad Press, New York, 1992.

2/Nixon's Piano, Kenneth O'Reilly, *The Free Press,* New York, 1995, page 295.

3/Ibid., page 294 and 295.

4/Stephen Lesher, *"Jackson State a Year After,"* The New York Times Magazine, March 21, 1971, page 25.

5/The data was compiled by a *Congressional Quarterly* study on votes in the U.S. Senate.

6/*St. Louis Globe Democrat:* Rep. William Clay Emerging As Leader of House Blacks, by John Beckler, Associated Press Writer, February 15, 1971, page 1.

7/Ibid.

8/Frederick Douglass, *The Washington Star,* September 22, 1893, page S-2.

9/William L. Clay, *Just Permanent Interests,* Amistad Press, Inc., New York, 1992, page 117.

10/Congressman Charles Diggs, Meet the Press, live television broadcast, Sunday, May 23, 1971.

11/Congressman Augustus Hawkins, Ibid.

12/Congressman William L. Clay, Ibid.

13/Ossie Davis, Ibid.

14/Congressman Julian Dixon (D-Cal.).

5

"Put a little man in a big position and he will bring it down to his size every time."

—Old proverb, author unknown

Agnew: Barnacle on Nixon's Ship of State

Agnew epitomized the phenomena of a low potential-high achiever, being in the right place at the right time. Despite substantial evidence of serious flaws in character, little knowledge of how government functions, lack of management skills, a Republican candidate, was elected governor of Maryland with support of many Democrats. Benefitting from indignant independent whites and outraged minorities, he defeated the acknowledged favorite, Democrat George P. Mahoney in an upset victory.

Overwhelming support received from liberals, independents, and blacks in the 1966 contest was a vote of protest against the negative, racist campaign conducted by Democrat Mahoney. Adopting the racist suggested slogan that "A man's home is his castle," Mahoney implied that whites had a right to prevent blacks from moving into their neighborhoods.

Agnew seized on the remark, accusing the candidate of being sympathetic to the goals of the Ku Klux Klan and others who spewed bigotry and preached hatred.

However, Agnew's victory was no indicator of his commitment to fair housing or other civil rights measures. A month into his administration, he supported a weaker, less effective of two different housing bills considered in the state legislature. Shortly afterward, two hundred students from Bowie State College held a peaceful protest rally outside his office in the State Capitol. He ordered their arrest and closed down the school.

Agnew's real temperament was displayed in his contemptuous attitude toward black leaders. In the wake of Dr. Martin Luther King, Jr.s' assassination and subsequent riots in Baltimore, he invited over one hundred black leaders to the governor's office on the pretext of discussing a strategy to address the causes for the disruptive behavior. Instead of outlining plans to alleviate conditions contributing to the violence, he administered an insulting, condescending, tongue-lashing lecture.

Before a battery of television cameras, he castigated the leaders as culprits and silent partners in burning of the city. Characterizing them as cowards, he admonished the group:

> *Look around you and you may notice that everyone here is a leader (except)
> ...the ready mix, instant type of leader...the circuit-riding, Hanoi-visiting
> type (implying H. Rap Brown and Stokely Carmichael)...Some weeks ago, a
> reckless stranger to this city...characterized the Baltimore police as 'enemies
> of the Black man.'*

But when white leaders openly complimented you for your objective, courageous action, you immediately encountered a storm of censure from parts of the Negro community.[2]

Playing to the cameras, he continued the scolding:

> *You met in secret with the demagogue [Carmichael] and others like him and
> you agreed that you would not openly criticize any black spokesman regardless of the content of his remarks. You were intimidated by veiled threats; you
> were stung by accusations that you were "Mr. Charlie's boy," by epithets like
> "Uncle Tom."[3]*

In the midst of the tirade, Parren Mitchell, the head of the antipoverty program, led a walkout. Twelve blacks and a bevy of newsmen remained to hear his final vituperative condemnation.

His well-publicized performance projected him into the national limelight, elevating his status to an instant hero for those who insisted Negroes were too uppity, too aggressive, and too disrespectful of authority. Within days a new racial piranha was accepted with open arms by bigots residing in every nook and cranny of the country.

Selected V. P. Running Mate

Two years after Agnew's election to governor, Nixon's chief speech writer, Patrick Buchanan, recommended him for Vice President because of "his appeal" to white voters angered by the sit-ins, picket lines, boycotts, and protest marches. According to many, he fit the profile of a candidate capable of promoting the Party's southern strategy. He mollified southerners whom Nixon had promised to name a running mate that would not be offensive to their beliefs.

However, not all top political advisers and financial supporters of Nixon were enthusiastic about the prospect of an inexperienced candidate on the ticket. Some were reluctant to forgive him for forming a draft Nelson Rockefeller committee. When Rockefeller withdrew his candidacy and later, rather than support Nixon, Agnew ran as a favorite-son candidate of Maryland. Despite the affront, Nixon was convinced the acid-tongued rabble rouser would booster the ticket, and selected him as the running mate.

On the campaign trail, Agnew's insensitivity toward legitimate protest became an embarrassment to Party moderates. His uncanny ability for insulting minorities and unsophisticated, public statements negatively impacted the Party's carefully planned strategy to increase minority and independent voters' participation. On "Meet The Press," he accused anti-war demonstrators of being under the control and direction of the Communist Party, USA. Later, he launched a blistering attack on the civil rights movement, asserting that it went too far the first day it began.

Zeroing in on minorities and foreigners as favorite targets, he said at a rally in Chicago that when looking at a crowd, he didn't see Negroes, Italians or "pollacks." In Tennessee, asked by a reporter why he avoided campaigning in the ghettos, he responded that when you have seen one slum you have seen them all. On a plane flying to Hawaii, in a loud voice, he referred to a Japanese reporter as a "fat Jap."

Spokesman for Silent Majority

Agnew claimed to represent an indignant, fearful "Silent Majority," who themselves were too intimidated to speak out against calamitous liberal policies. He described the muted throng of disillusioned citizens as an overwhelming number of quiet, respectful, law-abiding citizens wanting to be represented by no-nonsensical officials that did not tolerate disrespect for law and order. In boisterous, picturesque language, he evoked images of cowered voters secretly yearning for elected officials to get "tough with street hooligans and their violent acts."

The strategy was clear: anyone opposing Nixon and Agnew's positions on race, welfare, and the war opposed time-honored values of the country. Coining a catchy phrase 'silent majority' was a clever devise used effectively to stop George Wallace from splitting the white vote. The Alabama governor's candidacy was perceived as jeopardizing the GOP's ability to secure voters opposed to integration.

Nixon's southern strategy was in peril because Wallace's entertaining, cajoling, vaudeville-type road show was a source of hemorrhaging for the carefully planned campaign to capture southern votes without losing northern support. Wallace's crude exploitation of racial fears, appealed to rural town residents in northern states and blue collar workers in industrial centers. Nixon was able to blunt that appeal by convincing more of them that he understood their silently endured pain.

In one of the country's closest election, Nixon and Agnew were victorious over Democrats Hubert H. Humphrey and Edward Muskie. Wallace, running on the American Independent Party ticket, was a distant third with almost 10 million votes.

Agnew-the Administration's Intimidator

Vice President Agnew became a poster-child for curtailing freedom of speech, a soap box orator for conservative extremism, and a bull horn cheerleader for blasphemous radicalism. The list of victims vilified by his intemperate remarks and verbal barbs, included educators favoring desegregation of public schools, activists against the war in Vietnam, non-violent demonstrators protesting discriminatory employment, egg-heads in academia, and civil rights advocates promoting affirmative action.

He chastised television and radio commentators who disagreed with Nixon's prosecution of the war, asserting that the media's failure to mold public opinion around the President's war policies 'aided and abetted' the enemy.

CBS president Dr. Frank Stanton called Agnew's attack an: "unprecedented attempt to intimidate a news medium which depends for its existence upon government licenses." NBC's president Julian Goodman said that Agnew's attack was an appeal to prejudice and ABC's president Leonard H. Goldenson emphasized his network's confidence in the people to judge.

Intimidated or not! Fearful of retaliation or not! Indignant or not! Their rhetorical bravado, in unprecedented fashion, failed to materialize into courageous network outrage. The week following their slamming of Agnew's attack on free speech, 250,000 protestors marched in the nation's Capitol against the President's fraudulent proposal for peace in Southeast Asia. All of the major networks and their associate affiliates refused to cover the newsworthy event.

Spiro Agnew — A Loose Cannon

Agnew, an enigma to the civil rights community, masqueraded as America's super patriot, arguing for return to law and order, and zealously preaching the dangers of permissive society. His verbal chants couched in racist jargon, conjured up frightening implications that assisted in stifling and stalling the drive to abolish racial and sexual discrimination. He once bragged that "Dividing the American people has been my main contribution to the national political scene."[4]

Social justice had no place in the new order he sought. Supreme Court Justice Thurgood Marshall, personally offended by Agnew's endorsement of racial discrimination in housing, stated:

Agnew bothered me as much as Wallace, Faubus, Thurmond, and the Southerners ever did. Americans knew that they were bigots posturing for Southern

*constituencies. But Agnew was speaking to the nation with the prestige of the
vice president and the White House.[5]*

Attacks Black Leaders

In his usual haphazard, bombastic fashion, Agnew chose, of all places, the soil of Black Africa to lash out at American's black leadership. His personification of profound ignorance and his unique talent for race baiting were never more in evidence than in his uncivil diatribe against black leadership.

Traveling from the Congo to Spain aboard Air Force One, Agnew, the 'outer space cadet' observed that black leaders in America could learn much from three African leaders (Jomo Kenyatta of Kenya; Emperor Haile Selassie of Ethiopia; and President Joseph D. Mobutu of the Congo) whom he met for the first time on his brief official visit. He praised the African leaders as:

> *...dedicated, enlightened, dynamic and extremely apt for the task that faces them...This quality of leadership is in distinct contrast with those black leaders in the U.S. who arrogated unto themselves the positions of leaders, spending their time in querulous complaint and constant recrimination against the rest of society instead of undertaking constructive action.[6]*

In gratuitously advising blacks to emulate African leaders, the incorrigible, felony-prone Vice President conveniently ignored the history of the African leaders in their rise to power. Looking into his analytical crystal ball, he added a postscript, "Many black people in the United States are tired of this constant complaining and carping [of] Negro leaders."[7]

The response to the 'Neanderthal man of conservative politics' was immediate, cutting and equally bare-knuckled. He was bombarded with criticism from congressmen, civil rights leaders, ministers and newsmen.

Columnist William Raspberry of the *Washington Post* wrote:

> *Show me a black leader in the United States and I'll show you a Black Caucus. [They engage in 'carping and complaining'... because they sought, and were refused for 14 months, an audience with the President.[8]*

Rep. John Dent (D-Pa) ridiculed Agnew's 32-day round-the-world diplomatic trip to ten nations as a fruitless mission despite an entourage of 141 aides, bullet proof Cadillacs and $3,000 daily hotel bills. On the House floor, Dent read from a Newsweek article, "Aside from hacking up the local golf course, his main outing (in Kenya) was to a nearby hunting lodge, where in company with his private physician and his pretty, red-haired secretary, he watched two rhinos copulating."[9]

The Reverend David Abernathy of the Southern Christian Leadership Conference said, "I just think Mr. Agnew has done it again. ...(He) put his foot in his mouth to take away attention from the real issues in the country."[10]

Roy Wilkins, executive director of the NAACP, said, "It has become evident that one of the impossible tasks of this country is to try to find out what Mr. Agnew means."[11]

Members of the Congressional Black Caucus offended again by another of Agnew's insulting outburst, joined in the criticism. Chairman Diggs, speaking to the House, said, "The Vice President seems unaware that the matter of black leadership is not within his province to decide..."[12]

Representative John Conyers of Michigan said, "...Mr. Agnew's ill-founded outburst represents the maneuvering of a demagogue, searching for a scapegoat...Mr. Agnew is to be pitied."[13]

Congressman Stokes added, "[His remarks were those of a back room politician intent upon hacking up his political adversaries..."[14]

Congressman Charles Rangel of New York said, "I find it preposterous to ask black Americans to be "grateful" like black African leaders who are putting forth their finest diplomatic etiquette to get more foreign aid."[15]

I was in no mood to be kind or gentle. My remarks were scathing, caustic:

"Admittedly, our Vice President is a clown, but his tricks are no joking matter...he is seriously ill...has all the symptoms of an intellectual misfit. His recent tirade is part of a game called mental masturbation...[He] is an intellectual sadist who experiences mental orgasms by attacking, humiliating, and kicking the oppressed."[16]

Ford Demands Apology

House Minority Leader Gerald Ford claimed to be deeply hurt by my remarks. The following day, taking umbrage at my candid statement, he lashed out, saying, "I cannot imagine somebody in this body…using language of that kind on the House floor in reference to the second-ranking member of the U.S. Government…It seems to me that the gentleman from Missouri, Mr. Clay, for having used that language, owes an apology to the Vice President."[17]

Ford's demand was hilarious to those with knowledge of my background. I once spent weeks in jail for refusing to apologize to a bigoted judge. What intelligent person would contemplate my apologizing to a political juggernaut? My position was that Agnew owed an apology to black people and all our leaders.

"Vice" President an Appropriate Title

Agnew constantly accused opponents of lacking integrity, honesty, and moral character, but apparently lacked each himself. Under indictment for bribery, extortion, conspiracy, and tax evasion, he pleaded no contest (guilty) in October 1973 to a single charge of federal income tax evasion. The judge, pursuant to a previously arranged deal between Agnew's criminal lawyers and the Justice Department, sentenced him to 3 years of unsupervised probation and fined him ten thousand dollars.

Forced to resign in disgrace, he avoided prosecution for more onerous acts, including accepting cash kickbacks from contractors during his term as Baltimore County executive and governor. Some of the illegal payments were delivered to the basement of the White House during his time as vice president. His shameful behavior reflected badly on the image of American officials throughout the world. One leader of a third world 'banana Republic' scornfully referred to him as truly a "vice" president in charge of vice. His political demise was a proper ending of an ignoble political saga.

NOTES

1/An Old Proverb, author unknown

2/Jim G. Lucas, Agnew: *Profile in Conflict*, Award Books, New York, 1970. Pages 54-55.2651

3/Ibid., page 55.

4/Nixon's Piano, Kenneth O'Reilly, *The Free Press,* New York. 1995, page 287.

5/*Dream Makers, Dream Breakers, The World of Justice Thurgood Marshall,* by Carl T. Rowan, Little, Brown and Company, Boston, 1993, page 353

6/Agnew, *New York Times*, July 18, 1971, pg 1.

7/Ibid., page 1.

8/William Raspberry, *Washington Post* editorial comment, Friday, July 23, 1971, page A23.

9/Congressman John Dent (D-Pa), *Congressional Record*. 21 July 1971.

10/Abernathy, *The Washington Post,* July 19, 1971, page A3.

11/Wilkins, *The New York Times,* July 18, 1971, page 17.

12/Congressman Charles Diggs, *The Congressional Record,* July 21, 1971, page 26513.

13/Ibid., Conyers, page 26514.

14/Ibid., Stokes, page 5.

15/Ibid., Rangel, page 26516.

16/Ibid., Clay, page 26517.

17/*Saint Louis Post Dispatch*, by Lawrence E. Taylor, July 23, 1971, page 1.

18/Letter from Rep. Louis Stokes (D-Oh.) To President Richard M. Nixon.

19/Rep. Jack Kemp (R-N.Y.), nominating remarks, 1 972 Republican Convention, Miami, Florida.

6

"In 1976, Gerald Ford wound up in there [the White House]
by accident, and increasingly people thought he was an accident."[1]
— Thomas Atkins, Secretary
Mass. Community and Development

Unlikely, Unexpected, Uneventful Presidency

Gerald R. Ford, Minority House Leader, came into national prominence when President Nixon recommended him to fill the position of Vice-President vacated by a disgraced, disgraceful Spiro Agnew, convicted criminal.

Ford's confirmation was a foregone conclusion based on a rather general consensus that the country demanded a seemingly honest, non-controversial, un-offensive person to replace the bodacious, feloniously inclined Agnew. The nation while anxiously awaiting impeachment and conviction of the President for high crimes, removing him forcefully from office, unfortunately gave great deference to his choice as a successor.

The soft spoken, unimposing Ford met the meager criteria as an adequate replacement established in the public psychic and validated by a physically exhausted and mentally drained Congress. Political figures of both Parties were ecstatic that the divisive Watergate entanglement was coming to an end. To them honesty, industry and integrity were the most critical qualifications to reestablish citizen confidence in the highest office.

The nomination of Ford, a non-descript congressman, unalterably aligned with the business community, generated token opposition, but vigorous arguments from those seeking a higher standard.

His position on several issues prompted spirited debate.

Liberals accused him of secretly securing confidential documents from the Department of Justice, including raw data of a derogatory nature about Supreme Court Justice William O. Douglas, and later making the unconfirmed, information public. Ford then led the effort to impeach Justice Douglass for an impeachable crime, of all things, financial improprieties. The hearings faltered for lack of credible evidence and no public vote was taken by the House Judiciary Committee.

Ford was accused of personally profiting from information gathered as a member of the Warren Commission investigating the John F. Kennedy assassination and using it in his published book "Portrait of the Assassin." He used classified top secret information gained during the investigation which was a criminal act.

Labor leaders attacked his near unanimous siding with the Chamber of Commerce and other business interests in supporting anti-union legislation, and lambasted his record of consistently voting against programs to enhance the status of the sick, uneducated and poverty-stricken.

Atrocious Civil Rights Record

Ford's opposition to civil rights and anti-poverty programs was a minimal factor for a majority of Congress in assessing suitability for the presidency. Ignoring his record of consistently voting against civil rights, some based their support on frivolity and humor. Rep. Clarence Long (D-Md.) stated, "I am going to vote for Ford. He is wrong much of the time, but he is decently wrong. I think decency and stability are the most important considerations." [2]

Ford's limited background for the office was called into question by Rep. Rangel (D-NY) who made light of the juvenile assertions uttered as qualifying experiences. He praised the House for reducing the qualifications for Vice President to a level attainable by almost everybody in the country, saying, "It seems to me that what we are concerned with is honesty and integrity and I am certain that this will open the doors to many people who aspire higher office." [3]

No critic was more candid than the Reverend Robert Drinan, Congressman, a Catholic priest from Massachusetts. Sweeping aside the generous accolades invented to portray Ford, and the ingenious discovery of a fictitious record characterizing him as a paragon of virtue, Drinan went for the jugular, stating:

> Congressman Ford opposed the creation of the food stamp program in 1957, the establishment of the Office of Economic Opportunity's antipoverty program in 1964, and the creation of the Medicare program for the elderly in 1965.
>
> Congressman Ford voted against federal aid to public schools in 1965 and 1969. He voted against rent subsidy programs in 1965, against model cities' funds in 1967 and against the child care conference report in 1971.
>
> Congressman Ford has consistently voted in favor of any proposed law which would prevent pupil transportation to accomplish desegregation or to reduce racial imbalance.[4]

Fifteen of 16 CBC members, and numerous other black elected state officials echoing similar charges also challenged the nomination. Clarence Mitchell, the esteemed, respected NAACP lobbyist for more than 30 years, described Ford's activity in a most unusual manner, saying that as a congressman, he established "a narrow gauge approach to civil rights. He opposed such legislation in its early stage and only voted for it when passage was inevitable."[5]

Opposed Voting Rights for Blacks

Typical of Ford's duplicitous behavior on civil rights legislation was his joining Rep. William M. McCullouch of Ohio in a maneuver to undermine protections in the 1965 Voting Rights Act. The two offered a substitute designed to render it impotent and fatally cripple chances of it becoming law.

Attempting to offset criticism of his co-conspirator [McCollouch] for being against the voting rights of blacks, he shamefully stretched truth out of proportion, saying:

He [McCollouch] has been and always will be a staunch supporter of sound, constructive, civil rights legislation. There is no better champion of civil rights and voting rights legislation than the gentleman from Ohio.[6]

The amendment offered by the alleged "champion of civil rights" and Ford would have deleted legislative language prohibiting literacy tests and other devices used to deny blacks the right to register and to vote. The McCulloch-Ford substitute sanctioned the onerous practice of denying registration to anyone without a sixth-grade education.

Under the substitute, blacks would be tested by federal examiners to determine if they had 6 years of education or could pass the state literacy test. Whites would apply to state registrars, the same ones who refused to register qualified black voters with PH.D's because they allegedly could not pass a literacy test. What a dynamic duo, dancing the bigoted tango—one an alleged champion of civil rights, the other, a man of honesty, industry, and integrity fighting to deny millions of blacks in 9 southern states the right to vote.

Again in 1969, the ranking Republican member of the House Judiciary Committee refused to introduce President Nixon's proposal which was designed to emasculate the Voting Rights Act. Ford came to the President's rescue by offering the crippling amendment as a substitute bill. The measure would transfer enforcement of the Voting Rights Act provisions to state legislatures, the very ones that denied blacks the right to register. Emanuel Cellar (D-NY), chairman of the judiciary committee remarked,

"My colleague (Gerald Ford) says that black people have been included in the southern political process to such a great extent that State Legislatures will not reverse the trend"[7]

Ford's statement was farcical and disgraceful. Millions of blacks resided in Alabama, South Carolina, Arkansas, Oklahoma, Tennessee, Texas and Kentucky, but not one was elected to the legislature in any of the states. Only one black was elected in each of the other heavily black populated states of Louisiana, Mississippi, North Carolina and Virginia.

Conyers, Stokes, Mitchell, Dellums, Rangel and I spoke against confirmation. We objected to Ford's insensitivity to issues of critical importance to black Americans. We focused on the idiocy of allowing a discredited President on the verge of impeachment to name his successor. Conyers said:

We are now passing on a confirmation in one of the most unusual periods of America, one in which the President himself is under a cloud of such magnitude that for us to cavalierly consider this nomination in the ordinary course of the application of the 25th amendment is unreal.[8]

Ronald Dellums said,
"My constituents are discouraged by one of the most uninspired records on civil rights and civil liberties ever compiled by a Congressman."[9]

Stokes described Ford's record on civil rights as "abominable." He said:

As House Minority Leader he sought to gut the Voting Rights Act of 1965, take the fair housing provisions out of the Civil Rights Act of 1968, delete basic provisions from the extension of the Voting Rights Act in 1969 and cripple the Equal Opportunity Amendments of 1971[10]

The President's dismal record on civil rights was summed-up by Cong. Herman Badillo (D N.Y.) who said:

The record includes his [Ford's] July 9, 1965 vote to recommit the Voting Rights Act to the Judiciary Committee with instructions to report back a substitute crippling the provisions for Federal registrars and omitting the protection against intimidation and coercion; his July 25, 1965 vote to recommit the civil rights bill in order to delete fair housing provisions; his December 11, 1969 vote to gut the extension of the Voting Rights Act of 1965 by substituting for the straight 5-year extension, a bill which deleted the basic provisions of the 1965 law preventing States and localities from nullifying minority votes; and within the past 2 months, his vote to deny citizens of the District of Columbia the right to vote for their mayor.[11]

I said Ford represented mediocrity as a legislator and lacked inspirational leadership befitting an occupant of the vice-president's office. Recalling a meeting with Speaker Carl Albert, Majority Leader Tip O'Neil, Minority Leader Gerald Ford and twenty-seven

(27) Bishops of the AME Church who came to the Capitol opposing a plan to destroy the Office of Economic Opportunity, I was shocked to hear Ford tell them he was "philosophically opposed to special programs for any segment of the population."[12]

That statement was a moment of truth for me. It defined a politician who believed the federal government had no obligation to address the negative, adverse effects of its past racist policies.

Rep. Andrew Young (D-Ga.), the only CBC member to support Ford's nomination, said:

> *I am casting a vote of faith and hope that he [Ford] will be a uniting and stabilizing force in a nation beset by division and crisis.*

> *...his ascension to the Vice-Presidency will facilitate either the resignation or impeachment of the present occupant of the White House...*

> *...out of my own southern experience, I have confidence that people can overcome past parochial views and develop a broader perspective which takes into account the interest of all of the people.*[13]

After six hours of exhorting Ford's non-existent virtues and counter-condemnations, the Minority Leader was anointed to become the next Vice President by a vote of 387 Yeas, 35 Nays, 11 Not Voting.

Presidency Besmirched by Nixon Pardon

On August 9, 1974, Nixon resigned and Ford became the first President in modern times to serve without voter approval in a national election.

Two weeks after installation, Ford and the CBC assembled in the Oval Office of the White House allegedly to discuss mutual concerns. The session was nothing more than a clever ploy to prevent the same internationally negative publicity leveled against Nixon for not honoring a CBC request to dialogue about dire conditions facing black Americans.

Leaving the meeting, Andrew Young said while he rated Mr. Ford "a compassionate conservative," the White House meeting in itself was no more than a "gesture."[14]

He recommended Nelson A. Rockefeller as his choice for Vice President. Four months later, the Congress approved the selection.

For a month, the country experienced a sigh of relief that the presidency was in safe, if not competent hands and pledged support to the new chief of state. But the honeymoon with Congress and the American people abruptly halted September 8, when Ford granted Nixon "a full, free and absolute pardon" for all crimes committed while President.

During confirmation hearings, Ford said the American public would not stand for a new President quashing possible prosecution if Nixon were to resign. Later, he said although he would have the power to pardon, he thought it unwise and untimely to make that commitment until any legal process had been undertaken.

But Nixon, vulnerable to felony charges concerning his activities in the cover-up of Watergate crimes, was never given the opportunity to prove his innocence. Before the Special Prosecutor had the opportunity to determine if sufficient evidence existed for an indictment, Nixon was pardoned and the American people were denied knowledge of the truth, despite the latest Gallup poll showing 59 percent of them opposed granting him immunity to prosecution.

Opposed School Desegregation

As a House member, Ford consistently supported legislation to undermine the ability of courts to comply with the constitutional mandate of school desegregation. He was an outspoken advocate to cut off funds to the Justice Department in cases involving busing in desegregation cases. He supported illegal freedom of choice school desegregation plans and voted for constitutional amendments to ban school busing.

Continuing his hostility toward desegregation, he toyed with the idea of asking the Justice Department to seek a review to overturn Brown v. Board of Education. In the spring of 1976, he and his erstwhile solicitor general, Robert Bork, prepared a brief supporting anti-busing.

Addressed NAACP Annual Convention

In 1975, Ford spoke at the NAACP's 66th annual convention in Washington, D.C., saying "I come as President of all the people to talk about common problems and common sense approaches, about what we can achieve together."[15] Urging delegates to support fiscal restraint as the key to fulfillment of equality for minorities, he said, "too many of those whom the programs [Great Society programs] sought to help--the poor, the elderly and the disadvantaged–are now bearing the inflationary burden of the Federal Government's spending spree."[16]

The 3,000 delegates responded with politeness and courtesy but were not impressed nor beguiled by his 13 minute address. Neither were black leaders and the media. The *New York Times* described his request for black support of budgetary policy restraint in cutting programs for the poor as "unconvincing." George Meany, president of the AFL-CIO who spoke after the President, called Ford's economic policies "cruel and fraudulent." He declared hard won victories against racism "can be neutralized by the disastrous economic policies of this [Ford] Administration."[17]

I described Ford's remarks as "giving a dissertation on economics, asserting that to whip inflation, we have to eat less, freeze to death, walk instead of ride and wear a 'feel good' button."[18]

The NAACP Board Chair, Margaret Bush Wilson, in her keynote address to the convention, cited Ford's recent vetoes of employment and housing bills, accused the Administration of being "indifferent and unresponsive to the humiliation and suffering that millions of American are enduring."[19]

Mrs. Wilson, the first female chairperson of the NAACP Board said, "The Ford administration has thus helped create a state of cynicism and despair among black Americans at a time when their difficulties have become more complex than ever."[20]

Campaign to Undermine Affirmative Action

In September 1977, President Ford's Office of Federal Contract Compliance Programs (OFCCP) suggested sweeping and substantial changes in regulations governing the awarding of contracts. His Department of Labor argued their new rules would consolidate, thus improve equal opportunity enforcement provisions. The deceptive declaration was rhetorically offensive and insulting to intelligent persons.

The proposal l) raised the level for contracts covered by affirmative action compliance from a contractor with 50 employees and contract of $50,000--to l00 employees and a contract of $l00,000.00; 2) increased from $l million to $10 million the contract amount for pre-award compliance review; 3) encouraged contractors to delay review and compliance proceedings; and 4) abolished specific criteria of affirmative action plans.

Clarence Mitchell of the NAACP was correct, Mr. Ford did have "a narrow gauge approach" to civil rights.

Ford Vetoed the Hatch Act Bill

Ford's hostility was not limited to civil rights. It also extended to federal employees. My Hatch Act Reform bill passed the House by 288 to 119 and the Senate 47 to 32. It permitted government employees the right to participate voluntarily in the political life of the country and to ensure protection for federal workers from direct or indirect political pressures from supervisors.

Ford vetoed it, and the House failed to override.

NOTES

1/Thomas Atkins, V*oices of Freedom, An Oral History of the Civil Rights Movement from the 1950s through the 1980s,* Henry Hampton and Steve Fayer, Bantam Books, New York, 1990, page 616.

2/Clarence Long, *Congressional Record,* December 6, 1973, page 39812

3/11/Charles Rangel, *Congressional Record,* December 6, 1973, page 39812.

4/Cong. Robert Drinan (D-Mass), *Congressional Record,* December 6, 1973, page 39879.

5/*Lion In The Lobby: Clarence Mitchell, Jr.'s Struggle For The Passage Of Civil Rights Laws*, by Denton L. Watson, William Morrow and Company, New York, 1990, page 731.

6/House, Gerald Ford (R-Mich), 89th Cong., 1st Sess., *Congressional Record* (9 July 1973), pt 12: 16214.

7/Congressman Emanuel Cellar Congressional record, December 11, 1969, page 38514.

8/Congressman John Conyers, Confirming the Nomination of Gerald Ford to be Vice President, Congressional Record, December 6, 1973, page 39825.

9/Ronald Dellums, Congressional Record, December 6, 1973. Page 39844.

10/Louis Stokes, *Congressional Record,* December 6, 1973, page 39885.

11/Congressman Herman Badillo, *Congressional Record,* December 6, 1973, page 39849.

12/Congressman William L. Clay, 13 October 1976, Chase Hotel, St. Louis Missouri, delegates A.M.E convention.

13/Congressman Andrew Young, St. Louis *Globe Democrat*: Black Caucus, Ford stoke fires of friendship, by Edward W. O'Brien, August 22, 1974, page 1.

14/Congressman Andrew Young

15/Gerald R. Ford, Public Papers of the President of the United States (Washington, D.C.: Government Printing Office, 1977), 902.

16/President Gerald R. Ford, 66th Annual NAACP Convention, Washington, D.C.

17/Meany–James M. Naughton, *"Ford Asks Blacks' Support on Economy,"* New York Times, 2 July 1975, page 30/

18/Clay, "shell game", in speech at Loretta-Hilton Theater in St. Louis, Missouri.

19/Marg. Wilson, *Washington Post*: NAACP Keynoter Blasts Ford's Indifference, by Harold J. Logan, 1 July 1975, page A6.

20/Ibid., Margaret B. Wilson.

7

We are indisputably the group in America that is the razor's edge. Those who possess an arrogance of power must not be rewarded for deserting those who put them in power. [1]

– Congresswoman Cardiss Collins (D-Ill.)
September 22, 1980, Birmingham, Ala.

James Earl Carter—On a Collision Course with The Congressional Black Caucus

CBC Chairperson Collins' stinging reproach was aimed at President Jimmy Carter during his heated 1980 campaign for reelection. Her hostile tone reflected the feeling of other Democrats inside and outside of Congress, especially CBC members. A month prior to her admonishment, Rep. Hawkins (D-Cal.) wrote to Carter:

"In recent months, we have repeatedly drawn attention to the clear relationship between the [Carter] Administration's current economic policies, and the economic demise of black communities." [2]

Speaking before 3000 American Postal Workers Union delegates three months before the election, I accused Carter of advancing a host of shop-worn Nixon-Ford initiatives that the Democratic Congress in the past had routinely rejected.

During the Democratic National Convention, Rep. Ron Dellums was nominated for president from the floor. Following a brilliantly delivered speech before the delegates, he declined to seek the nomination. In withdrawing, he took a swipe at the President, stating:

> *Carter thinks he can out-Reagan Ronald Reagan. But I saw Reagan in California, and I can tell him that you don't beat Reagan unless you put up a positive alternative.*

> *Carter thinks he can take the right wing of the Democratic Party and make it win by stretching it farther over to the Republicans.[3]*

The ominous warnings echoed the general attitude of the President's most devout supporters. There was a wholesale lack of enthusiasm about his chances for re-election within the Congressional Black Caucus. An undercurrent of negative opinion among labor leaders, feminist, minorities, and federal workers added to his other woes. His critics accused him of actively advancing the agenda of the political right and economic conservatives.

James Earl Carter 39th President

James (Jimmy) Earl Carter, governor of a southern state with a history of denying equal rights to its black citizens, virtually unknown to African Americans outside of Georgia, ironically was the overwhelming favorite of black voters in the 1976 Democratic primaries and the general election. Their support propelled him to his Party's primary nomination and election to president in the general.

Carter on Ethnic Purity

Carter's campaign for the presidency in 1976 was almost torpedoed by potential black supporters before it got off the ground. His utterance of a racially insensitive remark about scattered-site, subsidized government housing, temporarily caused blacks to question his commitment to equality. Responding to a reporter's question, he defended "ethnically purity" in preserving neighborhood housing. Commenting on patterns of heavily concentrated European and Asian immigrants in urban neighborhoods, he stated:

> *I don't think government ought deliberately try to breakdown an ethnically oriented community-deliberately by injecting into it a member of another*

race. [4]

Congressman Morris K. Udall, also a Democratic presidential candidate, charged:

> *[Carter was practicing] the politics of racial division. Ethnic pride (should not) require the government to ignore the needs of America's minorities or encourage exclusionary housing patterns.* [5]

Another Democratic presidential candidate, Senator Henry M. Jackson (Wash.) said, "Carter's ethnic purity remark is amazing." [6]

Both the CBC and Vernon Jordan of the National Urban League wired telegrams to Carter demanding to know the accuracy of the statement and to hear his explanation.

Carter apologized, insisting he supported federal and state open-housing laws and government action to enforce equal opportunities in new housing.

A much stronger written statement of atonement satisfied black religious and political leaders who rallied to his defense. Coretta King, Rev. Ralph Abernathy and Mayor Coleman Young of Detroit issued statements of support. Rev. Martin L. King, Sr. stated that an apology was sufficient, saying he had never found a man who had never made a mistake.

The promotion of Carter's candidacy was so professionally done that several explosive racial issues surfacing during the campaign failed to spark contentious disaffection in black areas. Instead of arousing rancor, his membership in an all-white church, ended in solidifying minority resolve among African American religious leaders. Typical response to his gadflies was the reaction of St. Louis ministers accusing President Ford of staging the scheme to embarrass Carter.

Reverend Moses Javis, pastor of the West Side Baptist Church, speaking for a group of ministers, said, "The problems to be solved in this campaign are not church membership but getting housing, jobs and (better) health." [7]

Carter won the Democratic nomination with substantial black voter support and went on to defeat President Gerald Ford by a narrow margin in both the electoral and popular vote.

Supporters Disappointed With Performance

But the President was unprepared for the ensuing confrontation with civil rights leaders and some members of the Congressional Black Caucus.

In the early days of his administration, battle lines were drawn. Seemingly, Carter was genuinely concerned about addressing inequities against the elderly, sick, and minorities, but like so many other southerners, thought the problems could be resolved without consultation or input from the affected groups. His 'Father Knows Best' attitude was demonstrated in his failure to seek expertise in developing policies and advice in making appointments. It was a source of tension that lingered throughout his entire term of office.

The CBC's relationship was similar to the experience of riding a roller coaster at the carnival. On day, it was up—the Administration's support of Youth Employment, favoring a (CETA) bill that targeted assistance to low-income groups; and promoting expansion of 400,000 public service jobs. The next day our harmony thermostat dropped many degrees. Carter's stubborn refusal to vigorously support passage of Hawkins-Humphrey Full Employment Act and the Administration's vacillation on other issues, left many reeling in uncertainty and disbelief. One day, he ordered the Department of Commerce to enforce the 10 percent minority set-aside requirement for public works contracts. The next, he refused to issue a statement advocating passage of the Martin Luther King Holiday Bill.

Caucus members were shutout of the decision process. We had very little interaction in discussing appointments and no effort was made to reach agreement on structuring programs, or coordinating legislative strategies.

It was believed that his go-it-alone position on issues important to minority constituents, stemmed from a background as a small town politician unaware of the sentiments, sensitivities, and expectations of people not enamored by southern custom, or easily impressed by policies amounting to tokenism in resolving questions of racial inequities.

Administration positions were heavily influenced by the prevailing and passé thought that gradualism was still a legitimate concept for dealing with racial inequality. But this attitude had not been an acceptable blueprint for handling complex racial and gender situations in sections outside the conservative South for years.

Andrew Young Appointed U.N. Ambassador

One month before inauguration, Andrew Young requested CBC members meet with Carter to convince him that he (Young) could be used more effectively in a cabinet position other than ambassador to the United Nations. Young disagreed with Carter's assessment that the appointment was a significant break-through, and a great reward to African American voters for their election support.

We requested and were granted an audience at his home in Plains, Georgia, assuming that in the session, Carter would solicit our views on national policy and recommendations for key appointments.

As six of us were entering Carter's home, Ed Bradley of CBS's "60 Minutes" shoved a microphone in front of Rep. Dellums and asked what he thought about Young accepting the position of ambassador. Unaware of his acceptance, we were momentarily startled. After confirming the veracity of Bradley's assertion that issue became moot.

At the meeting, I presented a proposal developed by the CBC to reorganize and strengthen the machinery for enforcing federal job discrimination laws. Carter, reacting favorably to the idea, told us to prepare the plan in more specificity. The preliminary draft circulated, called for formation of a super enforcement agency with the power of cease-and-desist orders against employers who discriminated. It combined the equal employment sections of the United States Civil Service Commission; the Office of Federal Contract Compliance in the Department of Labor; the section of the Department of Treasury that enforced laws against discrimination in Education and Welfare; the section of the Department of Justice that filed anti-discrimination lawsuits against state and local governments.

During the meeting, Carter announced the appointment of Patricia R. Harris--the first black woman Cabinet member. He had not discussed his intention with any member of the Caucus and did not infer any future appointments would be discussed with us.

Carter Administration Reviewed By CBC

After two years in office, the CBC analyzed Carter's performance, citing achievements and documenting his shortcomings. It was necessary to have a factual report because several Caucus members, playing the role of loyal Party supporters, gingerly danced around critical issues impacting negatively on blacks and constantly defended Carter's misguided priorities toward them. The lengthy report was balanced and objective. A summary was made public September 29, 1978:

Employment
Unemployment nationwide was six percent by official figures, while it was 12.3 percent for blacks. For black teenagers, it was 36.3 percent. Carter was credited and condemned for attempting to address the problem through traditional, non aggressive government programs.

Civil Rights and Affirmative Action

Civil rights leaders concerned that Carter's choice of a southern conservative, Griffin Bell as Attorney General, to run the agency responsible for enforcement of all civil rights laws, would stymie efforts to eliminate discrimination.

Fortunately, Bell was not the reactionary ideologue envisioned by these leaders. He and the Justice Department responded effectively to enforcement of the laws and made important strides in increasing the number of blacks in key staff positions at the Department, including the number of attorneys.
Education
Carter supported an increase in funding of fifteen percent for the Elementary and Secondary Education Act, but was unsympathetic to the critical needs of black colleges in financial crisis.

International Relations

The Administration engineered an internationally recognized solution leading to independence and majority rule for Namibia, aided efforts to repeal the Byrd Amendment which permitted the importation of chrome from racist Rhodesia, led the fight against the Helms and Ichord Amendments that opposed lifting sanctions against the repressive Rhodesian government.

On the minus side, the Administration rejected most of the 12 points for action regarding apartheid in South Africa that the CBC recommended.

Urban Policy and Welfare Reform

The Administration declared intention to put together a coherent policy directed at urban revitalization, expressed a need to target assistance on poorer areas, and recognized the importance of employment in the improvement of entire cities. No such plan materialized or crystallized.

Miscellaneous Achievements

Carter was praised for successful congressional approval of a plan to reorganize federal equal employment agencies in a manner consistent with the plan presented by the CBC at Plains, Georgia, and applauded for his Solicitor General's submitting a brief in the Bakke case supporting the use of race-sensitive measures in affirmative action.

He pardoned almost 10,000 young men who evaded the draft during the unpopular Vietnam War, and overcame stringent Republican opposition to create the Department of Education.

Miscellaneous Omissions

Carter was admonished for failure to make a major speech to the nation emphasizing moral commitment to the principle of affirmative action; and panned for his limited number of black appointments to top administrative positions, particularly absence of blacks in top economic policy-making jobs.

Ignored Leadership in Appointments

The Administration continued on its course of making appointments to key positions without consulting or seeking the advice from local leaders or congressional supporters. One incident that personally incensed me was the announced intention to appoint Barry M. Locke to a high-level position in the Department of Transportation.

Locke, while executive director of Bi-State Transit in St. Louis, was guilty of racial discrimination in hiring, ignoring minority-group contractors, and providing poor service to black user areas. An investigation by the U.S. Transportation Department's civil rights enforcement section verified that service to black neighborhoods was less reliable, more crowded and of poorer quality than that provided white areas.

I revealed evidence to the Administration of numerous racially biased acts by Locke, including the charge by an employee of the agency that Locke solicited him to fraudulently award a contract to an unqualified firm in return for cash payments.

My charges were sufficient to embarrass the Administration into withdrawing Locke's nomination. He then moved on to head the transportation department in Boston, Massachusetts. There he continued his criminal activities and was eventually convicted of bribery and sent to prison for extortion in the handling of contracts.

Hawkins-Humphrey Full Employment Act

Rep. Hawkins and Senator Humphrey, co authored H.R.50, better known as the "Hawkins-Humphrey Full Employment Act." Hawkins was architect and chief engineer in promoting passage of the bill in the House. He was responsible for drafting the nuts and bolts provisions of the Bill and presided over 200 hours of hearings where noted economists, fiscal officers, labor leaders, and corporate executives testified. In rallying support for the Bill, he made many public appearances.

The bill simply and concisely stated that every American who was able and willing to work should have the opportunity. Further, the bill required the government to establish policies to provide those jobs in the event the private sector could not, and also committed federal resources to the endeavor as national policy to achieve its goal.

The measure was co sponsored by 69 members of the House. Carter questioned the cost of the bill as excessive, insisting on endless compromises, and weakening amendments in exchange for his support.

Concerned about the 12 million unemployed seeking work, I challenged his negative position toward the bill. At a noon rally on the lawn of the Kiener Plaza in St. Louis, I said:

"We want the Hawkins-Humphrey full employment bill this Administration, this year, and that's the message I deliver to the President. I thought we had settled this issue last November (with his election)." [8]

The president contended the country could not afford $50 million in funding the program. Insisting on amendments that met his satisfaction, the Act became a hollow replica of its original version. The crippled legislation was enacted and signed into law by Carter, but no president since, including him, implemented its discretionary provisions to use the resources of the Federal government to create policies that reduced unemployment.

In 1979, Carter had an opportunity to implement provisions of the law but refused. He was criticized by supporters as Keyserling stated, "of being in flagrant violation of the Humphrey-Hawkins Full Employment Act." Hawkins termed the president's action a violation of "the letter and spirit of the law," and Senator Jacob Javits of New York joined them in demanding a review of Carter's unrealistic time table for reducing unemployment.

Lukewarm To King Holiday Bill

Congressman Andrew Young, Mrs. Coretta King and Martin Luther King, Sr. introduced Carter to influential black leaders and vouched for his fairness in matters of race. They guided him through political mine fields in northern communities, praising him as a true advocate of civil rights, and arranged for his presence in the most effective covenants of political exposure in black America – pulpits of northern protestant churches. Their credibility among black ministers was instrumental in propelling Carter ahead of other equally acceptable Democrats seeking the nomination.

Yet, the greatest disappointment to proponents of a Martin Luther King Holiday Bill was the lackadaisical, non-existent support from President Carter. His attitude was so negative that Coretta King openly criticized him for failing to support the bill. Reverend Joseph Lowery, president of the Southern Christian Leadership Conference (SCLC) and Bill Lucy, Secretary-Treasurer of the American Federation of State, County and Municipal Employees AFSCME), publicly chastised him for his neutral stance.

While the president publicly conveyed the impression of neither supporting or opposing the bill, Administration operatives actively worked behind the scenes for its defeat. During the final days of the 95th Congress, a substitute to Rep. Conyer's Holiday Bill was offered by Rep. Robin Beard (R-Tenn) calling for celebrating King's birthday on the third Sunday in January. The odorous, meaningless amendment nullifying the paid holiday aspect of the Holiday Bill, passed 207 to 191.

Administration lobbyists were conspicuously absent in front of the House chamber during debate. Hamilton Jordan, chief aide to Carter, reportedly called legislators from Georgia, Alabama and Mississippi stating the legislation was not a priority issue for the President. If true, Jordan worked the list remarkably well. On the key motion offered by Beard, nine of eleven congressmen from the President's home state of Georgia cast votes for the crippling amendment. Wyche Fowler and Billy Evans were the two Georgians to oppose the Beard proposal.

Unkept Promises of James Earl (Jimmy) Carter

This was not the first time the CBC disagreed with Administration policy or with Carter. It was no different than that with other chief executives—not the first confrontation with an occupant of the White House, and predictably would not be the last. We sharply disagreed with Johnson's Vietnam War policies, with Nixon's assault on programs for the poor, and with Ford's pardon of Nixon.

Carter Conspired to Defeat Hatch Act

Nor was it the first confrontation that I had with Carter. During the 1976 campaign, he reached out to groups, using whatever tactic necessary to get their support. At the Democratic National Convention, nominee-Carter testified before its platform committee in favor of including a provision to support Hatch Act Reform.

At the American Postal Workers Union's national convention he had pledged that if elected, he would sign the bill. He pledged in writing to all federal employee union organizations that he favored the bill to lift the yoke of political oppression from their shoulders by granting them the right to actively participate in politics.
A year before Carter's election, both houses of Congress passed Hatch Act Reform by large majorities but Ford vetoed the bill and the Senate narrowly missed overriding it.

Immediately after inauguration, I reintroduced the bill and the House passed it. But Carter persuaded Senator Abraham Ribicoff (D-Con), chairman of Post Office Committee, not to report the bill out for a vote. Ribicoff, previously a staunch advocate of the legislation, assigned the bill to the subcommittee chaired by Senator Sasser of Tennessee who also supported the Bill in previous sessions. He held one perfunctory hearing and let the measure die in committee without a vote. Amazingly, their support for the measure dissipated after Carter's election.

Congressional Black Caucus 1978 Dinner

The Washington Hilton Hotel site for the 1978 Annual CBC Dinner held at the largest ballroom in D.C. apparently was too small to accommodate all desiring to attend. In the previous two years, more than $300,000 annually received in the mail for tickets to the 3,000 capacity ballroom, was returned.

As dinner chairman, I chose an additional hotel, equipped it with interchangeable piped-in cable television which enabled dinner guests at both ballrooms to enjoy the same program. To make the site more attractive to supporters who might view their seating at the second site negatively, half of the CBC members were scheduled at each hotel. Additionally, the entertainment was divided. Stevie Wonder was staged at the Hilton Hotel; Natalie Cole and Shirley Caesar at the Shoreham ballroom.

We invited President Carter to address the audience at the Shoreham for 15 minutes, and Senator Kennedy to appear at the Hilton for 15 minutes. Carter refused-demanding to be at the Hilton Hotel. We granted his request. Instead of honoring our request to limit remarks to 15 minutes, he held the microphone hostage for one hour, 20 minutes.

Recognizing celebrities in the audience and inviting them to join him on stage, Carter conveyed the impression that the evening was in his honor, and paid for by the presidential re election campaign committee. However, overtime expenses amounting to almost $30,000 for stage hands, television technicians, waiters, cameramen, security personnel and musicians in two hotels were paid by the CBC, not the Carter Re election Committee.

A Tribute to Barbara Jordan

On the same program, the Caucus paid tribute to two dynamic women, Yvonne Braithwaite Burke and Barbara Jordan. Both political pathfinders announced they would not seek re-election. Burke vacated her seat to campaign for Attorney-General of California. Jordan was retiring from public office to accept a professorship at the University of Texas School of Law.

Burke, former chairperson of the CBC, played a key role in securing legislation to ensure equal employment opportunity in the construction industry for minorities. The "[Yvonne] Burke Amendment]" tied federal funds for the building of the billion dollar Trans-Alaskan pipeline and mandated awarding of minority contract set asides and enforcement of affirmative action programs.

I had the privilege and honor of saluting Jordan, saying:

Barbara Jordan is the embodiment of the E.F. Hutton commercial-when she speaks, people listen. They listen not only in the halls of Congress and the inner sanctums of the oval office, but also in the towns and hamlets of America...They hear a voice so powerful, so awesome, so imposing that it cannot be ignored and will not be silenced. Tonight, members of the CBC proudly pay homage to the BLACK ROSE OF TEXAS, Barbara Jordan.[9]

Firing of Andrew Young

Carter, defending Andrew Young who was under attack from various sources, received a standing ovation at the 1978 CBC Annual Dinner when saluting Young as,

"a man who is not afraid to speak out when he sees something wrong...I don't know of anyone who has done more for our country throughout the world than Andy Young. As long as I'm president, and Andy Young is willing to stay there, he'll be the United Nations Ambassador."[10]

A short time before the next annual dinner, Carter under pressure from Jewish groups, fired Young as ambassador. The harsh penalty was exacted for Young's meeting secretly with representatives of the Palestine Liberation Organization (PLO). He was the scapegoat in the discredited policy dictum. John Gunther Dean, Ambassador to Lebanon, was authorized to meet with senior PLO leaders during the same period by Secretary of State Cyrus Vance and was not disciplined. Between 1978 and 1981, he had 35 separate meetings in violation of the pledge Secretary Henry Kissinger made and Carter honored that the U.S. would not negotiate with the Palestinians until they recognized Israel's right to exist. Somehow, Young's act was more egregious and warranted dismissal.

Carter and CBC on Collision Course

CBC members found themselves consistently in serious disagreement with Carter's evolving policy dictums. We openly expressed opposition to his controversial measures. We convened press conferences and issued press releases making clear that his patronizing treatment of African American concerns was reprehensible.

Relations between the Caucus and Jimmy Carter, while never very harmonious, worsened after his disrespectful performance at the CBC annual dinner. It was not surprising that shortly thereafter, the CBC's first southern regional conference in Birmingham, took on the flavor and aura of presidential politics. Congressman John Conyers announced on opening night that he would organize a dump President Jimmy Carter campaign. He told a local news reporter, "The facts are that President Carter has not lived up to his promise. He doubled-crossed us."[11]

Ben Brown, deputy chairman of the Carter-Mondale re-election committee, felt obliged to rebut Conyers' remark. He said, "I didn't come here to respond to Congressman Conyers' statement. We were coming anyway. But we're not at all surprised that he would make the statements he has made."[12]

But the debate intensified as caucus chairperson Cardiss Collins followed Conyers in attacking the Carter Administration. She stated:

> *We have thrown down the gauntlet against the President's cuts in the domestic employment, education and health programs. We are opposed to cutbacks in federal programs that assist our senior citizens and our youth.[13]*

The harsh criticism leveled at Carter, the titular head of the Democratic Party, by veteran members of the Caucus revealed the low esteem in which he was held by some who witnessed his activities on a daily basis.

Credit for Appointing Black Judges

Although most members of the CBC did not have an amiable relationship with President James Earl Carter, we praised him for the number of black federal judges appointed. In four years, he named two dozen more blacks to the federal bench than the combined total appointed by all Presidents from George Washington through the John F. Kennedy administration. Prior to his record setting appointments of 28 judges, Lyndon B. Johnson held the record with eight black judges.

Carter selected minority judges to serve in every district of the country-north and south, east and west, urban and suburban. I recognized his contribution in a speech on the floor of Congress, saying, "The black community is appreciative of the judges appointed by President Carter. His appointment of 25 (at the time) blacks to the Federal district courts is worthy of praise.[14]

Civil Service Reform

The President described civil service reform as the 'legislative center piece' of his domestic policy and his Director of the Office of Personnel Management, Scottie Campbell, launched a campaign to rewrite the rules for government workers without regard of their long negotiated rights. Catering to the conservative mantra that government was a major problem in what ailed America, the President and Mr. Campbell proceeded to blame 'incompetent' federal employees instead of 'ineffective' government policies for inflation, unemployment and other deficiencies in the system.

They developed a bill and convinced the chairman of the full Post Office Committee, Robert Nix (D-Pa), to bypass normal House procedure in removing me from the process to consider the legislation. In an unusual, unprecedented maneuver, the bill was not assigned to my subcommittee where it would receive a full and fair hearing. Instead, Nix announced hearings would be held at the full committee level rather than referring the bill to subcommittee. This procedure, short-circuited hearings that might have exposed pertinent factors embarrassing to the President and politically explosive for the committee chairman. The same evasive scheme was used often by southern chairmen to defeat civil rights initiatives.

Nix appointed Morris Udall (D-Ariz.) to manage the bill in full committee. He held several perfunctory hearings and with the support of all Republican committee members forwarded the bill to the full House. But the bill encountered a firestorm of opposition when it reach the chamber for consideration.

Ignoring advice of Democratic colleagues, and the knowledge of those most familiar with the subject, the Administration proceeded to "develop" its 'anti-labor-relations' proposal. The President's advisors reached an agreement with the largest Federal employee union, the American Federation of Government Employees (AFGE) that was soundly criticized by all other Federal employee unions. Democratic committee members who had been active with respect to Federal employees matters, particularly Bill Ford (D-Mich.), James M. Hanley (D-N.Y.), Patricia Schroeder (D-Colo.) and I were highly critical of the proposal and crafted a compromise bill to protect the established rights of federal workers.

As chairman of the subcommittee with jurisdiction, I adamantly opposed any effort to undermine job protections by lowering the threshold for firing workers and reducing the right to appeal in the process. Our compromise bill eliminated the President's undesirable features: thrust to reduce long-standing statutory protections enjoyed by employees, dilution of due process rights, and reduction of proof required to discharge workers.

The President personally placed telephone calls to members of Congress stating that my action threatened passage of the bill. His observation was accurate. That was precisely my intent.

Carter called my close friends, Louis Stokes, William Ford (D-Mich.), and Harold Ford (D-Tenn), asking Stokes to lead the floor opposition against the amendment. Stokes replied:

> *"I'm sorry Mr. President, not only do I support the amendment, I intend to speak for it. Clay is on the floor at this very minute preparing to bring it up for a vote. Why don't you call him?"[15]*

Although the President found time to call my friends, he told Bill Ford he was too busy negotiating a Mid-East peace plan at Camp David with Israeli Prime Minister Menachem Begin and Egyptian President Anwar Sadat to converse with me   Each time Nix and Udall attempted to pass the so-called reform measure, I threatened to offer an amendment to repeal political restrictions on federal workers (Hatch Act Reform).

Realizing that I had the votes to prevail, they withdrew the bill. The President's version of civil service reform legislation never passed.

In the next election, Nix was opposed for a second time by a dynamic young Baptist minister, William H. Gray, who lost two years earlier by 339 votes. During the election campaign Carter promised that in the event Nix lost, he (Carter) would appoint him to a position at the Committee on Aging. This time, however, Gray easily defeated Nix by 11,651 votes.

Again the President reneged on his word. Instead, he gave the job to Jerry Waldie, a former Congressman from California.

CBC Opposes Carter Budget

The Congressional Black Caucus denounced Carter's budget in bitter terminology, stating its members were shocked, appalled, and unalterably opposed to the cuts. We met with him in February 1979, advocating for the millions who stood to suffer most from his announced economic policies. We expressed three basic concerns (1) We are deeply and unalterably opposed to the cuts in the domestic social budget (2) The majority of Americans oppose the spending cuts in programs designed to help young adults, the elderly, handicapped and the poor (3) We warn that the National Black Leadership Round Table (200 black organizations) are mobilizing a national protest in opposition to your proposed budget.

Carter held his ground, contending it was necessary to balance the budget in order to protect the poor against high inflation. He denied his solution to fight inflation by imposing high interest rates would entice high unemployment by choking off capital for business expansion. The CBC agreed inflation was a serious problem, yet cited the Administration's own studies concluding that withholding $15 billion in federal expenditures would decrease inflation by only a scant 0.2 percent.

The CBC did not oppose the concept of a balanced budget, but believed it could be achieved by eliminating pork barrel subsidies, the closing of tax loopholes, and the freezing of wasteful military expenditures.

I charged that black voters interpreted his campaign message as

"A commitment to balance the economy, balance the scales of justice, balance the disparity between the rich and the poor, balance the inequities in the tax structure. They (black voters) supported him believing his policies would enable them to balance their own budgets."[16]

Carter Defeats Kennedy in Primary

The Democratic primary election contest between President Carter and Senator Ted Kennedy ended before the Caucus' next annual dinner. Infighting among CBC members taking sides created a chasm. Some advocated giving Carter carte blanche access to the Caucus apparatus in his bid for re election. Others were determined to deny him such preferential treatment.

Never before had the Caucus come as close to dissolving than during this period. Carter was accused by some of displaying a cavalier attitude toward Caucus issues and sneering at individual Caucus member's proposals. His supporters were personally accused by colleagues of overlooking broken promises. Others possessing neither extreme dislike nor unrestrained love for Carter, were displeased by what they conceived as hypocritical positions on matters of grave interest to the black community. The challenge to CBC's unified leadership was in jeopardy. Members alienated by the President's attempt to build a black power base independent of our organization, were in no mood to quietly acquiesce.

Georgia's state campaign committee for Carter's re-election unveiled its slogan in the primary, "No, Not One" at a rally attended by the President's wife, Rosalyn. It ignited another political fire storm. The saying was a throw-back to a battle cry of the 1950s for activists fighting to preserve segregation.

Rev. Ralph Abernathy of the Southern Christian Leadership Conference (SCLC) called it offensive. State Senator Julian Bond attacked it as an insult to black people. Attorney Pitts Carr said its use was another example of the incredible insensitivity of the Carter people toward blacks.

Hostility toward the President was similar in other parts of the country. The Cleveland press asked Stokes why he supported Kennedy's candidacy, his answer was:

> *It gives me a chance to tell some of the things he [Carter] has not done in my congressional district.*[17]

Stokes was riled by Carter's attempt to manipulate church leaders in Cleveland. He wrote 250 pastors attacking Carter's invitation to the White House as a "blatant appeal" to win votes, saying:

In 1976, the black ministers of this city were very instrumental in Mr. Carter's election...In 1980, with high unemployment, the plight of black people in Cleveland is worsening. It is very important that Mr. Carter realize that a community which gave him 95 percent of the vote had a right to expect him to keep his promises. [18]

Stokes continued,

"I hope you will give serious thought to the fact that it is President Carter who has just sent to Congress his balanced budget for fiscal year 1981, which has over $16 billion in cuts in programs such as CETA, nutrition, food stamps, school lunch programs, LEAA, health, education, and Counter Cyclical Aid for cities. It is a budget which the Congressional Black Caucus has described as an "unmitigated" disaster for minorities, the poor, and the disadvantaged." [19]

Middle East Peace Agreement

In 1978, Carter through tough, around the clock negotiations successfully set the framework for peace in the Middle East. The result of his effort was referred to as the "Camp David Accords." The next year, Prime Minister Menachem Begin of Israel and President Anwar el-Sadat of Egypt signed a treaty at the White House.

Neither envisioned the difficult days ahead nor saw the historic agreement as a panacea for settling the deep-seated division for the area's hostilities. Sadat antagonized other Arab leaders that were giving his country financial aid and was later assassinated. Begin faced opposition from right-wing zealots against the withdrawal of Israeli troops from the Sinai Peninsula-leaving Jewish settlements unprotected.

Both Begin and Sadat earned Nobel Peace prizes in 1978. President Carter was honored with the Prize several years later.

American Hostages in Iran

Sixty-three Americans were taken hostage at our embassy in Tehran by students who supported the anti-American ayatollah Komeini. They demanded the return of Shah Muhammad Reza Pahlavi, the deposed former leader of Iran who had come to the United States for a cancer operation. Carter attempted a dramatic, unsuccessful rescue of the hostages. The U.S. military helicopter collided with a transport plane in the Iranian desert killing eight and injuring more.

Eleven hostages were released because of ill-health. The fifty-two remaining were held 444 days and released on January 20, 1981, the day Ronald Reagan took the oath of office for President.

Carter, A Man Of Peace And Honor

After leaving office Carter became a source of inspiration, an icon of concern and compassion for the suffering, a model for other Americans to emulate. No former president in U.S. history has impacted the world with such decency and dignity, imbuing hope where none existed than James Earl Carter.

He has been a dominant force in lessening world tensions, spreading democracy through overseeing honest elections, and bringing about peaceful solutions in areas of conflict. He has devoted his life to a mission of good, of healing, and of addressing poverty, oppression and sickness.

NOTES

1/Congresswoman Cardiss Collins (D-Ill.) Washington Hilton Hotel, Washington, D.C., September 22, 1980.
2/Congressman Hawkins' Press Release, 7 July 1980, Los Angeles, Cal. *Congressional Record*, February 12, 1980, Volume 126, No. 21, 96th Congress, Second Session.
3/ Gary Wills, "Why Dellums Spoke Out at Convention," *Washington Star*, 22 August 1980, page A-7.
4/Jimmy Carter, *Facts on File World News Digest, Politics:* Carter Apologizes-Rues ethnic Purity mark, 17 April 1976, page 260 DZ.
5/Ibid, page 260 DZ
6/Ibid, page 260 DZ
7/Reverend Moses Javis, *St. Louis Globe Democrat*, 3 November 1976, page 1.
8/*St. Louis Post Dispatch:* "Clay Tells Rally He'll Push Carter To Support Jobs Bill," by Ann Telthorst, date unknown.
9/*Just Permanent Interests*, page 186.
10/*St. Louis Post:* "Carter backs jobs bill", Washington (AP), Sept 1978.

11/*Birmingham News,* 26 May 1979, page 1.

12/Ben Brown quoted in *Birmingham News*, 26 May 1979, page 1.

13/Collins, ibid., page 1.

14/Congressman Clay, House floor speech.

15/ *St. Louis Post Dispatch*, 'Bill Clay: I'm A Counterpuncher,' 14 July 1981, page 11a.

16/Speech to American Federation Government Employees, St. Louis, Missouri, 21 June 1980, Roadway Inn.

17/Louis Stokes, *Cleveland Plain Dealer*: Carter Calls Stokes, Who is Backing Kennedy by Thomas J. Brazaitis. May 1980, Page 1.

18/*Just Permanent Interests*, Amistad Press, New York, 1992, page 309.

19/Stokes, Ibid.

8

"It does, indeed, appear to be the case that no black official since Adam Clayton Powell has been so maligned as Congressman William Clay."[1]

– Mary R. Warner, Chairperson
Committee on the Status of Minority Elected Officials
National Association of Human Rights Workers

Warner wrote that perhaps no other official had spoken out so pointedly and firmly to fight the attack being waged. He (Clay) charged that the government was involved in a conspiracy to undermine and eliminate outspoken black leadership and challenged those who disagreed to explain why 50 percent of all blacks in the U.S. House of Representatives were under investigation for criminal activity and not 50 percent of all white Representative.

It was a government sponsored conspiracy in every sense of the definition: a premeditated collusion to deprive a person or persons of their rights and privileges.

Media and Government Harassment

During my early years in Congress, harassment of office-holders by the media was common occurrence. Unfounded allegations designed to eliminate ideological adversaries, or diminish their effectiveness as political voices, were often made by reactionary elements. Serious charges of misconduct surfacing in news editions with quotes from unnamed sources provided the usual method of maligning opponents. Failure to reveal sources gave liars and cowards a platform that made a mockery of the hallowed concept of press freedom.

Politicians are often advised not to engage in dogfights with those who buy ink by the gallons. But I was not easily susceptible to unsolicited threats, especially ones advocating surrender to media badgering, intimidation and extortion. My mental metabolism reacted to assaults on my free speech rights with tenacious indignity. My confrontational political activism left no room for compromise on issues of racial equality.

Techniques of Character Assassination

I refused to be intimidated by manipulative journalists writing outlandish articles, quoting unidentified sources, citing undocumented data, reporting questionable accounts of criminal activity by elected officials. Nebulous accusations against labor leaders, civil rights advocates or anti war protestors became the basis for prompting official government investigations.

Despite strenuous protests, the innuendo, half-truths, false statements lacing slews of printed words and repetitive television commentaries, continued to be aired. Ambiguous circumstances and frivolous accusations evolved into inescapable images of guilt. In many instances, questionable allegations were quietly, unceremoniously dropped. By then the damage was done: impeccable characters tarnished, promising careers halted, sterling reputations destroyed. In the process, family and children were traumatized, neighbors and friends embarrassed.

Even more obnoxious, the culprits who maligned them succeeded in diluting the credibility and influence of legitimate, innocent persons without producing credible evidence of wrong doing.

Facts Twisted To Fit Cynical Purpose

The endless saga of petty persecutions against black elected officials, including myself, was a prototype of the abuses used to victimize elected officials throughout the nation. The implication was that black members as a group were more criminally inclined, less principled, more corrupt, less moral.

St. Louis Globe Democrat publishers, Richard Amberg and his successor G. Duncan Bauman, the primary architects of massive resistance to extending equal rights to minorities in Missouri and surrounding states, embodied the salient, prevalent characteristics of dishonest news reporting. Their racially biased news articles and inflammatory editorials fomented hatred that engendered racial animosity among a sizeable group of whites.

I found myself in a twenty-five year battle, fighting for political survival with editors and reporters to salvage my reputation, constantly fighting for political survival. News stories and editorials covered my activities in a fashion normally reserved for incorrigible criminals or subversives threatening national security. Every statement I made was analyzed through a negative, biased prism, and scrutinized for every possibility of twisting into personal embarrassment or condemnation.

The campaign to drive me out of politics became an all-consuming obsession for the *Globe's* employees. Several ex-reporters who embellished non-newsworthy events into front page sensations, admitted that when the name of Bill Clay was mentioned there was disruption and confusion among editorial board members and senior staff. In the newsroom, typewriters automatically self activated in ideological panic.

One investigative reporter said the standing order from "on high" demanded that distortion, ridicule, and misquote should accompany every word or deed attributed to me. Ordinary everyday occurrences made the presses roll overtime: the way I teased my Afro-bush hair style, the easy fitting dashiki I wore. The way I smiled was always described as a sneer.

I was the 800 pound 'black' gorilla in the newsroom that the publishers did not create, could not destroy, and never understood.

Amberg's death in 1967 ended 10 years of bitter confrontation between us. His heir apparent, G. Duncan Bauman became publisher and launched a campaign more intense than the icon of racial hatred preceding him.

Globe Democrat: **Community Conscience** **(Identifies Particulars Against Clay)**

The new publisher became a self-anointed guardian of community values, and his personnel moonlighted as interpreters of moral standards. These patriotic town criers, in tainted ethical garb, waged relentless ideological warfare against the infidels: individuals, corporations and institutions that strayed from their myopic view established as puritanical standards of conduct. Their preoccupation with cleansing St. Louis of perceived corrupt political influence, readily reflected an overreaching bias in every article concerning activity of persons of my philosophical leanings.

The publisher's compelling neurotic motivation with destroying my effectiveness produced weird accusations that implied involvement in crimes and ethical lapses only he could envision. During my first 10 years in Congress, the newspaper devoted extensive coverage of my involvement in assorted and nefarious schemes: padding government payroll, falsifying congressional travel, diverting political contributions for personal use, engaging in illegal narcotic trafficking, importing a hit man to kill my opponent, consorting with gangsters, evading federal income taxes, refusing to represent the interests of white constituents, and promoting racism against white people.

Federal and local agents of government became private detectives without compensation from the newspaper, assisting in attempts to substantiate the bogus charges.

I became the target of criminal investigations by the Department of Justice, the Internal Revenue Service, the U.S. Attorney, and the Drug Enforcement Agency. Acting in collusion and conspiracy with the *Globe Democrat* and other journals, the Feds pursued the baseless charges with reckless abandonment.

Twenty-four hours before the 1974 primary election, the *Globe* printed a photograph on its front page, showing two individuals with extensive criminal records and me. The half inch headline stated, "Hoodlum Support for Clay." An editorial endorsing my opponent failed to mention the photograph was given to the newspaper by the Metropolitan Police Department. It was taken by a commercial photographer for a fee along with similar photos of 400 others at a political fund raiser years earlier.

One person in the photo had been dead three years. The other had been in prison for two years. An unidentified person had been excised from the photograph. The front page editorial stated:

> *This newspaper is convinced that William L. Clay's tenure in Congress has been a disgraceful affront to all the citizens of the 1st District, black and white, and Clay should be beaten in his attempt to return to the U.S. House of Representatives... The Globe Democrat, joined by two of three black newspapers, the Sentinel and the American, have cited numerous practical reasons for recommending Clay's rejection.[2]*

Abused Prosecutorial Authority

The campaign to end my political career was not confined to the *Globe Democrat*. Others allied with the publisher joined in conspiratorial tactics to defeat me. Elements in the media, the business community, the judiciary, and the Justice Department participated in a concerted effort to publicly ridicule and embarrass, and if possible to send me to the penitentiary.

In 1974, the Chief Prosecutor of the U.S. Crime Task Force in St. Louis, Liam Coonan, in opening remarks before a jury trying State Representative John Conley, promised it would hear evidence against an elected official for illegally trafficking in drugs, saying he would prove that William Clay (the one) met with an undercover agent and arranged to sell narcotics. Within hours of this mind boggling revelation, the *Globe* was on the streets with a lengthy story detailing the specifics of an alleged drug deal between Congressman Clay and an undercover agent.

The source for the prosecutor's unconscionable, irresponsible allegation was the word of a small time hoodlum with an extensive arrest record who had been convicted of murder, robbery, narcotics, burglary, and grand larceny. He was on the government's payroll at $100 weekly as an "undercover agent," commissioned to entrap others involved in criminal activity.

This was the third trial of the accused state representative and the first time the name William Clay appeared. The trial ended in a hung jury. Conley was convicted in the second trial but the verdict was overturned by a higher court on appeal.

At the conclusion of the trial, sources in the media alleged that Judge James Meredith called Coonan into his chamber and reprimanded him for injecting my name into the trial without offering evidence to substantiate the nature of my involvement. He also allegedly threatened to bar the prosecutor from trying any case in his court if he conducted himself like that again.

Samuel Dash, former Chief Counsel of the Senate Watergate Committee and Professor of Law at Georgetown University, in an unsolicited, spontaneous statement, said the assertion by Prosecutor Liam Coonan in open court was: "improper and an abuse of prosecutorial discretion. It is a poor prosecutor who names an individual when the prosecutor does not have evidence of culpability."[3]

When I protested the wild, irresponsible injustice to the Attorney General, a top official of the Justice Department told the media that I was the person and he had documented evidence of my involvement. His accusation was contradicted by John R. Bartels, Jr., Director of the Drug Enforcement Administration (DEA) who stated: "Clay is not nor has he ever been under investigation" for narcotic trafficking by this agency.

For eighteen months, I carried the label of a drug pusher like an albatross around my neck. My wife and children were looked at with that suspicious eying of guilt by some associates.

Numerous requests to produce the claimed evidence went unheeded. In disgust and frustration, again I wrote Attorney General Edward Levi stating,

> In flagrant and total disregard for what I consider my constitutional rights of citizenship, and my legislative responsibilities as a U.S. Congressman, various sections of the Department of Justice began conducting a witch hunt against me. It appeared that the recent, over zealous activity of Department of Justice agents was, and is designed to create or manufacture, if possible, a case involving me in the illegal trafficking of narcotics.[4]

I stated that "Anyone who says I am involved in narcotic traffic, including a U.S. Attorney General and members of the *Globe Democrat* are damn liars."[5]

Levi rejected my request for a meeting to discuss the matter. After thirteen months, eleven letters, and repeated phone calls without a substantive response, I enlisted the aid of congressional colleagues. My concern was not for special consideration, but fair consideration.

Determined to be heard on the evidence, not speculation or prejudices of a government attorney, biased newspaper articles, or a punk criminal, I enlisted eighty four (84) members of congress to sign a letter to Attorney General Levi, demanding that he: 1) admit or deny that the William Clay accused of peddling narcotics was the congressman; 2) justify his thirteen month refusal to answer questions from reporters and Congressman Clay about the case; 3) conduct a full and thorough Grand Jury investigation of the allegations, and (4) if evidence existed indict and try the Congressman for the offense in a court of law.

A meeting was scheduled with Attorney General Levi as a result of the letter. In attendance was House Majority Leader "Tip" O'Neill, and Representatives Louis Stokes, Barbara Jordan and Charles Rangel.

Levi did not impanel a Grand Jury but conducted a full scale investigation. Several dozen persons, already imprisoned for selling narcotics, were interviewed. Some were offered reduced sentences or freedom if they could prove my involvement in drug trafficking. At least fifty drug dealers and police informants were questioned about my possible association with known drug merchants. The U.S. Attorneys' office in Saint Louis, the Saint Louis Police Department and the *Globe* were asked to submit evidence of my involvement in narcotics. None was forthcoming.

The Justice Department and its Republican Attorney General, clearing me of any involvement in drug activity, wrote:

As you [Congressman Clay] are aware, last January you requested that the Department of Justice initiate an investigation into certain allegations that you were involved in illegal narcotics activities in the St. Louis area.

The Criminal Division has just concluded its inquiry into these allegations. I have reviewed the final report and I am now in a position to inform you that our investigation does not substantiate these charges. You will be pleased to know, therefore, that we are closing our files on this matter.[6]

Four days later, on June 16, 1975, a press conference was called by Republican Attorney General Levi to publicly declare that no evidence existed to: "tie Congressman Clay with illegal drug trafficking".[7]

Call for Apology

An editorial in the *Chicago Defender* titled "Bill Clay's Vindication," stated:

Rep. William 'Bill' Clay has always had a reputation as a tough fighter. Recently, he proved that he not only can stand the heat, he can give it to.

An ordinary person might have caved in when a major newspaper, the FBI, the Justice Department and the Drug Enforcement Administration combined to press charges of involvement in narcotic traffic. But Clay is not an ordinary person. He took on the whole establishment with the zest of a prize fighter in prime condition.

A fortnight ago, Clay was vindicated when the Justice Department closed its investigation... And the St. Louis Post Dispatch in an editorial called for the Justice Department to apologize to Clay for smearing his reputation.[7]

Clay Sought Impeachment of Attorney Coonan

I asked the House Judiciary Committee to impeach Attorney Liam S. Coonan. In a sharply worded letter to Chairman Peter Rodino, I stated: "Coonan accused me of the gravest crimes without corroborative evidence or pursuit of a formal indictment." I quoted from the American Bar Association's "code of professional responsibility" which said that a public prosecutor had the "duty to seek justice, not merely to convict."[9]

In the House chamber, I informed my colleagues: "U.S. Prosecutor Liam S. Coonan has prostituted his oath of office, brought shame to the Department of Justice and cast serious doubt on the impartiality of our system of criminal justice...Coonan attempted to frame me on a 'trumped up' narcotic charge. I use the harsh word "frame" because there is no other in the English language which is more descriptive of the vile, unconscionable act of this despicable employee."[10]

The inquiry was the most expensive of the investigations. The government tapped my telephones at home and my congressional office, bugged my hotel rooms and district office, and kept 24 hour surveillance while I was in St. Louis.

Padding the Payroll

In July 1974, the *Globe Democrat* charged me with padding my payroll with friends and associates who were ghost employees. When the federal government indicated it was to conduct a preliminary inquiry, I insisted on a complete investigation and voluntarily made available all records to substantiate my claim of innocence.

Eight of my employees were investigated during a seven month period. I appeared before the grand jury on four separate occasions, giving more than a dozen hours of testimony, provided all documents requested and answering every question asked.

During the course of the investigation, my administrative assistant was indicted and pled guilty of placing his sister-in-law on the payroll for two years without her showing up for work. He was sentenced to three years in prison.

The incident of alleged criminal activity of 'padding my payroll', lasted eight (8) months. The estimated cost was more than $800,000.00 in federal and local law enforcement funds. It involved the government bringing almost 100 witnesses to testify.

No evidence was found to substantiate the charge against me and another letter from the justice department informing me that the Grand Jury cleared me of any implication in the affair.

Campaign Contributions Investigated

In 1975, the *Globe Democrat* assigned two indefatigable reporters to uncover any suspicions of criminal conduct or rumors of derogatory information about me. They searched official files, interrogated friends, enemies, cohorts, and government officials.

Doggedly inquiring of my political and personal activities, anything mentioned that approached illegality or indiscretion, no matter how unreliable the source or insignificant the issue, appeared in print. Allegations were made without identifying accusers, merely stating that it came from a source wishing to remain anonymous.

Based on flimsy, sometimes comical accusations of wrongdoing, a story appearing in the *Globe Democrat* prompted the FBI to investigate the possibility of my converting campaign contributions to personal use. Responding to the foolish charge, the agency dispatched agents to interview labor leaders and other contributors to my re election campaign and somehow their responses were leaked to the media.

I accused FBI Director Clarence Kelly of being retained by the *Globe Democrat* as its private detective agent, and invited him to interrogate me before accepting as fact an article in a discredited scandal sheet. In response, he sent two field representatives to ascertain my side of the controversy. After properly identifying themselves, one took out a small card and began to read my Miranda rights as the subject of a criminal inquiry. I took offense to the procedure and informed him to leave my office at once.

Later that day, Director Kelly sent two other agents in search of the facts. Knowing it was the story in the newspaper which caused the investigation, I asked the FBI to produce the document which prompted suspicion of criminality. He brought out the official report all members of Congress are required to submit to the Clerk of the House of Representatives.

He stated that I received contributions from D.R.I.V.E., C.O.P.E., N.A L.C., and several other initialed organizations but failed to report them. I took his copy of the report, pointed out that each donation was listed under official names of the groups. Together, we meticulously established such organizations as DRIVE (Democrat, Republican, Independent, Voter Education Committee), COPE (Committee on Political Action (AFL CIO), NALC (National Association of Letter Carriers), SEIU (Service Employees International Union). Two embarrassed, red-faced FBI agents admitted the mistake, turned off their recorder, quietly zipped their brief cases, and sheepishly left my office.

On August 11, 1975, another official of the Justice Department, Assistant Attorney General in the Criminal Division, Richard L. Thornburgh became a Pen Pal joining our literary club and wrote:

> *"We have determined that no further action is warranted on allegations that you and your campaign committees did not report some 1974 political contributions."[11]*

Government Sues Clay for $186,000

The *Wall Street Journal* printed a front page article by staff reporter Jerry Landauer, alleging that I falsified travel records and billed the government in excessive amounts. Titled: "How a Congressman Bilked Government for Phony Travel," the headline itself rendered a verdict of guilty. I was accused of receiving reimbursement for travel back to my district while remaining in Washington D.C. Throughout the article there were personal opinions of a demeaning nature and derogatory adjectives usually found in political smut sheets. The 'news article' was written in editorial style, and implied that I stole thousands of dollars from the taxpayers.

The *Wall Street Journal* copyrighted the article and syndicated it nationally on its day of publication, coordinating it to appear in the *Globe* and other conservative leaning papers simultaneously. All three national television networks played the story as their evening lead. The *Saint Louis Post Dispatch* ran an editorial the next day quoting verbatim from the Journal without first ascertaining the facts. The editorial of the liberal newspapers curiously challenged me to disprove the charges instead of the government proving them.

One of the more prominent charges was that on April, 18, 1974, I could not have possibly been in St. Louis because reporter Landauer cited me as making a speech in Los Angeles. The *Post* referred to that instance in its editorial, writing, "If Mr. Clay actually made both trips-it would seem that the phony travel issue loses its force." And so it not only lost its force but its credibility within a matter of hours.

After a personal telephone conversation with the editor of the

Post Dispatch, many of the inconsistencies in the article became apparent. I suggested he check his personal calendar for the day in question about my being in Los Angeles and call me back. Thirty minutes later he did, and informed me that on April 18, 1974, indeed I was in Saint Louis meeting with him and his editorial staff. So much for professional investigative reporting!

On my birthday, April 30, 1976, the prestigious *Wall Street Journal* ran a follow up story implicating nine other members of congress in the same travel bilking plot. All nine members were white, four from the Saint Louis area. However, the article was not syndicated nationwide, not the lead story on any of the national television networks, not front page news in the Saint Louis press including the *Globe Democrat*, nor was it a subject of harsh editorial treatment by either the *Globe* or *Post Dispatch*.

The Congressional Black Caucus took issue with the *Wall Street Journal* concerning the manner in which it handled the two stories. Congresswoman Yvonne Brathwaite Burke (D Calif), Chairperson of the Caucus in a press release stated:

The *Journal's* article attacking Representative Clay used a totally different style than an April 30th article questioning travel expenses collected by other Members of Congress. The *Wall Street Journal's* focus on Congressman Clay while de emphasizing the allegations against other Members as individuals, raises serious questions about disparate treatment of black political leaders.

The act of singling out Bill Clay for a special front page story accusing him of falsifying travel vouchers, and then several weeks later lumping together nine non black Members of Congress who were accused of substantially the same thing, makes one wonder about the objectivity of the *Wall Street Journal*.

The *Journal* story concerning Representative Clay was filled with derogatory and demeaning language, including such statements as "Clay bills government for phony travel trips." and "Cost of government has doubled since Clay came to office." The April 30th article on the nine non black Members did not resort to such loaded phrases of personal attack.[12]

Several weeks later, a freshman law student from a New York college sued me. He filed under a seldom used federal statute allowing citizens to financially benefit a percentage of the money collected from those who filed false claims against the government. The Justice Department immediately rushed into court, amended the petition and charged me with knowingly filing 89 false expense claims. They asserted that I owed the federal government $186,000.

Curiously, the federal government did not file legal actions against the nine white members accused by the same reporter of violating the same law. Neither did the hyper incensed law student file legal briefs against them.

Confronted with the cost of legal procedures and the full weight of the Justice Department, presented me with a difficult but not insurmountable task. I had to resort to the painstaking, time-consuming task of reconstructing my travel for the last five years and producing documentation to substantiate my where a bouts.

Before the issue was resolved, I produced evidence of plane tickets, gasoline records, highway motel receipts, credit cards, checks proving my travel for all but 8 of the 89 trips. In addition, I produced receipts for 97 trips paid by personal monies to verify the validity of my travel claims.

After presenting my case, my learned Pen Pals at the Justice Department conceded the folly of the obnoxious charges and offered to drop the suit. Considering that I had already spent considerable money in attorney fees, and recognizing that pursuing the case would cost more in defense expenditures than the settlement offered, I agreed to pay the federal government $1,754 for eight trips undocumented (less than one 1% percent) of the $186,000 alleged amount I was accused of pilfering. The settled amount came to $30 per month over a five year period.

The irony is the federal government owed me $2,500 for official travel which I discovered during my record recounting was owed me and never reimbursed.

One of the *Globe Democrat* reporters who made most of the untrue accusations against me was rewarded by the Justice Department that hired him as an Assistant U.S. Attorney in the St. Louis Federal District.

After the travel fiasco, I thought it would end the newspaper's obsession with attempts to jail or defeat me for reelection and I could get back to focusing on constituent problems. But my adversaries were indelibly wedded to the idea that I deserved incarceration or defeat.

Investigated for Criminal Tax Evasion

The infamous *Globe* seemingly out of desperation, instructed another of its government subsidiaries-the Internal Revenue Service (IRS)-to look into my affairs. In an editorial, it suggested the IRS investigate my income tax returns, stating: "Any irregularities in expenditures and receipts certainly should be a concern of IRS, whether they involve Clay or the beneficiaries of political payments."[13]

Less than six weeks later, a new set of letter writers, essayists at the Internal Revenue Service, feeling slighted, notified me that an official investigation was underway. After thirty years of filing tax forms and never being called to explain any deduction or expenditure, I suddenly found myself the subject of a criminal inquiry for evasion of income taxes. For obvious political reasons, the U.S. Prosecutor saw fit to seek an indictment without first asking me to respond to those questions which gave him "deep" concern. His precipitous action resulted in the harassment of many of my associates. Within a month, a subpoena was issued for all my congressional payroll records, expense accounts and personal congressional bank transactions during the previous five years. Simultaneously, subpoenas were served on all financial institutions with whom I did business, and on many of my relatives, and friends, as well as my present and former staff employees.

So detailed was the search that Revenue agents went to the homes of persons whose checks had shown up in my account six years earlier. Some of those transactions were in the paltry sum of $10 and $15. Agents asked them if the checks were payments in return for services my office performed.

Family members, friends, and political associates were also

harassed. IRS agents visited the homes of my personal friends as late as 10:00 p.m.

After nine months of the charade, it dawned on me that all the subpoenas were dated the same day in August. Normally grand juries in Saint Louis, as a tradition dating back prior to air condition, did not sit during the dog days of August. In checking the record, none had been impaneled for this occasion.

Based on the newly discovered evidence, my attorney entered a motion to quash the subpoenas and all records attained through this fraudulent process. The federal judge, furious that he had been duped into signing the subpoenas by the prosecutor, agreed, issuing an order confiscating all records, sealing them and prohibiting the IRS from using information gained for civil or criminal prosecution. He stated: "Government shall make no civil use of the testimony or documents produced before the grand jury..." without first obtaining a court order.

But the Internal Revenue was not easily discouraged. Three weeks later, prolific writers at the IRS sent a message informing me that it intended to proceed in a civil case if my wife and I would sign the enclosed form voluntarily waiving our rights and granting permission for them to use the subpoenaed documents. I immediately contacted my attorney who sent them a blistering telegram expressing outrage at their audacity.

The investigation lasted more than two years. The IRS interviewed more than 200 individuals who had business transactions with me. Some experts estimated the cost in excess of $550,000.00.

The Dreadful Fear of Gerrymander

There were two attempts in ten years to gerrymander the district I represented. Both times I went into the federal courts asking that they preserve established boundaries that made it possible for a minority candidate to have an equal opportunity to be elected. Both times, I was successful.

On another occasion, three days before a hotly contested election with a white candidate, the registration rolls of my congressional district were purged of 20,000 black voters. I solicited an injunction which resulted in a court order keeping the polls open five hours past the usual closing time. Eligible voters who had been arbitrarily and capriciously stricken by the election board were allowed to cast ballots upon presenting utility bills or other documents to polling officials showing proof of residency.

Due Process and Free Speech Prevail

If I had been guilty of the numerous charges of gross violations of law, and yet never arrested, indicted, tried or convicted, then something must have been gravely wrong with the judicial system.

Suggesting what it might be, I issued a press release attacking the Saint Louis community for allowing publisher Bauman free reign to intimidate individuals and stymie free expression, writing:

> *It's frightening to see the kind of power that a bigot like G. Duncan Bauman holds in this community. He has not only cowered public officials, but has intimidated the moral community as well. High ranking church leaders are so afraid of him that they prostitute themselves and their religious principles in an effort to curry favor from this demonic creature...This man is against everything that the moral leadership proclaims to abhor and he is opposed to all they have sworn to support.[14]*

Testifying before a committee of the Congressional Black Caucus, Lu Palmer explained the problem and power of the press in its relations to black people. He said:

> *"The press has gone through a period of so-called objective journalism which was never objective at all. Then we moved into a period of so-called interpretive journalism which was not interpretive at all. Both of these phases simply allowed whites in the press to continue their insidious control over the minds of our people."[15]*

Some in Media Helped Save My Career

Trashing the role played by the *Globe Democrat* and the *Wall Street Journal* is not an indictment of the media as a class. I readily admit that without the assistance of honest editors and dedicated reporters my career would have been destroyed years prior by unscrupulous yellow journalists working for cynical press operatives. The black press in St. Louis played a major role in my successful fight to keep the government and mass media from destroying my career. Eugene Mitchell, Nannie Mitchell Turner, and Howard B. Woods of the Argus, Vaughan Chatman of the People's Guide, Floyd Edmonds of the Crusader answered with facts, unsubstantiated allegations of irresponsible, fraudulent charges. Three *Post Dispatch* reporters, Robert L. Joiner, Robert Adams and Lawrence E. Taylor, performed exceptionally well in establishing facts about the untrue accusations of those attempting to smear me.

When the ordeal was coming to a favorable close, the *St. Louis American* wrote, "Not since Adam Clayton Powell has a black legislator been the focus of such controversy and investigations as faced William L. Clay."[16]

Media Had Its Deep Throat

December 18, 1974, in a House statement titled: "Deep Throat of Newspaper Industry," I said on the floor of the House of Representatives to my colleagues:

Mr. Speaker, in every field of human endeavor there are those who abuse the rights and privileges extended for the benefit of all. The field of journalism is no exception. There are those publications that have interpreted the constitutional guarantee of freedom of the press and the Supreme Court ruling of libel and public figures as a mandate to vilify and crucify those who would dare philosophically to disagree with the publishers and editors.

One such muckraking newspaper is the St. Louis Globe Democrat. Its' reputation for yellow journalism is widely known throughout this country. Mr. Speaker, the St. Louis Globe is almost completely void of truth, decency, and morality. Any story appearing on its pages remotely resembling the truth is purely coincidental.[17]

Congressional Committee Testimony
(Reform or Abolish Grand Jury System)

In testimony before a House subcommittee, I asked the serious consideration of legislation to reform or abolish the grand jury system entirely, stating its original intent was to protect the innocent who had been accused falsely. I contended that

In recent years, grand juries have been composed almost exclusively of society's financial and social elite who routinely disregard the interest of the ordinary individual. Prosecutors use the juries as personal tools to harass, intimidate and frame those who espouse radical causes or differing political opinions."[18]

I testified that Prosecutors developed elaborate arrangements with press persons trying to convict the accused in the court of public opinion by leaking derogatory, unsubstantiated testimony for the purpose of discrediting and destroying the accused. The accused is not permitted legal counsel while appearing before the grand jury, not afforded the basic constitutional right to be confronted by his accusers, nor is he allowed to cross examine his accusers. I said,

"In the present anti crime hysteria, a grand jury indictment becomes synonymous with guilt. Most grand juries are pawns in the hands of unscrupulous prosecutors who select what evidence will be considered, which witnesses will be called to testify, who will be granted immunity and, which charges will be leveled.[19]

I described grand juries as rubber stamps for the system and advised that if evidence of a crime exists, that evidence should be taken before the court in a preliminary hearing and give the accused the right to cross examine.

Negative News Coverage No Deterrent
To Political Advancement

My life long struggle with the *Globe* did not reap the most productive benefits desired by its publisher. The continuous flow of negative news coverage and editorials failed to cripple my influence as the newspaper's impact in the black community became nil.

In the white community, I was portrayed as a race hating monster who ignored the needs of white voters. Creation of that image, for many years, temporarily placed limitations on my ability to effectively establish coalitions with certain segments of the broader community. But, eventually, senior citizens, working people, civil libertarians, environmentalists, women's organizations, and poor people of all races acknowledged my concern and began to show appreciation for my leadership. Subsequently they rejected the biased reporting of the newspaper.

Jake McCarthy, a columnist for the *Post Dispatch* summed up the lack of influence the newspaper had on my political fortunes, in an article titled "A Personal Opinion:"

> *Clay's popularity seems to be riding high despite the publicity barrage against him. At a recent dinner sponsored by the St. Louis chapter of the National Association of Social Workers, Clay rose to introduce the principal speaker, Congresswoman Barbara Jordan of Texas. As he went to the rostrum in the Khorassan Room of the Chase Park Plaza Hotel, the full house gave Clay a standing ovation. One Clay associate noted, accurately enough, that this was an assemblage of middle class black and white social workers and their spouses, not a band of precinct workers from Clay's twenty-sixth Ward.*[20]

Steve Hartman, jacket and book designer for a publishing company wrote, "Clay survived the on-going" fight with the daily that waged a campaign to ensure his loss in every election, and without compromising his principles or softening his attacks on racist and racism, won 15 consecutive times, and the newspaper eventually folded.

President Nixon's Enemy List

While the sordid mess of governmental lawlessness in the Watergate affair was slowly untangling, it was revealed that President Nixon had compiled an enemies list comprised of American citizens who disagreed with his policies and politics. Included on the list were corporate executive, educators, lawyers, former cabinet members, insurance executives, labor leaders, civil rights advocates, publishers, editors, 10 members of the U.S. Senate and 18 members of the U.S. House of Representatives. I, Bill Clay, was one of them.

The President's enemies were subjected to numerous kinds of harassment by government agents acting in official capacities.

Those who struggled to end racism, sexism, poverty and discrimination were designated as enemies. Disagreeing with Nixon's philosophy and ideology was the standard for measuring patriotism and defining insurrection. In his psychic, he saw nothing wrong in unleashing the awesome power of government on those he identified as enemies of HIS democracy.

As an aside, I must note that percentage-wise the rate of involvement in squeamish, sordid, even criminal activity is generally the same for all professional groups. Incorrigibles are found lurking in every field. The difference lies merely in the public's perception that politicians are more corrupt because media coverage of felonious activity engaged in by doctors, lawyers, judges, educators, and businessmen is not exploited to the same extent.

The notoriety of their deeds is not harped on until other professionals are driven from their occupations. Carl Holman, Executive Director of the Urban Coalition summoned up the situation accurately when he declared, 'The media (has) the power of approval or disapproval. (It has) the power to treat people and causes as fads.'[21]

NOTES

1/The Dilemma of Black Politics: A Report on Harassment of Black
Elected Official, by Mary R. Warner, Voter Education and
Registration Action, Inc., 400 First Street, Suite 105, Washington,
D.C., July 1987, page 42.
2/*St. Louis Globe Democrat:* Hoodlum Support For Clay,   August 5, 1974, page 1.
3/*Just Permanent Interests*, page 328.
4/Letter from Congressman Clay to Attorney General Edward Levi, January 1975.
5/*St. Louis Argus,* January 30, 1975, page 9.
6/In a letter dated June 12, 1975, Deputy Attorney
General Harold Attorney Harold R. Tyler,
7/*St. Louis Post Dispatch:* U.S. Drops Criminal Inquiry Into Clay's Travel Expenses, by Shelia Rule, 9/17/76. page 1.
8/*The Chicago Defender*: Bill Clay Vindication, July 10, 1975, editorial page.
9/Letter to Peter Rodino, Chairman House Judiciary Committee.
10/house chamber
11/*St. Louis Post Dispatch:* Rep. Clay Is Cleared In Inquiry, August 11, 1975, page 1.

12/Congressional Black Caucus Press Release, dated May 15, 1976.

13/*St. Louis Globe Democrat,* March 13, 1975, editorial page. 14/Press release by Rep. William L. Clay

15/Congressional Record, U.S. House of Representatives,   December 18, 1974, 567-669 39254 U.S. Government Printing 1975, Washington, D.C

16/*St. Louis American*, April 8, 1976.

17/U.S. House of Representatives, Wednesday, December 18, 1974, article "Deep Throat" of Newspaper Industry.

18/Testimony Before House Committee

19/Ibid.

20/Jake McCarthy, "Personal Opinion," *St. Louis Post Dispatch*

21/ Carl Holman, Executive Director of the Urban Coalition, 6 March 1972, Cannon House Office Building, Washington, D.C.

9

Internal Politics of U. S. House

The awesome responsibility of Congresspersons is not limited to legislating matters of grave national and international import, but also involves setting standards of personal conduct regulating behavior of its membership, establishing rules for maintaining in-house order, and developing procedures for normal housekeeping duties to keep the body functioning smoothly.

The Committee on Standards of Official Conduct (Ethics) determines if member activity violates any laws, regulations, House rules or reflects unfavorably on the institution.

The House Administration Committee oversees the daily functions of dispensing job-related perks, privileges, and gratuities incidental to regular salary, awarding office space, assigning parking spots, management of restaurants, barbershops, staff allotments, members travel to-and-from districts, home district office facilities, and election challenges against individual members.

Hays/Thompson Fight for Chairmanship

My first real encounter with a powerful committee chairman was in 1971 when I was rejected for a seat on the House Administration Committee. Wayne Hays, chairman of the committee, informed me that it was an internal struggle for control of the committee between him and Frank Thompson of New Jersey and I happened to be caught in the cross-fire.

He accused Thompson, a member of the Education and Labor Committee, of attempting to usurp his power as chairman, and explained that members of the committee I was on already had disproportionate representation on the Administration Committee. He was correct in that assertion. Six of the 15 Democrats on the committee were members of our Education and Labor Committee.

To Post Office and Civil Service

Hays enjoyed great latitude and absolute power in chairing the committee. He was sometimes accused of using that authority in an arbitrary and vindictive manner. To prove his opposition was not personal, he noted that two years prior I indicated a preference for the Post Office and Civil Service Committee. Acknowledging my continued interest, he arranged for the appointment which proved valuable in placing me on a fast-track for several subcommittee and full committee chairmanships.

In 1976, Hays, accused of placing a female on his payroll who performed no official duties, under a barrage of media criticism, resigned his seat. Next in line according to House seniority rules, I inherited his vacated office in the Rayburn Building, located on the 3rd floor in the northwest corner, situated in a dead-end corridor. The swank quarters had a beautiful view of the Washington Monument visible from a small balcony outside the spacious suite. It was one of the much publicized office 'hideaways' that senior members occupied. The elevator opened in front of the office door. Visitors finding themselves in this very private, secluded section were either coming to the office or were lost. After inspecting the office, I requested that the property manager leave all the furnishings, including a large ornate, hand-carved desk, prominently enhancing the decor. My request was summarily rejected with a hearty laugh, as I was informed the desk was an antique belonging personally to Congressman Hays and valued at more than $20,000.

Twist of Fate Makes a Majority Leader

The contest between Richard Bolling of Missouri, Philip

Burton of California, and Jim Wright of Texas for majority leader in 1976 turned into a donnybrook that held Democratic Caucus members and the media in animated suspense for days.

Bolling of Missouri, a liberal and veteran of 28 years in the House, was author of two books on reforming the Congress, and had chaired the bipartisan committee to reform the committee structure. Because of his interest in basic institutional reform, he was endorsed by the *New York Times*, St. Louis *Post Dispatch*, the Kansas City Times and other dailies. Burton of California, Caucus Chairman, a liberal with strong ties to old line Democrats and southerners, was considered the favorite for the position. Wright of Texas, a cautious, serious legislator had broad based support across the south, west and the northeast. Considered a middle-of-the-roader and in some circles a conservative, he was not given much chance to win.

I found myself innocently embroiled in the midst of the contest. My support was sought by Bolling the dean of my state delegation, Burton, a traveling companion and a member of the same committee, and Wright, a friend and adviser whose mother lived in my congressional district and supported my candidacy. I endorsed Bolling.

Bolling and Burton vied for support of liberals and moderates while Burton and Wright divided the conservative members. Wright picked up some support in the Northeast because he had organized support for New York City when it faced bankruptcy. Others sup ported him because as a member of the Public Works Committee, he aided in funding for buildings, bridges, dams and federal buildings in their states.

Under the rules, if one candidate failed to get a clear majority, the two highest vote-getters faced each other in a run-off. Assessing the situation, Burton, the front runner and excellent vote counter, concluded Bolling would defeat him in a tete-a-tete race. Feeling comfortable with his lead, he persuaded enough of his supporters to vote for Wright who ousted Bolling by three votes.

Fascinating! Intriguing! High political drama! A liberal (Burton) supported a conservative (Wright) to defeat a liberal (Bolling). But in an ironic twist of fate, Bolling, after losing, retaliated by persuading his liberal friends to cast their votes for conservative

Wright who in turn defeated liberal (Burton) by one vote. Wright's victory put him on a track eventually leading to House Speaker.

Dellums on Armed Service Committee

An early mission of the CBC was to spread the organization's influence by winning seats on all House committees. Blacks served on eleven of the twenty-one standing committees, however none were on the major "exclusive committees" of Appropriations, Ways and Means, and Rules. No CBC member was assigned to another key committee Armed Services which Ron Dellums sought.

Congressman Wilbur Mills, chairman of the Committee on Committees, responsible for determining assignments, informed Dellums that Rep. F. Edward Hebert (D-La.), chairman of Armed Services, would accept any black member recommended by the Black Caucus except Dellums.

The alleged reason for opposing Dellums was his effort to reduce military spending, and to find peaceful solutions to the world's problems. According to Rep. Jim Corman (D-Cal.), Hebert claimed Dellums was a radical from Berkeley and his placement on the committee would be a: "significant security breach."[1]

Dellums sought the help of Phil Burton who told him to immediately contact Stokes, chairman of CBC and demand an immediate meeting with Speaker Carl Albert (D-Ok.). He said, "Lou Stokes is a great guy, nice and polite. You need him, but you also need someone who can be angrier than Lou will be, somebody who'll play the bad cop. You need Bill Clay as well."[2]

Albert invited majority leader Tip O'Neill, and Wilbur Mills to the meeting. Stokes in presenting the reason for Ron's place on the committee, said, "Mr. Speaker, this is a matter of principle to us...The CBC has made a collective decision to have Ron serve... Black people throughout the country recognize him for his leadership in this area."[3]

Speaker Albert said that he would go back and attempt to convince committee members to change their minds. But that did not end the exchange. Stokes made it clear that black members were adamant about Ron sitting on the committee.

The gauntlet was thrown down. At that point, I charged that Hebert's ultimatum conveyed a message that "southerners" still hanging on to their ante-bellum notions would decide which blacks qualified to speak for our race. I made it known that the only reason for denying Dellums was racism, and stated "If you don't put Ron on the committee, the CBC will call a press conference and denounce the Democratic leadership in Congress as racist. I said, "There's no other possible explanation for excluding this brother."[4] Dellums was appointed to the committee the next day.

Members Convicted in ABSCAM Sting

The biggest congressional scandal during my tenure of office, ended with convictions and prison terms of six House members and one Senator. The 1980 entrapment of members by an FBI sting operation (the ABSCAM), charged them with accepting $50,000 each from undercover government agents posing as Arab sheiks, asking their congressional influence in legislative matters.

Michael 'Ozzie' Myers (D-Pa.), despite his criminal conviction by a federal jury in 1980, was nominated in the Democratic primary for reelection. But the House displayed its disgust when more than two-thirds of its members voted to expel him. It was the first time since 1861 that the House of Representatives expelled a member. Three were expelled for support of rebellion when they joined the Confederate Army during the Civil War.

Indiana 8 Election Recount

The Congress is responsible for investigating disputed elections. I played a role in adjudicating one of the closest disputes of its members in the 20th century.

On election night, Frank McCloskey, a Democrat, was unofficially ahead of Republican Richard McIntyre by 72 votes. But, after a hurried, partisan and suspicious contested recount, the Republican Secretary of State certified his GOP opponent, McIntyre, the winner by 34 votes. A second recount supervised by Republican state officials increased his lead to 481 votes.

The campaign was filled with controversy. At one point, more than 4,800 ballots were disqualified because of a technicality. The errors made by state election officials, not the voters, disenfranchised McCloskey's most avid supporters. Twenty percent of the ballots cast by African Americans were not counted. The unfairness and possible illegality of the action cast suspicion on the election process and recount procedure.

The Democratic controlled U.S. House, refused to seat McIntyre. Congressman Bill Ford recommended to the Speaker that he appoint me to a special investigative task force to determine the factual results of the election in the 8th District of Indiana.

Speaker Tip O'Neil appointed me to the House Administration Committee specifically to assist in resolving the disputed election. I joined Congressmen Bill Thomas (R-Cal.) and Chairman Leon Panetta (D-Cal.) on the investigating committee. The General Accounting Office (GAO) secured the ballot boxes to protect against tampering. The Special Task Force journeyed to Indiana on weekends to recount the votes according to rules established by the GAO. Before a resolution was reached, the process involved more than 200 hours of congressional debate, 100 hours of deliberations, testimony and travel by our task force, and four months of partisan wrangling. The recount of 233,000 votes gave McCloskey a 4-vote margin of victory.

Debate on Seating McCloskey

The recommendation on a committee vote of 2-to-1 for seating McCloskey riled every Republican. The resolution declared McCloskey duly elected from the Eighth District of Indiana. Since 1933, the House had resolved 102 contested elections. It was one of the closest and most bitterly contested.

I said in floor debate that the single guiding principle of the committee was to ascertain accurately as possible the will of the citizens of the Eighth Congressional District. In my opinion the task force achieved that end. Unfortunately, some Republicans voiced dogmatic assertions and bold accusations that the election was stolen. In rebuttal, I stated, "Partisan politics taken to such extreme serves neither Mr. McIntyre nor Mr. McCloskey, the Republican Party nor the Democratic Party, this body nor the country. If there is to be dispute, let it be based on the facts."[5]

On May 1, 1985, McCloskey was seated by a Party-line vote which precipitated a disruptive demonstration. All 190 Republican members marched out of the House chamber in protest and held a rally on the lawn of the Capitol where they vowed to disrupt normal House procedure.

Despite the furor and explosive outrage of the Republicans, the action of the House in seating McCloskey was validated and vindicated. Five years later, I took the floor of the House to announce that Ferman Yearby, Republican Party chairman for Spencer County, Indiana pleaded guilty to conspiracy in the buying of votes in the 1982, 1984 (McCloskey/McIntyre election), and 1986 elections. He was sentenced to 3 years in jail. Seventeen other individuals, including two former treasurers of the county's Republican Party were convicted of vote fraud crimes committed in the same elections.

The Demise of Speaker Jim Wright

In 1988, Newt Gingrich (R-Ga.) filed a complaint with the House Ethics Committee against Speaker Jim Wright, alleging four counts of misconduct. He was joined by 71 Republican members who later admitted two of the accusations questioning Wright's oil investments were in error. The remaining charges involved royalties the Speaker received from sell of his book, "Reflections of a Public Man".

In the atmosphere of media overreaching and public hysteria, every facet of Wright's public and private life came under scrutiny. The inquiry was broadened as the 12 member Committee on Standards of Official Conduct (Ethics) looked into alleged accusations of a real estate deal that netted the Speaker $50,000, improper use of a business associate's condominium, influencing federal bank regulators on behalf of two Texas savings and loans, and use of staff as ghostwriters for his book.

Wright relinquished the Speakership in 1989, bitterly denouncing the treatment accorded him in the investigative process as a climate of "mindless cannibalism."

Gingrich's fellow colleagues elevated him to the No 2 leadership post, the Republican Whip.

Sgt-at-Arms Check Cashing Scandal

In March 1992, the U.S. Attorney's office in Washington, D.C. opened an investigation related to allegations of criminal conduct involving the House Sgt-at-Arms. The nation's newspapers and talk show hosts demanded disclosure of banking records to determine if there was criminal wrongdoing. For months, the media was consumed by speculation of improprieties.

Charges were waged without merit or substance. Rules of federally chartered banks were applied to the Sgt-at-Arms which was not a bank, but a facility instituted by the Treasury Department to pay Congressional salaries. The entity provided no savings accounts and paid no interests on deposits. The average daily cash on hand was in the millions. The entire amount belonged to members of Congress and were not covered by the Federal Insurance Deposit Corporation or protection from embezzlement.

I was accused by the media of writing checks of $9,000.00, $16,000.00, $30,000.00 among the hundreds of alleged overdraft instruments attributed to other members. I voluntarily appeared and testified before the House Ethics Committee, providing substantial evidence that not one of my checks constituted an overdraft. According to stringent banking rules even if the Sgt-of-Arms were a bank, the law clearly showed checks covered on the same day are not a violation.

Like most members, I kept money in an interest bearing account at the Wright Patman Federal Credit Union, located 100 yards from the Sgt-at-Arms. Each time a check was presented for payment, I was informed and immediately called the credit union for a hand delivered transfer to cover the overage. If it were a regular bank protection against thief, it would have been covered, interest rates would have been paid on savings and automatic transfer to cover overdrafts would have been made.

In closing, I stated that deposits made at any time during the bank's normal hours must be credited the day made.[6]

Despite arguments of legality, there was a simple question of basic fairness. I insisted "Historically, there were no rules, no regulations, no laws prohibiting the loose practices of the Sgt-at-Arms and it is now too late to debate whether or not there should have been more strict enforcement."[7]

I concluded that

"In each instance of proof provided, there is a showing of sufficient payments transferred from my savings account to my checking account on the same day the checks were presented. However, the policy of the Sgt-of-Arms was to record them the next day."[8]

There was no evidence that the checks did not arrive the same day and it would be highly unusual that a deposit traveling by inside mail or by messenger from the Rayburn Building to the Capital took more than one day. In addition, I stated: "I can't prove that those deposits arrived the same day. Neither can you disprove. But I submit, according to long established principles of law and of fairness, I don't have to prove it."[9]

End of Check Cashing Scandal

In a letter from Office of the U.S. Attorney General, hand delivered to my office by a FBI agent, I was notified that after

"complete review of your account [Clay's] at the House banking facility and the documents associated therewith...On the evidence we have reviewed, I have concluded that there is no basis for pursuing a further inquiry regarding possible criminal violations concerning your account."[10]

The clearance letter was based on a review of more than 300 member's accounts over a 39-month period for overdrafts.

Gingrich Destroys All Caucuses

When Gingrich became Speaker in 1995, one of his first acts was to lessen the influence of caucuses. His proposal targeted liberal and moderate leaning organizations. The groups slated ranged from the Democratic Study Group (DSG) that provided research to Republicans and Democrats and was considered an excellent vehicle for analyzing legislation, to the most prominent legislative service/research group: the Congressional Black Caucus.

Gingrich's widely discussed motivation also called for elimination of the Hispanic Caucus and the Women's Caucus. To accomplish his goal, he found it necessary to destroy all 25 Legislative Service Organizations (LSO) as the caucuses were designated.

House Democratic Minority Leader Richard Gephardt opposed the move, stating the Congress would be rendered "less informed, less effective and less able to serve the American people in ways that matter."[11]

During debate, I stated caucuses are "a very efficient way of operating to make sure there is the right expertise for focusing on issues of national import."[12]

Going to the extreme, Tom Tancredo (R-Colo) introduced a rule change to prohibit race-based caucuses. If accepted, it would abolish the Black, Hispanic and Asian Pacific groups.

An outraged Ciro Rodriguez (D-Texas) stated, "His proposal to silence the collective voice of minority members is shocking and offensive."[13]

The proposal was so radical that it never gained traction even among Tanecredo's Republican colleagues.

Leadership Becomes Dictatorship

Gingrich successfully changed House rules supposedly to create a business-like system of efficiently administering and streamlining the operation. In effect, the drastic rule changes adopted by the majority resulted in the transfer of most power to the Speaker. He became a czar, vested with unlimited authority to eliminate seniority, diminish the influence of chairmen, arbitrarily change the scope, jurisdiction and responsibility of committees, and to deny committee membership to those not in ideological sync with him.

Under the new rules, a small group of Gingrich's insiders wielded influence, punishing those who expressed ideas and thoughts contrary to the leader's agenda.

The Republican reorganization abolished several committees, including Post Office and Civil Service. The important role of 3 million federal and postal employees were down-graded and legislation relative to their interests were transferred to subcommittees of various other committees. Eliminating committees was declared a major reform when Republicans were fighting to win control of the congress.

Caving-in to the folly, Democrats arrived at their own decision to eliminate the Post Office Committee. In weeks leading up to losing control of the House, Democrats believing we would retain a majority, started its own reorganization.

A behind the scene struggle was waged by those who recognized the importance of the Post Office Committee and also the dilemma facing Democrats if it was abolished. Circumstances presented a timid Democratic leadership with a wrenching, divisive issue.

Bill Ford (D-Mich.), chairman of the Education and Labor Committee did not seek reelection. I was poised to replace him as chairman. Patricia Schroeder (D-Colo) was next in line to become chairman of the Post Office Committee that I was vacating.

The dilemma--abolishing the postal committee meant women would continue to be shut out of chairmanships. It was predicable that feminist and advocates of fairness across the nation would organize in great numbers and raise much hell to prevent the affront to a highly, qualified, talented female legislator.

Toppling of Speaker Newt Gingrich

Gingrich spearheaded charges against Speaker Wright and successfully forced his stepping down. Later, he was faced with the same predicament after being named Speaker. He became the subject of complaints before the Committee on Standards of Conduct (Ethics) alleging violations of House rules on: outside income earnings, gifts from individuals with direct interests in pending legislation, failure to report political campaign contributions, and abuse of

Congressional franking privileges in promoting a private business venture.

Facing the possibility of indictment, he stepped down.

Livingston: 'Not A Saint'

The selection by the House Republican Conference of Bob Livingston (R-La.) in 1998 to replace Gingrich was short lived. In seeking the position, Livingston told a reporter inquiring about his past: "I am running for Speaker, not sainthood"[14] He was named Speaker.

Larry Flynt, publisher of *Hustler* magazine, implying there was dirty linen in someone's closet, announced the payment of $1 million for evidence of a member of Congress or a top government official who was engaged in adultery.

Within days after Livingston uttered the 'Saint Hood' statement, he resigned after admitting he had "on occasion strayed from my wife."[15]

If those representing Americans at the highest level of government are imperfect or fail to measure up to the ideal expectation of voters, H.L. Mencken's admonition is apropos of remembrance when he dismissed the American electorate as a "boobocracy," easily diverted by the empty symbols that cynical politicians dangle before them.

NOTES

1/*Lying Down With The Lions,* Ron Dellums and H. Lee Halterman, Beacon Press, Boston, 2000, page 100.

2/Ibid., Rep. Phillip Burton, page 101.

3/Ibid., Rep. Louis Stokes, page 1025/Ibid., Rep. William L. Clay, page 102

4/Ibid. Rep. William L. Clay, page 103.

5/Congressional Record, May 1, 1985, page H2773, U.S. Printing Office, Washington, D.C.

6/Congressman William L. Clay, Sr., Testimony before House Ethics Committee, 30 July 1987.

7/Ibid.

8/Ibid.

9/Ibid.

10/Letter from Office of U.S. Attorney General.

11/*St. Louis Post Dispatch*, 12/7/94, page 3A

10

For laws to be just – consciousness and fairness, not expediency – must be the controlling factor. [1]

– William L. Clay, Sr.

Although I didn't win all the skirmishes, I was one of the liberals in Congress that formed a road block to conservatives attempting to roll back protection of laws that mattered to those whose "general welfare" was usually ignored by society as a whole.

It is amazing that conservatives have been able to intimidate many in both political parties to fear being identified as liberals. It's shocking that so many average people whose lives would be a disaster buy into the gross propaganda campaign that there is something sinister, something evil about liberal policies. Most middle class elderly Americans should realize that they would be existing in abject poverty if conservatives had succeeded in defeating legislation to create Social Security. Their health problems would not be attended if conservatives in Congress had prevailed in defeating the Medicare Care Legislative Act. Liberals pushed through Congress the Student Loan Program despite almost total opposition of conservatives. Most children of poor parents would not be educated through Pell Grants if it was left up to conservative.

My legislative initiatives were in defense of these and other programs that benefited the majority of taxpaying citizens. It was a record I take great pride in acclaiming.

My Legislative History

Composition of the U.S. Congress reflects the concept of 'melting pot' much the same as any segment in American life. Its members spring from vastly different cultures, racial groups, ethnic backgrounds, religious preferences, ideological commitments, philosophical persuasions, and educational attainment. It's an amalgamation of multifarious interests representing a variety of customs, habits, experiences, disciplines and religious differences.

It's miraculous that such distinctly diverse individuals, sometimes representing competing and adverse forces are able to navigate around thorny issues and achieve legislative solutions to many of the nation's divisive issues.

Passing legislation requires an ability to comprehend the interest of other colleagues, to respect their opinions, and to recognize the special egos of staffers who play key roles in the orderly processing of bills.

I particularly relish the honor of successfully sponsoring, co-sponsoring and managing legislation of 295 bills that became law-an accomplishment most never achieve. Some attach amendments to bills, but giving birth to complete policy changes which become the law of the land is a rare accomplishment.

Legislative enactment, except on rare occasion, belongs exclusively to the prerogative of the majority party and the whims of its chairmen. Chairmen and subcommittee chairmen possess the clout necessary to make things happen. Therefore, they pass most of the major legislation.

Even Republicans who later became Speakers of the House-Gerald Ford, John Rhodes, Robert Michels—were unable to pass legislation of great national import during the 42 years Democrats controlled the House,

My motivation for championing the cause of society's underrepresented, in a sense America's untouchables, was in part inspired by the sage advice of a conservative, Winston Churchill who said, "Humanity rather than legality must be our guide."[2]

My Early Initiatives
Earnings Tax Withholding

In 1971, I passed my first free standing bill. It was minor when considered in context to the overall legislative scheme, but of great importance to its limited number of beneficiaries. It allowed cities and townships to withhold earning taxes from the pay of federal employees. The prohibition against state and local entities attaching federal wages was originally part of a law to protect employees from unscrupulous creditors filing frivolous garnishments and other unreasonable suits.

Inability to legally collect city earnings taxes bi-weekly, in small increments from payroll checks, created horror stories for some. Failure to pay for several years, accrued obligations in thousands of dollars in back taxes when adding interests, fines, and court costs. Passage of the bill was warmly greeted by federal employees needing relief, and city officials needing finances.

Rent Subsidy for Public Housing

I introduced the bill that placed a limit of 25% of income on residents in public housing. During a House/Senate conference, the language of my legislation limiting the rent was incorporated. The provision reduced the rents of 215,000 of the 800,000 families living in the housing units. Calling for the cap was prompted by the payment of a disproportionate share of income for substandard housing. The infamous Pruitt-Igoe housing project in my congressional district exemplified the notorious, unsanitary, unsafe living conditions existing in public housing units that were built to replace slums. In city after city, because the government refused to provide proper maintenance, the units were worse than the private housing replaced but the rental fees were unconscionably steep for services provided.

The final legislative version became known as the "Brooke Amendment." It was a combination of a bill originally introduced by Edward Brooke (R-Mass), the first African American elected to the Senate by popular vote in 1966, and an identical bill introduced in the House by me.

Sickle Cell Legislation

Accompanied by Dr. Accie Mitchell, a board member of the Research Foundation for Sickle-Cell Anemia (SCA) in Los Angeles and Dr. Elmer Anderson also from Los Angeles, I was the first to testify in support of legislation for funding the prevention of sickle cell anemia. Senator Edward Kennedy's (D-Mass) committee chairman convened the hearing in November 1971.

I testified that SCA was the most neglected disease in the nation. The average total cost per patient who had a severe SCA crisis was too steep to be borne by most sufferers.

The legislation sponsored by Kennedy and Jacob K. Javits (R-N.Y.) was the beginning of the long, successful battle to address the problems of SCA. I recommended funding $25 million for testing, education, and the creation of facilities to conduct research for the prevention and cure of the disease.

President Nixon supported the measure, recommending that Congress appropriate a similar amount to deal with the problem.

Minimum Wage for Domestics

During the drafting of a bill to increase the minimum wage under the Fair Labor Standards Act in 1971, I inserted language providing coverage for several million domestic workers who were excluded in the original 1936 law. With the help of Phillip Burton (D-Cal.), chairman of the subcommittee, the amendment was included. The bill increased the wage from $1.60 to $2.20 per hour. Nearly one-third of domestics working full-time the previous year earned less than seventy cents an hour. Half of them were paid less than $1.00 an hour.

We covered over-time pay for Federal, State and Local government employees in the same bill.

ERISA

In 1974, I was a member of the subcommittee that developed the Employee Retirement Income Security Act (ERISA) which protected private pension benefits. We amended ERISA in 1989 to require financially sound employers to pay retirees their full pension benefit. It was common for workers to retire after 30 or 40 years, expecting to receive their earned retirement compensation only to learn that the company had spent the funds in operating expenses.

The legislation required that the funds be placed in a safe trust to be used only for retirement.

Later, I also managed efforts in the House to amend ERISA and the Age Discrimination in Employment Act (ADA), requiring those who continued to work beyond normal retirement age to earn pension credits up to the maximum of the plan.

Plant Closing Protection

The Workforce Investment Act which I sponsored provided federal job training to workers dislocated because of trade policies. I inserted a provision in the Act (a Plant Closing Notification) that required employers of 100 or more to give 60 days notice when there is a factory closing or mass layoff or pay the equivalent to each worker.

Prior to my legislation, more than two million workers a year lost jobs due to layoffs and closings of companies that abruptly moved to low-wage states or foreign countries.

Five Year Vesting

I was in the vanguard of the effort to reduce the maximum vesting period from ten years to 5 years for participating in a pension plan. At the time of enactment, only 30% of retired women were drawing from their own retirement plans. Women seldom worked the necessary 10 years for the same company to qualify for pensions. Starting work right out of high school, women usually quit after giving birth, or after marriage and many remained home for an extended period. Returning to the workforce, they seldom were rehired by the same employer so they had to start over, investing in a new retirement plan.

Women's Retirement Equity Reform Act

I introduced the Women's Retirement Equity Act which was passed by Congress and signed by the President. The Act prohibited discrimination against women by private pension plans. It lowered the participation age from 25 to 21 and the vesting age from 22 to 18; provided that previous service could not be disregarded unless five consecutive one year breaks-in service occurred and that one year maternity or paternity leave would not be counted as breaks-in-service. It required pension plans to honor qualified domestic court orders awarding a share of a pension to divorced spouses.

COBRA Provisions

I was the primary sponsor of the Single Employer Pension Plan Amendments (SEPPA) which became Title XI of the Consolidated Omnibus Budget Reconciliation Act of 1985 (COBRA). It required employers to guarantee enrollees continued access to group health insurance for workers who lost their jobs, surviving spouses, divorced spouses, and dependent children. The Continued Access to Group Health Insurance Act provided 18 months of continued health insurance coverage if job lost was due to termination, reduction of hours, or death of a spouse.

Family and Medical Leave Act

I was the key sponsor of the first bill that President Clinton signed into law, the Family and Medical Leave Act. Passage of this major legislation gave workers a legal right to take off in cases of emergency without losing their jobs. Congresswoman Patricia Schroeder was a major factor in soliciting support for its enactment. She was an untiring promoter, energizing others to join the campaign for enactment.

The legislation provided 12 weeks of unpaid leave for birth or adoption of a child, to care for a seriously ill family member or for one's own illness.

Representing the House, I spoke in the Rose Garden of the White House Lawn on the occasion of the bill signing. At the time of my retirement in 2001, the law had given more than 21 million workers the opportunity to take leave without fear of losing their jobs.

Hatch Act Reform

The landmark Hatch Act Reform legislation guaranteed Federal and postal workers the right to participate in the political process the same as other citizens. The law makes it unlawful for employees to use official authority for the purpose of interfering with elections, confers protection against coercion and intimidation without compromising the integrity of our Merit System; and makes it possible for federal workers to exercise the right of free speech for redress of grievances as enjoyed by all other Americans.

Davis-Bacon Protection

Throughout my career, I was a prime participant in opposing effort to repeal requirements that contractors pay workers locally prevailing rates for federally financed construction work. From 1995 through 2000, I was the floor manager in fighting to preserve the provisions of the Davis-Bacon Act and successfully blocked all attempts to weaken its enforcement.

Miscellaneous Bills

Other legislation that I played a major role in passage include:
• PENSION PLAN TERMINATION: prevents employers from terminating healthy pension plans in order to use assets for other purposes such as corporate takeovers.
•CLASSROOM SIZE REDUCTION: President Clinton's proposal and a House-Senate Federal Budget agreement funded 100,000 new teachers in high poverty areas reduce class to no more than 18 students in grades 1-3.
•STUDENT LOAN INTEREST RATES: allowed the government to guarantee student loans at 3 or 4 percent as opposed to the 7 or 8 percent charged by private lenders. Resulted in a $11 billion savings to college students.
•INCREASED FUNDING FOR PELL GRANTS: resulted in substantial increased funding for Pell Grants and successfully

fought in committee and later as floor manager to repel Republican efforts to underfund the program.

•CAPITAL FINANCIAL ACT: provided $375 million in federal loan guarantees for construction and renovation projects at Historical Black Colleges and Universities Act (HBCUs).

•CARL D. PERKINS LAW: reauthorization provided $1 billion over four years to teach vocational and technical skills to secondary and post secondary students.

•POLYGRAPH REGULATION: prohibited the use to screen workers and mandated the announcement informing the caller that his/her conversation may be monitored.

•CONNIE LEE PRIVATIZATION BILL: empowered the organization to enter into contracts as a private, for-profit business. It became the first federally authorized Government Sponsored Enterprise (GSE) to voluntarily relinquish government support and convert fully to a state-chartered general purpose company. The proceeds from the sell of its stock was used to upgrade and enhance the learning environment of elementary and secondary school students in the District of Columbia.

•AMERICAN FOLKSONG and FOLKLORE: re-authorized funds for the program that had enriched the nation in folk-song and folklore for more than 60 years.

It was the conservatory of ex-slave narratives, Native American chants and rituals, gospel, and the blues. The bill's passage was important so that citizens could enjoy in the future, the richness of these cultures, and their musical and storytelling contribution to the American mosaic.

The Center is a research facility providing a resource of more than one million items that are used on daily basis by scholars and others seeking to learn more about our diverse American roots.

•AMERICAN INDIAN NATIONAL MUSEUM: established within the Smithsonian Institute on the National Mall and provided for the construction of a new museum in New York City to preserve the priceless collection of Indian artifacts of the Heye Museum.

•AMERICANS WITH DISABILITIES ACT of 1990: protected employment and public access rights of our disabled community (floor manager).

.

A Vision Fulfilled

Some bills I developed, promoted, and steered through the House, died in the Senate or were vetoed by a President. Two such important legislative initiatives failing to pass the Senate were the Striker Replacement Bill, and the Double Breasting Bill. The first would prohibit the replacement of striking workers by Scabs who cross picket lines to take their jobs. The second would prohibit the same company from establishing two entities--one for bidding on union contract jobs, the other for non union jobs.

Another bill I was unable to enact was introduced by Senator Kennedy and me. It would have halted the resurgence of sweat-shops, and amend provisions of law that did not adequately deter the exploitation of human labor. We were unsuccessful in holding manufacturers and contractors in the garment industry jointly liable for violations of the minimum wage and overtime provisions of Fair Labor Standards Act, and to provide civil penalties for their failure to maintain payroll records.

I am proud of my role in preventing conservative lawmak-ers from turning the clock back on worker's rights in other areas as well. They tried to repeal the overtime pay of workers and failed. They tried to bring back company unions and failed. They tried to raid worker pensions and failed. They tried to snuff out union de-mocracy and failed. They tried to kill the minimum wage increase and failed. They tried to torpedo the work of the National Labor Relations board and failed.

My vision for America did not vary much after I first real-ized that our country was great but could be greater--that it could and should grow and mature. At a very young age, I established a fundamental sense of values due in large measure to the influence of my father. It was predicated on following a course of action that would guarantee justice, equity and equality for all. The philosophy was the driving force, the steering column in the diesel engine pow-ering my legislative pursuit. I believe that every person should live in a decent home in a safe neighborhood, receive a quality educa-tion in order to realize his/her fullest potential, get a job commen-surate with his/her skills and abilities, and receive the best medical care possible regardless of income. My record reveals that I always put this concern ahead of any political endeavor.

These were valid concerns and exemplary ideals when I was a young man and are fitting pursuits today. Preservation of the environment, protection of consumers, promoting equal access to education, advancing workers' job security and defending civil rights are causes sutured together by common thread to improve the quality of life. Enhancing the dignity of every individual is a worthwhile vision for America.

I viewed my legislative obligation as not only championing the causes of Society's neglected, unrepresented, and under-represented who were seeking a slice of the pie, but also making sure they were at the table to decide how the pie was sliced. Throughout my career, I was an uncompromising advocate for the full rights of working people. My legislative actions were motivated by a deep desire to share the benefits of our nation's great economic prosperity with the men and women who make the economy function.

NOTES

1/William L. Clay, Sr. (D-Mo.)
2/Winston Churchill, text and date unknown

Thru The Years

Hard Fought Battle for Congress - Clay is Victorious
Clay announcing his victory, L. to R.: daughters Michell and Vicke, wife
Carol and son Lacy

Srabble, a family affair in the Clay household

Bill Clay in his newly assigned Congressional Office

Clay Family ready for move to Washington, D.C.

Clays boarding plane to attend 1st congressional swearing-in

NEW CONGRESSMEN joining the old line-up to make a historic nine colored members in the House of Representatives are Democrats Wil-liam Clay, 1st District, St. Louis; Mrs. Shirley Chisholm, 12th District, Brooklyn, first woman of her race in the Congress, and Louis Stokes, 21st District, Cleveland. (AFRO Staff Photo by Cabell)

Making history – 3 African Americans elected to Congress same day

Forming the Congressional Black Caucus

CBC Members: L. to R. John Conyers, Chas. Diggs, Bill Clay, Louis Stokes, Chas Rangel, Parren Mitchell, George Collins, Walter Fauntroy

Original members of Congressional Black Caucus after historic White House meeting with President Nixon

Rev. Leon Sullivan, founder of Opportunities Industrialization Centers of America (OIC) being honored by Congessional Black Caucus

Clay gesturing to Congressman Ronald Dellums...Congressman Harold
Washington (seated) and other members of congress
enjoy the point made

Supreme Court Justice Thurgood Marshall honored by the
Congressional Black Caucus

Clay and President Carter exchanging stories

White House meeting: Clay, President Carter, Congressman James
Hanley and Ralph Metcalfe

Speaker 'Tip' O'Neil greeting St. Louis ministers. Cong. Walter Fauntry
to his left and Bishop Wilie Ellis is next to him

House Speaker John McCormick welcomes Clay to Congress

Speaker Thomas Foley recognizes Bishop Frank Cummings of St. Louis

Speaker Jim Wright welcomes Rev. Jarvis and family to the
House chamber where he opened the session with prayer

White House signing of Clay's Family and Medical Leave Act
VP Gore, President Clinton, Congressman Bill Ford and Clay

Clay speaking at White House Signing of his Bill to
reform the Hatch Act

Hillary Clinton in Clay's Capitol Hill office discussing strategy for
passage of Universal Health Care Program

President Clinton signing Clay sponsored Education Bill

Clay greets President Anwar Sadat of Egypt

Clay meeting with Cuban President Fidel Castro

Clay, Pope John Paul II, Congressman Bill Richardson
and President Clinton

President Nelson Mandela, South Africa

Congressman Clay's granndson Michael Alexis at White House signing of Hatch Act Reform. L. to R.: President Clinton, Clay, Vice President Gore, Senator John Glenn

Clay with Charles Shaw and Ronnie White whom he recommended for federal judgeships. Shaw was confirmed.

Clay, Congresswoman Juanita McDonald and President Clinton

White House meeting on Education Bill. Senator Kennedy (partially hidden), Congressman Bill Goodling and Senator James Jefford

Clay and Humphrey

Clay and President Clinton, V.P. Gore, and White House Assistant Leon
Panetta after meeting on Clay's Family and Medical Leave bill

Lacy Clay succeeded his father in 2001 and is now serving in his tenth year as a member of the United States House of Representatives

Political Servants: Congressman Bill Clay (seated), State Senator Lacy Clay and Alderman Irving Clay

Congressman Lacy with President Obama and House
Speaker Nancy Pelosi

Lacy and Mom celebrate news of his first election to Congress in 2000

Congressman Clay campaigning with Vice President Joe Biden

Miscelaneous & Honors and Awards

Introduction of "Just Permanent Interests" at University of Missiouri at St. Louis (family members)

President Marshall Grigsby confers honorary doctorate of laws on Clay
at Benedict College in South Carolina

Speaker Tom Foley congratulating Clay at book signing. Looking on L.
R.: unidentified, Publisher Charles Harris, Bill Giles, Bob Moses,
behind speaker

Clay at dedication of Molecular Sciences Building in his name at
University of Missiouri in St. Louis

Dedication of Child Development Center in honor of Congressman Bill
Clay at Harris-Stowe University. L. to R.: Lacy Clay, Bill & Carol Clay,
President Henry Givens, Congresswoman Maxine Waters

Dedication of the
William L. Clay, Sr. Early Childhood Development Center. Far right:
President Henry Givens, Harris Stowe University, and
Congresswoman Maxine Waters

Induction to International Walk of Fame in Atlanta, Georgia.
Shoes of "picket line" Bill Clay
Former U.S. repre-sentative "Bill" Clay poses with his star on the "St. Louis Walk of Fame" in University City. Clay, the first Afri-can - American U.S. Congressman, passed 295 bills during his 32 years in the House of Representatrives and became the 114th star on the "Walk of Fame," which honors prominent citizens of St. Louis. (Photo by Wiley Price)

Dedication of the William L. Clay U.S. Post office in St. Louis. Congressman Lacy Clay and Russ Carnahan at ceremony

President Givens dedicating Bill Clay NASA's Science and Technology Center at Harris Stowe University

Cleveland Mayor Carl Stokes, Comedian Flip Wilson,
Carol and Bill Clay

Naming street in St. Louis after Dick Gregory. Comptroller John Bass
and Clay holding ladder

Heavyweight Champion Muhhamed Ali

Clay with heavyweight champion Evander Holyfield

Clay addressing labor rally on Capitol steps

POWER OF PRINCIPLED POLITICS

Clay meeting with former employer Joseph Ames, Sec. Treas. AFSCME

Chairman of Postal Committee Bill Clay discussing postal legislation
with former president of APWU Moe Biller and Bill Burrus,
current president of APWU

Vice president Al Gore promoting Clay's Striker Replacement Bill. L. to R.- Clay, Sen. Kennedy, Gore, Cong. Owens, Sen. Stabenow, Labor Sec. Robert Reich. In rear; Senators Wellstone and Rockefeller

11

"Fact-finding is more effective than fault-finding." [1]

– Carl Louis Becker

Despite public perception based on misleading media stories and hysterical readers parroting the hyped-up propaganda that ridicule foreign travel as congressional junkets, fact finding missions are important aspects of congressional responsibility that serve the national interest.

Foreign Travel and Congressional Responsibility

I took a course in comparative government at Saint Louis University for one semester under the tutelage of professor Kurt von Schuschnigg, former Chancellor of Austria. The night before Austrians were to vote in plebiscite deciding unification with Germany, Adolph Hitler's army invaded the country, took control of the government, and ousted Von Schuschnigg.

The professor, a colorful, popular, enlightened instructor, stressed the importance of interlocking relations with other countries. At the time, I had no idea that someday the responsibility of assisting in the formulation of policy affecting those relations would befall me.

The United States invests more money (taxes and private corporate financing) in foreign aid business ventures than any nation. Members of congress appropriate billions of dollars to fund embassies, military bases, hunger relief programs, medical assistance, health planning, safe drinking water facilities, and other projects critical to the mutual well-being of our country and recipient nations.

Secondhand knowledge, relayed by government employees

of State or Defense Departments do not and cannot accurately gauge for Congresspersons how the rest of the world reacts to, and is impacted by its policies.

Travel is a hot button issue because the media, exaggerating incidents and arousing anger in an unsophisticated public, makes it a boogey man. It is controversial only because gullible and disgruntled citizens feed on incendiary stories about non-issues that have little relevancy to disparate conditions at the foundation of their daily frustrations. Front page coverage alleging abuses of congressional travel at taxpayers' expense and many other non-important events allows editors to bury on page 10, articles of real significance of monumental abuses by their major financial contributors that should be of prime concern. The slight-of-hand allows for ignoring why its readers do not have adequate health insurance, sufficient retirement benefits or real job security. Exposing the unethical games played by corporate interests would embarrass these major advertisers.

The Value of Foreign Travel

Critics of congressional travel never mention that the job of the executive branch is to implement policy, not to make it. Foreign policy is shaped by decisions of Congress, in conjunction with the President, based on information received from agents in the theater of activity, or more preferable, by first-hand knowledge of the situation addressed. Personal interfacing with global neighbors is a critical component of making sound, policy.

Congress in a bubble, isolated from the real world, cannot intelligently create legislative policies in areas of: energy, arms sales, agriculture, space exploration, arms control, treaties, and trade agreements. Unfortunately, the executive branch and the congress are not always in sync when pursuing the same agenda priorities, do not always agree on the best way to resolve disagreement with other nations, and often have differing analysis of the impact of foreign aid programs.

Information garnered in foreign travel, educates, influences, and acquaints congresspersons with specifics of programs. It provides opportunities to examine, compare and incorporate the best features of other government's programs into ours. The alternative of policymakers not traveling is total dependence on information supplied by mid-management clerks in federal agencies who themselves travel the world on government expense accounts. They attempt to interpret for congress what priorities are needed, determine effectiveness of funded projects, and assess world opinions according to their own priorities, and sometimes personal biases.

Allegations that congressional travel is totally funded by American taxpayer's, in many instances, are deliberately misleading. Major sources of legitimate coverage of expenses are provided by private organizations with valid interests in improved international relations. The Aspen Institute, Rockefeller Foundation, Congressional Black Caucus Foundation, Heritage Foundation, Ford Foundation, and numerous other non-profit groups, underwrite many trips. Other underwriters are American businesses, workers associations, chambers of commerce, peace groups, educational conglomerates, and agricultural organizations that have foreign interests critically important to the welfare of the United States.

Foundations established by governments in Taiwan, South Korea, Israel, Brazil, Nigeria, China and others, sponsor congressional trips hoping for increased U.S. aid to deal with pressing problems of hunger, sickness, poor housing, poverty and improved infrastructure projects.

The House and Senate ethics committees must approve these trips in advance after determining the purpose and relevancy. There is nothing secret or sinister about the trips. In most cases, the media are informed prior to the travel.

Until recently, expenses for numerous congressional trips were underwritten by foreign governments from two sources, Counterpart Funds and Local Currencies. The funds represented monies that nations owed the United States from Lend Lease Programs established during and after World War II. Most countries were not making direct payments to reduce the indebtedness but were willing to pay for expenditures incurred by American officials while present in their countries.

They allotted local currencies to the U.S. State Department for paying salaries of embassy employees and for hiring local citizens to work in various U.S. programs. Money was available to pay rents of embassy personnel and purchase property for agencies as the United States Information Agency (USIA).

Congressional committees often purchased airline tickets in countries owing the U.S. money. The cost was charged to either Counterpart Funds or Local Currency accounts of the foreign governments, reducing what they owed the US government and was not paying. Upon arrival of congressional delegations, per diem for living expenses was drawn from the same funds.

Unjustified Attack on Travelers

Every large scale program in government, as in the private sector, is subject to abuse. Contrary to mangled images created by the media and tax-exempt watchdog citizen groups, congressional travel is seldom the luxurious vacation in exotic spots as portrayed by some journalists. Unfortunately, too many members are so intimidated by fear of unfavorable publicly, and subsequent adverse voter retaliation resulting from unfair news articles that they refuse to inspect first-hand overseas programs enacted by them.

Most trips are for brief periods, as congresspersons visit two or three countries in less than ten days. The schedule is tight and the workload rigorous. The hectic pace begins with a working breakfast around 7:30 a.m. during which members are briefed by the State Department. It is followed by meetings with the host country's elected leaders and government administrators to discuss specific policies. Field trips are conducted to review various U.S. funded programs in operation. Members usually return to the hotel at 5:00 p.m. to prepare for dinner with heads of state and other dignitaries. Seldom is time allotted for extensive sight-seeing.

Since America is a state of constant war and its people are conditioned to exist in a war mood, there is no criticism of congressional travel to military zones and theaters of active combat. But travel to desolate places like Guyana, Ethiopia, Somali, Bangladesh, the Sudan, to assess the need of providing assistance for hunger, disease, poverty and other human devastations, don't make front page stories ripe for sexy distortion. These trips are often described as 'junkets' by journalists sitting in newsrooms 3,000 miles from the scene and without knowledge of actual events. That bit of theatrics can only be labeled 'yellow journalism.'

During my time in office, ten (10) members died tragically while on official travel. The fatalities averaged one every three years. For a group of 535, it represented a higher percentage of deaths per person, per year of any similar sized group.

Congresspersons who died in the line of duty while on fact-finding trips, return visits to their districts, or campaign trips for reelection were: Hale Boggs of Louisiana and Nicholas Begich of Alaska in 1970, George Collins of Illinois in 1972, Jerry Pettis of California in 1975; Jerry Litton of Missouri in 1976, Leo Ryan of California in 1978, Larry McDonald of Georgia in 1983, George 'Mickey' Leland of Texas in 1989, Larkin Smith of Mississippi in 1989, and John Heinz of Pennsylvania in 1991.

McDonald, a passenger on a Korean commercial flight was killed when the aircraft drifted into Soviet Union air space and was shot down. Jerry Litton, his wife and two children were killed on election night when flying to Kansas City, Missouri to celebrate his Democratic Senatorial primary victory. In 1978, Richard D. Obenshain the nominee to replace Senator William L. Scott of Virginia was killed in an airplane crash. Mel Carnahan, governor of Missouri who won the Democratic nomination for the U.S. Senate, was killed in a plane crash on the campaign trail. His death came too late for his name to be removed from the ballot, but the voters of Missouri preferred him over Republican incumbent senator John Ashcroft. After the election, the Democratic Party selected his wife, Jean Carnahan to fill the vacancy and serve her husband's senate term. In 2002, Paul Wellstone of Minnesota, his wife and daughter died in airplane crash while campaigning for reelection.

My friend and subcommittee chairman on the Postal Committee, George "Mickey" Leland of Texas also died on a congressional trip. The plane crash killed him along with his staff while on a fifth trip to observe the feeding program of starving people in Ethiopia. Rep. Leland devoted much time addressing suffering in faraway, desolate villages where large numbers were dying of AIDS or starvation.

For eleven days, citizens of the world watched, prayed, and hoped that Cong. Leland and the 16 others would be found alive. But the massive search conducted by the U.S. government and European nations ended in discovery of the airplane, but no survivors. In 1978, Congressman Leo Ryan and four Americans were shot to death in Jonestown Guyana while on a mission of mercy to liberate his constituents from the clutches of a religious fanatic. Cult leader Rev. Jim Jones, pastor People's Temple of California, convinced 1000s of followers to join him in Guyana where he swindled them out of their personal properties, including welfare and Social Security monthly checks.

When Congressman Ryan arrived to investigate, he and four aides were shot by bodyguards of Reverend Jones. More than 900 followers, enticed by the deranged preacher, committed suicide by drinking kool-aid laced with cyanide.

Amazingly, those murdered attempting to rescue the victimized, were never accused of vacationing at a leisure resort or playing golf in a foreign country at taxpayers expense. A fellow colleague, Otis Pike of New Jersey wrote:

"The next time you hear about congressmen going off on junkets at the taxpayer's expense, remember Mickey Leland and Larry P. McDonald and Leo J. Ryan. Some congressmen occasionally risk their lives to do very good deeds."[2]

As chairman of committees with jurisdiction over important areas requiring global interrelations, I had the opportunity, duty, and responsibility to study critical world issues. In an official capacity, my colleagues and I visited industrialized nations, especially those militarily and economically strategic to the vital interests of the USA and our allies.

Legislatively related travel was extensive because committees I chaired or served on, covered matters similar to on-going programs in other countries. The Labor Management subcommittee handled about 60% of issues affecting workers; the Pension Task Force Committee had jurisdiction of ERISA, protecting the retirement rights of workers; the Federal and Postal Employees Compensation Committee; the ad hoc Committee of Non-appropriated Fund

Agencies: PXs and Commissaries.

The committees dealt with issues of funding education programs, student loans, postal organizations, overseas military schools, pension and retirement, government employees' relations, coal mine safety, workplace safety, health issues, fair labor standards. Often, we found foreign governments more advanced in specific programs, especially those relating to improved living standards, plant safety, and universal health care. In some countries educational and health care benefits were more extensive, more superior, and usually less costly than our own. We benefitted from sharing knowledge and technology.

Visiting areas of unbelievable poverty and deprivation, we witnessed what seemed like millions of our tax-dollars wasted by local leaders on inept attempts at addressing the problems. We encountered evidence about how and why our basic manufacturing companies continued to move overseas, leaving a trail of employees jobless. American companies that closed factories in the USA, opened sweat shops in Asia, Central and South America. They manufactured the same products but paid employees, in some instances, sixty cents a day for 12 hour shifts.

I cringed at the sight of 10 year old boys and girls making shoes in Korea, Taiwan, and Singapore that once were produced by men and women in my district, formerly the shoe capital of the world. Companies relocated there to take advantage of exploited child labor, inhumane slave wages, and inexpensive, unsanitary working regulations.

These non-competitive standards destroy the free trade market concept, and weighed heavily on my position that free trade must also be fair trade, with the labor playing field equal in both countries. A major factor in my view of global economics was that no country should be forced to lower its people's standard of living to compete with cheap products produced by exploited workers in other countries.

NOTES

1/Carl Louis Becker

2/*Houston Chronicle*, August 15, 1989, Otis Pike, "Leland should give pause to `junket' labeling," page 19a.

12

*"The only difference between Ronald Reagan and
Al Capone—Mr. Capone had at least one conviction."[1]*
— Congressman William L. Clay

Ronald Reagan's Southern Strategy

The policy dictums of Presidents Nixon, Ford and Carter constituted nuisances but not serious menaces to Government's continued struggle against impediments facing society's poor, uneducated, sick, elderly and racial minorities. But with the election of Ronald W. Reagan the progress of those constituencies were abruptly halted. His followers were blinded by mellifluous rhetoric of the charismatic leader who artfully painted a rainbow of ideological ignorance and intolerance to justify draconian measures in stripping away the "safety net" for the country's economically disadvantaged. They willingly supported the irreparable damage his policies did to their causes.

Reagan's budget policies slashed to the bare bones the Food Stamp Program that millions depended on for survival; cut programs designed to feed hungry children, housing for the poor; and job retraining for the Unemployed. He and his supporters surrendered to political expediency in rationalizing that an unconscionable increase in military spending made proper sacrificing vital life sustaining programs for the disadvantaged.

But nothing was more of a criminal nature than President Reagan and his aides setting in motion programs specifically designed to reverse historic advancement of civil rights, civil liberties and social justice. He surrounded himself with a cadre of economic bourgeois and conservative acting Neanderthals who like him, were dedicated to reshaping the social order by steering the country backward into an age of racial incivility. Claiming the advancement of rights for blacks and women was at the expense of white men, Reagan led the country's retreat into the abyss of mediocrity and reestablished many repressive controls that existed before the days of enlightened civil rights legislation.

He had no compunction about violating provisions of law in his obsessive desire to fight communism even if it meant using the resources of government to overthrow democratically elected heads of state as in the Iran/Contra scheme.

Reagan's Overt Plea to Bigotry

Reagan's entire campaign for president was well financed, well planned and well orchestrated far in advance of every event. Nothing was by accident or left to chance. Every word, every facial expression, every hand and body gesture had a specific purpose. Each was calculated to evoke a positive voter response. Surely, an occasion as important as when and where to officially initiate his southern strategy was not a matter taken lightly.

After winning the GOP nomination, Reagan kicked off his general election campaign in Philadelphia, Mississippi, launching a strategy to win southern states. His effort to sever the overwhelming stranglehold that Democratic presidential candidates traditionally held on the South was a legitimate concern of previous Republican aspirants. But no prior campaign's appeal to racial prejudices was as vulgar, intense, obvious and overt.

One of the most shameful, most insidious, most disgraceful acts displayed by an American political leader, was the site chose to kick off his 1980 general election campaign. The act defied all standards of decency and desecrated all codes of moral behavior.

That little town had earned a prominent position in the archives of barbaric racist atrocities for the infamous murders of civil rights workers James Chaney, Michael Schwerner, and Andrew Goodman in 1964. The three youths-two Jews from New York (Schwerner and Goodman) and a black (Chaney) from nearby Meridian-were assisting the Congress of Racial Equality (CORE) in establishing "freedom schools" for black children.

Elected officials in the area, defying the Brown v. Board of Education Supreme Court decision outlawing racially segregated schools, chose to close their public schools rather than comply with the law. They then developed an illegal scheme to teach only white students in church basements and store front facilities, illegally using tax dollars.

On a hot smoldering June day, the three were arrested, allegedly for a traffic violation, and subsequently released, according to the sheriff. What he did not admit was their release was in the dead of night on a lonely back road to a waiting mob of Ku Klux Klansmen.

In August, the FBI discovered bodies of the three youths buried in a swamp. They had been shot numerous times. Chaney was severely beaten, his bones crushed and broken. In December, eighteen white suspects, including the sheriff and his deputy were charged with conspiracy in the deaths.

They were released when federal Judge W. Harold Cox, an unabashed, self-avowed advocate of white supremacy with a long history of opposing the rights of blacks, dismissed the indictments. Judge Cox once publicly described blacks as "niggers and chimpanzees."

Three years later, a federal grand jury returned conspiracy indictments against the same eighteen. An all-white jury acquitted eight, declared a mistrial in the case of three, and convicted seven of conspiracy rather than the more serious charge of murder. Among the guilty were Sheriff Cecil Price and Sam Bowers, Imperial Wizard of the Ku Klux Klan.

Philadelphia, Mississippi, a town of 12,000 in the backwoods of Neshoba County, is filled with widely scattered dilapidated shacks, dusty clay roads littered with pickup trucks decorated with Confederate flags. It is located 30 miles from the nearest moderate size city of Meridian. The picnic or the town had no political significance whatsoever. Frankly, with only seven electoral votes, the state of Mississippi by itself was not a critical factor in the election of any President. But consolidating the support of like-minded bigots across all southern states painted an unambiguous picture difficult to misinterpret.

The symbolic significance of Reagan's location to declare his candidacy was equivalent to a political death charge detonating an explosive outburst in the ocean of racial intolerance. Verbal shrapnel exploded all across the South. The small hamlet with a big reputation was chosen to send a positive, but cynical, signal to bigots and reactionaries everywhere that racism under his administration would be openly condoned. It underscored everything nasty and abhorrent about racial injustice and issues exploited in campaigning for public office..

The attempt to foster racial division should have been met with massive cries of public outrage. Instead, it was silently accepted by the religious community, the mass media, and both political parties.

Three days before his appearance at the picnic, the Knights of the Ku Klux Klan, in a ringing endorsement of him, described the Republican platform as reading as if it "were written by a Klansman." Although the candidate denied soliciting the endorsement, his presence and remarks defending "states' rights" were the primary reasons given by the Klan for the endorsement. Inferring Southern states-rights sent a clear, coded signal to Klansmen and other bigots that no shame was attached to the town's image and its tragic involvement in the brutal murders.

Prior to Reagan's visit, the 106 year-old annual political picnic at the Neshoba County Fair had never played an important role in national politics. Several years later, in common political vernacular of "me too, monkey see, monkey do," other presidential aspirants Michael Dukakis, Jack Kemp and John Glenn made pilgrimages to the den of racist iniquity.

Eight Years of Famine

Reagan's southern strategy worked in defeating Carter. He won the South in unprecedented fashion. Showing appreciation for the Party's new converts, the GOP ushered in an atmosphere more hostile toward minorities than had existed for several decades. The President rewarded southerners, many of whom traditionally and systematically discriminated against minorities and women, by appointing them to key government positions. In a series of mean spirited acts and clever policy tactics, Republican leaders proceeded to undermine civil rights. Appointees to sensitive positions made good on the symbolic gesture at Philadelphia, Mississippi, announcing immediately after assuming authority that their first priority was to repeal the Voting Rights Act.

Two weeks after taking office, in a meeting with the Congressional Black Caucus, Reagan gave us assurance that in the present financial crisis, the burden of sacrifice would be shared equally by all. He stated that the poverty stricken, the disabled, the elderly could rest assured that the safety net of programs they depended on "is exempt from any cuts." But his promise that the federal budget would not be balanced on their backs, rang loudly with cynical hollowness.

In a television appearance the next evening, billed as a fireside chat, he enumerated $17 billion in budget cutbacks. Every dollar was targeted to slash programs enacted to assist the poor, aged, ill, unemployed, low income energy assistance, college student loans, the unemployed, food stamps, child nutrition, and Medicaid. He did not recommend one cent reduction in government perks for the upper middle class, the rich farmers, or the country club crowd.

By the end of his term of office, almost 32.5 million lived in poverty. Although the percentage of blacks in such conditions was astronomical, 22.8 million others suffered this indignity, mostly children.

The misconception that only blacks and Hispanics receive welfare assistance is a media creation. Two-thirds of the food stamp recipients are children, elderly, disabled, and white. Misery and suffering know no color, age, race, sex, or religion.

Reagan Changed the National Debate

My assessment of the Reagan years differed dramatically from those who were dazzled by his easy smile, upbeat persona, and superficial conversation. He had a wonderful capacity for mesmerizing the public. His greatest achievement, If you agree with his basic philosophy that government has only a minimal obligation to assist the average American, he was a great leader. But if you were on the other end of his draconian budget cuts, you were dazed by his gutter-like capacity for diverting and confusing the national debate.

His charming personality and masterful command of the language shifted discussion of priority issues of the 1960s and 1970s from abolishing poverty, eliminating bigotry, improving educational opportunity, caring for the sick to a debate encouraging divisiveness among the races and classes. He used his powers of mesmeric oratory to convince a naïve public that critical discussion centered around issues of capital punishment, abortion, forced busing, prayer in school, reversed discrimination, affirmative action, MX Missiles and a litany of other insignificant bumper sticker slogans.

The 'Great Communicator' sold a large segment of the public on the need for drastic changes in how federal dollars should be spent by repeating the nonsensical phrase: "Get government off our back." Ironically, this incoherent rhetoric resonated largely among many who finished college because government got on their backs with the G.I. Bill, with those who started businesses because government created the Small Business Administration that loaned them capital to finance their ventures, with the poor who were healthier because of Medicaid, and with the elderly who could afford to see doctors because government got on their backs with Medicare.

Reagan's illogical ranting that government was the problem, not the solution, appealed to many who lived healthy lives in better financial conditions because a caring government instituted Social Security. Sadly, the ones mostly buying into the argument that government assistance was intrinsically evil and counterproductive, were primarily individuals who would be subsisting on incomes comparable to that of peasants in third world countries without direct or indirect government help.

In recommending drastic domestic cuts, the President said the nation was teetering on the brink of economic bankruptcy, due to uncontrollable inflation, intolerable high interest rates, and unconscionable unemployment. I countered his remarks in a press release, declaring that

"To fight inflation, he [Reagan] proposes decontrolling oil which is inflation-

ary. To combat high interest rates, he supports tight control of the money supply which drives up interest rates. To tackle unemployment, he advocates elimination of public service jobs, and reduction of funding for retraining those who have lost their jobs."[2]

The administration's intellectual and moral gyrations were reflected in its ability to fine-tune regressive rhetoric of Dixie-crats. The new vocabulary of the suave, articulate, highly educated Reagan appointees was a sea-change from that of the old-line, race-baiting, southern-drawl speaking images implanted in the public psychic by the Eugene "Bull" Connors, George Wallaces, James Eastlands, and Theodore Bilbos. Reagan's chief operatives coined high sounding phrases: "freedom of choice", "reverse discrimination", "local control." Phrases as "states' rights", "federal intervention," "segregation forever," became taboo. The excision of more inflammatory, defiant terminology gave the appearance of decency to a fraudulently immoral scheme to halt any and all improved racial conditions.

Reduction in vital social programs exemplified a mindset that placed the failures of society on its victims. In floor debate, I accused the administration of distorted priorities,

"Twenty-three million Americans resort to food stamps for survival, 11 million suffer the indignities of unemployment, 8 million are afflicted by alcoholism and 4 million endure the torture of drug abuse, while the national debate centers around such trivia as school busing and prayer in public school."[3]

In opposing budget cuts that I contended were racially motivated, I stated:

"Human degradation transcends race and color. Hunger, disease, and ignorance don't know race. Six million people of all races, sleep on public sidewalks nightly, swollen bellies and tuberculosis indiscriminately debilitates blacks and whites, mental retardation knows no color barriers."[4]

Rejecting the highly media publicized image of Reagan's caring for the poor and afflicted, I added, "Anyone (like Reagan) who seriously assaults these people and attempts to destroy their programs without adequate replacements, is not compassionate.[5]

Reagan's policy adversely impacted the least financially stable. The number of working poor dramatically increased during his term of office. The number of full-time working poor who earned the minimum wage or less increased by 44 percent. The number of working poor in their years of prime employment increased by 47 percent. Those officially designated poor by government figures rose to 6.7 million.

While demanding that the Berlin Wall be torn down, the President constructed another barrier in the United States that shielded the poor from the tangible fruits of the most prosperous economy in world history.

Harsh Punishment for Air Traffic Controllers

The President's indifference toward workers, as revealed in his handling of the air traffic controller work stoppage, completely destroys the myth spread by political admirers that he was compassionate. His administration, in a shameful display of insensitivity, refused to consider the stressful burden of air traffic controllers: working more than 40 hours a week in tense situations with antiquated, unreliable equipment, and a host of other demeaning work rules.

In April of 1981, I introduced H.R. 1576 that recognized the difficult job and awesome responsibilities of the controllers. The proposal was meant to deal with their legitimate grievances. The bill would have adjusted working conditions in a fair and comprehensive manner. It called for reform to ensure their working hours were not excessively long, pay was commensurate with their responsibilities, retirement benefits were similar to others in hazardous positions.

It was apparent that President Reagan was more interested in destroying the union than considering the hardships of the workers.

When they walked off the job, he fired all 11,000, permanently replacing them with military personnel and traffic controllers with less experience. He then imposed a lifetime ban on their re-employment for any federal job.

It was a cruel act that adversely affected more federal workers than any other executive decision in history, and gave the green light for a wave of permanent replacements of strikers in the private sector that followed.

A few weeks prior to the work stoppage, the U.S. Senate and the House unanimously passed resolutions defending the right of a work stoppage by government employees. Members made beautiful speeches defending workers who protested and pleaded with the government to show understanding and compassion for the plight of its illegal strikers. They encouraged the workers to continue defying the government until their conditions improved and demands were met. Very noble gestures.

But two days after the air traffic controllers walked out, a majority in the Senate showed the hypocrisy of their commitment and reversed their position. They sent a letter to President Reagan asking him not to tolerate defiance by U.S. government employees.

In the first instance, the praise and support was for the actions of government workers illegally striking against a communist controlled government in Poland. It proved that their commitment to democratic values was only surface deep, not universal.

Right to Strike Legislation

I believe the right to strike is the most potent means workers can bring to bear in protecting wages and improving working conditions, regardless of what country and under what form of government they live. The right to permanently replace striking workers reduces that right to a right to be ignored and ultimately fired.

Nine industrialized nations, including Canada, Germany, Japan and France prohibit the permanent replacement of strikers.

In 1991, I introduced a bill to prohibit the permanent replacement of striking workers. Its purpose was to restore fairness to the collective bargaining process. Without the right to withhold services as leverage during negotiations, workers have little hope of management seriously considering their concerns. Passage was essential to restoring balance to our system of labor-management relations.

The bill passed the House on a vote of 247 to 182 in 1991, and again in 1993 on a vote of 239 to 190. Both times, it died in the Senate.

Reagan Opposed Affirmative Action

President Reagan, a vociferous opponent of extending equal rights to blacks and women, claimed legislation to accomplish that end was 'at the expense of white males.' He described efforts to establish equal treatment under the law as 'reverse discrimination' against whites and `preferential treatment' for blacks.

His top aides pursued ingenious strategies to evade court remedies in discrimination cases by attempting to neutralize the effects of the Voting Rights Law, frustrating efforts to desegregate public schools, and using delay tactics to avoid enforcement of the Fair Housing Act.

In January 1982, by executive fiat, the President rescinded an Internal Revenue Ruling which denied tax-exempt status to schools that discriminated on the basis of race or national origin. His action violated various existing federal anti discrimination laws. The effort to grant tax subsidies to private schools that overtly discriminated against minorities and women boldly defied the Supreme Court's interpretation of fundamental Constitutional guarantees of minorities and women.

Appointment of Civil Rights Adversaries

Reagan replaced members of the U.S. Civil Rights Commission who were dedicated to racial equality with political `mannequins' who refused to ferret-out and report instances of massive racial discrimination. Naming those opposed to minority rights to administer agencies as the Civil Rights Commission and the Equal Employment Opportunity Commission (EEOC) critically damaged the ability of those victimized by discrimination to receive adjudication. Oversight and enforcement of legally established prohibitions against discrimination were stifled, ignored or eliminated.

Clarence Pendleton and William Bradford Reynolds typified a long list of anti-civil rights agitators who were appointed to key government positions. Both attempted to repeal legal and administrative remedies developed in legislation and judicial opinions to fight racist policies.

As Chief of the Civil Rights Division of the Justice Department, Reynolds refused to investigate charges of school discrimination, voting rights violations and allegations of violations in the area of civil rights.

As Chairman of the Civil Rights Commission, Pendleton used his authority to ridicule civil rights laws, condemn affirmative action, and lash out at others who supported programs for women and minorities.

Clarence Thomas, a Reagan appointee as Chairman of EEOC, and Assistant Secretary for Civil Rights, was another leading advocate for diminishing the rights of minorities, women and the elderly. He attacked Supreme Court decisions extending protection of rights, including desegregated public schooling, affirmative action programs, and minority set-asides in licensing and contracting. He acknowledged and attempted to justify flagrant and intentional violations of a court order compelling timely processing of discrimination complaints.

Reagan Vetoed Civil Rights Bill

Reagan determined that public support for civil rights no longer existed and became the first president in modern time to veto a civil rights bill. In a case involving Grove City College, the ultra-conservative Supreme Court obviously misinterpreted the 1964 Civil Rights Law in declaring that an institution could continue to receive federal aid if one of its components was guilty of discrimination as prohibited by Title IX of the law. The Court, dominated by conservatives, mischievously ruled that the law permitted one entity of an institution to discriminate without jeopardizing financial aid to the parent school body.

In his veto message, Reagan falsely claimed the legislation would "expand the scope of federal jurisdiction over state and local governments and the private sector, from churches and synagogues to farmers, grocery stores and businesses of all sizes."[6]

The clever, licentious, creative mind of Reverend Jerry Falwell came up with the strategy for attacking the legislation on the basis of religious freedom. He contended in his usual uncharitable, unChristian manner that the bill would force churches "to hire a practicing active homosexual drug addict with AIDS to be a teacher or youth pastor."[7]

However, the Senate and the House disagreed and easily overrode Reagan's veto.

Judicial Appointments

Between President Truman's appointment of the first black federal judge and the end of President Carter's term, an increasing number of blacks were added to the judicial system. But Reagan's negative attitude toward minority appointees, brought the modest gains to a screeching halt. During his first term, he appointed 160 judges, two of whom were black. In eight years, he made 360 life-time judicial appointments, six of whom were black. A majority of the appointees, including the six black tokens, were conservatives who disagreed with the Brown v. Board of Education decision, and criticized subsequent case rulings based on the historic decision.

Three of the more radical conservative judges nominated by Reagan were to obtrusively biased for the Senate to confirm: Lino A. Graglia of Texas who often and publicly belittled black people in the courtroom; Jefferson B. Sessions III who was fond of telling racist jokes, and the notoriously outspoken anti-affirmative action Robert Bork who in one instance described the Public Accommodation Section of the 1964 Civil Rights Act as "a principle of unsurpassed ugliness."[8]

[8]Mary McGrory, A Hostile Legacy

Reagan also appointed to the Supreme Court: Sandra Day O'Connor, Antonin Scalia and Anthony M. Kennedy. He named William H. Rehnquist, a Nixon appointee, to the position of Chief Justice.

The new conservative wing under Rehnquist's leadership wasted no time in reversing many of the previous gains won by black people through court battles. In the City of Richmond v. Croson, it was ruled that the city had no authority to impose a percentage of contracts for minority owned businesses. Then, the court ruled in a series of opinions that (1) eliminated the 1866 Civil Rights Law as a basis for minorities to sue in harassment cases, (2) shifted the burden of proof from the employer to the employee in job-bias cases, and (3) allowed whites to challenge affirmative action remedies imposed by lower courts to rectify previous acts of discrimination.

The situation got so bad that Justice Harry Blackmum disagreed in one decision, stating, "One wonders whether the majority still believes…race discrimination against non-whites is a problem in our society or even remembers that it ever was.[9]

Signing Dr. King Holiday Bill

Reagan's signing of the Dr. Martin Luther King Holiday bill was interpreted by allies as a commitment to civil rights. The exaggeration illustrates the magnitude of historical revision taking place in the last half of the 20th century. Just two weeks before the White House signing ceremony, he restated opposition to the legislation.

The deed was not evidence of a lifetime adversary suddenly becoming an enlightened advocate of equality, but the realization of almost everyone who ever opposed the bill that there was no political mileage left in trying to stop its passage.

Enactment of a national Dr. King holiday, after 14 years of congressional effort, was a cause for major celebration on the part of those who championed the legislation. But by the time the bill reached Reagan's desk for signature, controversy surrounding it had subsided significantly. A majority of the states had passed their own paid legal holiday legislation.

The measure was so non-controversial that the Democratically controlled House passed it under a special procedure limiting debate to 20 minutes on each side (pros and cons), prohibiting amendments, and requiring a two-thirds majority for passage. Time reserved for the opposition was hardly used. The vote for passage was 338 to 90, more than the 2/3 needed to override a presidential veto.

In the Senate, Republican Majority Leader Howard Baker held the bill at the desk rather then assign it to committee which would have subjected it to crippling amendments or stalling tactics. He later permitted the House version of the bill to go directly to the floor for a vote without hearings or extended debate. Passage of the measure was a foregone conclusion. The Senate passed it 78 to 22, more than enough to override a veto.

Reagan Officials Subverted the Law

At the beginning of Reagan's presidency, the country faced difficult foreign policy situations in Central America and the Middle East. The pro-Western government of Shah Mohammed Riza Pahlavi was overthrown by a radical faction led by the anti-American Ayatollah Khomeini. Nicaraguans had become increasingly anti-American under the leftist leaning leadership of the Sandinista government. American hostages were held in Lebanon by pro-Iranian jihad groups.

Top officials in the administration with approval of the President, secretly schemed to free American hostages held in Lebanon. The clandestine arrangement was sinister warfare in flagrant, criminal violation of numerous federal laws specifically prohibiting 'direct or indirect' sales of military weaponry to Iran and use of funds for military operations in Nicaragua. The sale of munitions to Iran contradicted the Administration's policy of pressuring other nations to observe an embargo imposed by the United States of all military weapons to the Iranian Ayatollah Khomeini.

A nine-point plan, developed and organized by National Security Advisor Robert McFarlane and his successor, Retired Admiral John Poindexter, was the vehicle used to evade legal prohibitions imposed by Congress. The complicated, illegal scheme involved airlifting four C-130 cargo planes filled with military weapons from the Philippines to Iran; Danish ships, in collusion with top Reagan officials, transported five loads of arms and ammunition from Israel to Iran. The same officials then diverted cash from the sale of arms to Iran to supply arms to the Nicaraguan resistance (Contras) for its revolution to overthrow the legitimate Sandinista Government.

Lt. Colonel Oliver North, a deputy director for political-military affairs at the National Security Council was put in charge of executing the illegal policy.

Joint congressional committees investigating the Iran-Contra Affair learned the Enterprise, a dummy corporation, was established to funnel monies for the operation. According to the report, millions of dollars were improperly or never satisfactorily accounted for. About $3.8 million from the sale of arms to Iran went to support the Contra rebels, $16.5 million was used to purchase arms from various sources for sell to Iran, and an expenditure of $48 million by the Enterprise was never fully explained.

Agents of the dummy company took $6.6 million in commissions and other profit distributions. Almost $1 million went for covert operations sponsored by Col. North and $4.2 million held in reserves for future operations. A deposit of $1.2 million went in Swiss bank accounts, and several thousand dollars were used to pay for a security system at Colonel North's personal residence.

President Reagan Implicated

For seven months, Colonel North invoked the 5th Amendment time after time to avoid testifying before House and Senate committees about involvement in the Iran-Contra affair. Finally, granted limited immunity, he was forced to testify or subject himself to contempt-of-Congress for refusing.

For six days the committee interrogated him. Under oath he stated: "I assume the President [Reagan] was aware of what I was doing and had, through my superiors, approved." He claimed to have sent five memos to Admiral John Poindexter, the President's national security advisor, requesting permission to divert monies from the sale of arms to Iran for the purpose of funding the secret Contra War in Nicaragua.

Reagan had no compunction about violating provisions of law in his obsessive desire to fight communism even if it meant illegally using the resources of government to overthrow democratically elected heads of state.

News of the illegality involving Iran, the Contras, and the Reagan White House became public near the end of 1986. According to the Official transcript of the Joint Hearings before the Senate Select Committees on Secret Military Assistance to Iran and the Nicaraguan Contras, and the House Select Committee to Investigate Covert Arms Transaction with Iran:

> *"all covert operations must be approved by the President personally and in writing. By statute, Congress must be notified. The funds used for such actions, must be strictly accounted for."*[10]

The committee concluded that the common ingredients of the Iran and contra policies were "secrecy, deception, and disdain" for law. The Report stated:

> *"The action was not approved by the President in writing. Congress was not notified. And the funds to support it were never accounted for. In short, the operation was an evasion of the Constitution's most basic check on Executive action-the power of the Congress to grant or deny funding for Government programs."*[11]

In May 1989, Colonel North was convicted of destroying and falsifying documents, use of public funds to pay for a personal security system at his home and aiding in the obstruction of Congress. He was fined $150,000, given a three-year suspended sentence, and ordered to perform 1,200 hours of community service. In June 1990, Rear Admiral John Poindexter became the seventh former Reagan official convicted in the Iran-contra fiasco. He was convicted on five counts of conspiracy, obstruction of Congress, and making false statements to investigators. He was sentenced to six months in jail.

In September 1991, a federal judge ordered Iran-Contra charges against Oliver North dropped, the result of a legal technicality.

A Balanced Portrayal of Ronald W. Reagan

Eight years of Reagan's presidency left many disillusioned. An accurate description of his tenure came from the esteemed chairman of the House Energy and Commerce Committee, John D. Dingell (D-Mich). The thirty-three year House veteran capsulized his feelings about the President in a letter to an awestruck constituent who wrote Dingell in support of the television mini-series "The Reagans" produced by CBS. Dingell responded:

> *As someone who served with President Reagan, and in the interest of histori-
> cal accuracy, please allow me to share with you some of my recollections of
> the Reagan years that I hope will make it into the final cut of the mini-series:
> $640 Pentagon toilets seats; ketchup as a vegetable; union busting; firing
> striking air traffic controllers; Iran-Contra; selling arms to terrorist nations;
> trading arms for hostages; retreating from terrorist in Beirut; lying to Con-
> gress; financing an illegal war in Nicaragua; visiting Bitburg cemetery; a
> cozy relationship with Saddam Hussein; shredding documents; Ed Meese;
> Fawn Hall; Oliver North; James Watt; apartheid apologia; the savings and
> loan scandal; voodoo economics; record budget deficits; double digit unem-
> ployment; farm bankruptcies, trade deficits; astrologers in the White House;
> Star Wars; and influence peddling.[12]*

Many had the foresight to predict the calamity in store for the country at the beginning of Reagan's term, and challenged the shortsighted legislative measures that he offered for resolution of the problems. At the end, a majority of the public disagreed with his draconian policies, realizing his neglect was not confined to the poorest, defenseless elements in society. Despite the pros and cons and the propaganda campaign by the Republican National Commit-tee, the national rating of the great communicator was the lowest of any president since the beginning of recorded national polls.

At the end, the smiles of his avid cheering section turned to sneers as they realized what his policy initiatives caused in terms of human suffering. The measure used to chart misery, rose to mean-ingful, unprecedented levels: 30 million suffered at least on episode of unemployment, hundreds of billions of dollars lost in gross week-ly earnings, more than 200,000 mortgage foreclosures carried out, and over 40,000 businesses failed.

An aging population was told there would be cut backs in their benefits while the working poor were told to forget subsidized day care facilities, give up food stamp supplements, and continue working for a minimum wage that was not a livable wage.

Racist or Not! Civil Rights Hemorrhaged

It is not necessary to engage in academic argument whether Reagan was or was not a racist. His motives are insignificant and unimportant. The fact is that his policies, deeds, pronouncements, and actions had devastating adverse impacts on relations between the races.

In the closing days of Ronald Wilson Reagan's presidency, he professed to be aghast that many black citizens thought he was a racist. Mary McGrory, columnist of the *Washington Post* wrote that when he was leaving office: "blacks [were] conspicuously dry-eyed, while the rest of the country puddles up over his departure."[13]

McGrory stated that Reagan pretended to be baffled and hurt by criticism of blacks, but had apparently forgotten his record. She wrote: "He has adopted policies that have been consistently, even blatantly, hostile to black citizens. Then when they protest, he turns around and accuses them of prejudice against him."[14]

The columnist was mild in her treatment of Reagan compared to what many blacks thought. Remarks by Roger Wilkins, a civil rights leader and journalist reflected the typical sentiment of blacks when he called Reagan "an ignorant savage when it comes to black problems and concerns."[15]

NOTES

1/Rep. William L. Clay, Speech in St. Louis, Missouri.
2/Rep. William L. Clay, Press Release
3/Ibid., Clay
4/Rep. William L. Clay, Speech
5/Ibid. Clay
6/President Reagan's Veto Message
7/*Congressional Quarterly Almanac*, 1988 (Washington, D.C.: *Congressional Quarterly,* 1988) page, 67.
8/Mary McGrory, *A Hostile Legacy for Blacks, Washington Post,* 17 January 1989, A2.
9/Carl T. Rowan, *Breaking Barriers*: A Memoir, Little, Brown and Company, 1991, page 329.
10/Report Senate Select Committees on Secret Military Assistance to Iran and the Nicaraguan Contras
11/Ibid.
12/Letter to Constituents, from John D. Dingell, Member of Congress, 29 October

2003.
13/Mary McGrory, "A Hostile Legacy for Blacks," *Washington Post*, 17 January 1989, A2.
14/Ibid.A2.
15/Ibid A2.

13

Approaching Washington airport, the flight attendant announced, "George H.W. Bush is now President of the USA. According to FAA regulations, I must inform you to place your trays and seats in the original upright positions, fasten your seat belts and turn your watches back 100 years.[1]

– Congressman William L. Clay

George Herbert Walker Bush
A Politician with Many Contradictions

George H.W. Bush had an extensive, impressive background in government service: member of Congress, Ambassador to the United Nations, Republican Party Chairman, envoy to China, director of the Central Intelligence Agency (CIA), Vice President of the United States.

In this remarkable government career spanning 35 years, he refused to come face-to-face with a paradoxical conflict of duplicity in considering his stances on matters of race. Claiming abhorrence to all forms of injustice, he steadfastly opposed any specific proposal to ameliorate it. Throughout his distinguished career, he consistently opposed civil rights at every opportunity.

As legislator, administrator, and executive, he was a master-craftsman in masking hostility to equality. He never met a civil rights measure he could support without qualified reservation. Legislative initiatives and administrative dictums devised to alleviate oppressive conditions of segregation and discrimination were always sufficiently flawed, in his opinion, to justify objecting to the remedy.

In numerous instances involving denial of minority rights,

Bush's response was the same: deplore the horrible injustice, but decry trampling on the Constitution to eradicate it. In his biased, reactionary mind-set, proposals offered for rectifying racial injustices did not go far enough, went too far, or should have been considered at another time, in another context.

He was a virtuoso practitioner of subtle opposition to civil rights while feigning consternation, trepidation, and indignation at obstacles preventing blacks from achieving first-class citizenship. Yet, time after time, pretending to be in sync with the goals of the movement, he aided and abetted those who constructed insurmountable barriers to equal opportunities.

When his flights of fancy were challenged and his fantasyland narratives exposed as sugar-coated, racist obstructionism, he routinely voiced indignation, often became overwhelmed with self-pity, and accused critics of distorting his intentions. But there was little room for misreading the elasticity of his ethnical shortcomings.

Pursuing policies similar to those of his predecessor, he caused as much damage to halting the struggle to advance civil rights. Reagan smiled, joked, cajoled, uttering clever one-liners while undermining basic rights of the underprivileged and racially denied. Bush's deception differed in style and mannerism but was equally as effective. He engaged in unlimited, fallacious arguments to justify assailing civil rights and anti-poverty programs.

Typical of his lack of integrity and gross insensitivity to minority feelings was the exploitation of a racist television commercial that proved decisive in his election. Introducing it into his political campaign is one of three dramatic incidents highlighting his legacy to Black Americans. Veto of a civil rights bill and the nomination of Clarence Thomas to the Supreme Court being the others.

His 1988 political election committee fanned the flames of racism and capitalized on "white backlash" in producing one of the most demagogic advertisements in recent history. Associating his Democratic opponent, Governor Michael Dukakis of Massachusetts with the crime of an African American convict on furlough from a state prison was a cynical, unethical, racist tactic. Repeatedly showing the television clip of a black prisoner (Willie Horton) who raped a white woman and stabbed her fiancé while on furlough, was a provocative flash back to the days that inspired mob lynching and stirred latent emotions of deep seated racial bias.

The 30 second "Willie Horton" advertisement distracted voter's attention from Bush's unimpressive record and focused the debate almost entirely on race as the major issue.

It did not matter that a Republican governor introduced the furlough system into law, or that the parole board had absolute authority to grant prisoners weekend passes. It did not matter that a similar policy had been widely used in California when Reagan was governor. What mattered was Bush's refusal to denounce the canard as a despicable, dishonest manner of campaigning and disassociate himself from it.

Columnist Molly Ivins described the Horton commercial:

"a vapid, racist exercise featuring the flag and Horton, conducted while he [Bush] carefully concealed the extent of the savings and loan fiasco and lied about his involvement in the Iran-Contra scandal."[2]

Campaigning for re-election four years later, Bush had the audacity to become agitated when Congresswoman Maxine Waters (D-Cal.) called him a racist. He maintained his campaign was not responsible for the Horton ad because an independent political action committee ran it without his knowledge or consent. However, his miserable record of perpetual collision with the destiny of black people, made it difficult to accept the explanation as plausible.

Bigoted Record Speaks Loudly

Despite carefully orchestrated propaganda that lionized Bush as a man of courage who supported civil rights when it was perilous to his own career, truth and candor revealed the contrary. His behavior during his time in congress, appointed positions, and presidential days were filled with contemptuous disrespect for the rights of minorities. His tenacious defense of outdated mores justifying segregation, long after most intelligent people recognized the system's imminent demise, speaks in earsplitting loudness about his lack of integrity and non-commitment to a "colorblind society."

In the 1960s, television networks extensively covered brutalizing events, exposing the savagery of white mobs attacking helpless Negroes with bricks, clubs and dogs as they attempted to register for the vote or to desegregate all-white illegal public school classrooms. Bush ignored the mayhem and blamed the Supreme Court decision in Brown v. the Board of Education and its `forced busing' for precipitating the violence. The most far-reaching, racially-oriented legislation in modern history was enactment of the 1964 Civil Rights Act. Six years after it became law, Bush was still opposing the measure with missionary zeal. Appealing to the bigotry of white voters in a Texas campaign for the U.S. Senate, Bush repeatedly stated, "The Act was passed to protect 14 percent of the population. I'm also worried about the other 86 percent".[3]

When peaceful marches and other non-violent protests by blacks demanding the right to register and vote, he voiced no sympathy for their cause. When millions of television viewers looked on in horror as police billy-clubbed black adults as they peacefully demonstrated for the right to vote, the Congressman did not criticize their behavior. When City firemen in their official capacity sprayed elementary school children with high-pressure water hoses for supporting the registration drive, he was still unmoved. Yet, seemingly oblivious to the injustices, he found soul-searching reason to vigorously oppose the 1965 Voting Right Act, which was designed to guarantee the right of all to participate in the electoral process without fear of physical harm.

In this period of unrest, hundreds of counties in southern states had no black registered voters, even where the black population exceeded 50 percent. Lowndes County, Mississippi, where black citizens comprised more than 65 percent of the population, typified the general situation-Negroes held no elected office and less than 10 percent of those eligible were permitted to register by white registrars. Only 5% of blacks in the entire state of Mississippi had been allowed to register. In Selma, Alabama, 2.1% of the black voting age population was registered to vote. Fear of physical harm, even death and other intimidation caused the low registration numbers.

Bush opposed the Voting Rights Act, rationalizing that blacks did not need federal supervision to insure their ability to register and vote. He ignored reality. In Dallas County, Alabama, a community just outside the city limits of Selma, with a population of 29,515 adults, of whom 14,400 were white and 15,115 were black, only 383 blacks were registered compared to 8,216 whites. Nor was he moved to indignation by the slogan of the Alabama Democratic Party that endorsed his candidacy: "the Party of white supremacy."

In Bush's legal lexicon, widespread harassment, intimidation, and physical violence preventing blacks from registering and voting was insufficient to justify federal intervention into rights reserved to the states, despite amendments to the Constitution and laws enacted to the contrary.

What Was Bush's Position on Fair Housing?

Describing his 1968 vote for the Fair Housing Act as a profile in courage that jeopardized his chance for reelection is grossly distorted political hyperbole. The fact was that Bush only voted for passage after unsuccessfully leading an effort to kill the bill.

In 1967, the House of Representatives passed H.R. 2516, a bill aimed at protecting civil rights workers who were being beaten, gassed and killed for trying to register black voters and to desegregate public schools. After the bill passed the House, the Senate Judiciary Committee held hearings and reported it to the full body for consideration. The full Senate failed to act before adjourning for the Christmas recess.

Reconvening in January, a fair housing provision was added after a cloture vote of 65 to 32 ended a filibuster conducted by Senators Sam Ervin (D-N.C.) and Strom Thurmond (R-S.C.). To appease those who opposed fair housing, an anti-rioting amendment (which was pushed by Bush in the House) was accepted. The action was specifically aimed at H. Rap Brown and other black leaders whose incendiary speeches allegedly incited blacks to riot in numerous cities. The bill provided criminal penalties for anyone convicted of traveling in interstate commerce or using the mails, telephone, telegraph, radio or television with the intent `to incite, organize, or encourage a riot."

There was no evidence that interstate agitators prompted the 1965 riots of Watts, Los Angeles which lasted 6 days, left 34 persons dead, 1,000 wounded, and more than 4,000 arrested. Then the violent summer of 1967 saw riots in Newark (killing 23, wounding 1, 500) and in Detroit (killing 43, wounding 2,000). Again, there was no claim of outside militants inspiring the violence.

In that atmosphere, the House was presented a bill calling for fair housing as well as Bush's version of making it a federal crime to cross state lines for the purpose of inciting violence.

Bush found the fair housing legislation attached to the anti-violence bill distasteful and politically uncomfortable. He argued that the Act was unfair, and challenged the authority of Congress to impose restrictions on realtors and home owners.

Caught between the proverbial rock and a hard place, he dared not oppose the highly emotional and popularly driven effort to pass his own anti-rioting legislation. But the fair housing amendment fit his obsessive complaint about civil rights promotion always being at the wrong time and in the wrong place.

Six days before the scheduled vote, Dr. Martin Luther King, Jr. was murdered in Memphis, Tennessee. Within 72 hours, fiery uprisings erupted in 125 cities and civil unrest broke out on 50 college campuses. The U.S. Army and the National Guard found themselves pitted against an army of black insurrectionists with little respect for the property rights of cities, states and the privileged class.

White America was in a state of peril and disbelief, confusion, and bewilderment. For three days and three nights, Washington, D.C., the capital of the free world, burned. Dark clouds of smoke belched from fires lit in front of the President's residence and surrounding neighborhoods. Marines in sand-bagged bunkers and mounted machine guns protected the White House from the possibility of fire-bombing and sacking.

Bush Led Effort to Kill Fair Housing

In that climate, Bush, a disciple of profile in courage, used parliamentary tactics attempting to cripple and prevent passage of the Fair Housing Act. First, he tried to kill the entire legislation by organizing opposition to the rule that permitted a vote on the Senate bill. Unsuccessfully, he argued for the benefit of bigoted southern members that a subsequent rule would be adopted to allow a House vote only on the anti-rioting part. His motion was defeated as the House passed the rule with the fair housing provision attached on a vote of 229 to 195.

Bush who claimed to have placed his career in jeopardy, then offered an amendment to delete the fair housing section which virtually would have killed it. The ploy too failed. After exhausting a number of weakening amendments, he reluctantly voted for final passage.

Continuing to characterize his vote for the Fair Housing Act as one of courage and integrity, simply demeans the collective intelligence of people who can separate fact from fiction.

Opposed Extension of Voting Rights Act

When congressional liberals and moderates waged a crucial struggle to extend the life of the 1965 Voting Rights Act for 5 years, again the ultra-conservative Mr. Bush found hallowed ground for opposing the effort, supposedly because the Senate attached a rider to grant 18-year-old youth the right to vote. Young men of that age, drafted and dying in disproportionate numbers on the battlefield in the jungles of Vietnam were ineligible to vote in elections that decided who would make policy about war.

Uttering the customary, esoteric phrases in praising the worthiness of protecting the sacred right of black people to vote, Bush decried the Senate action to mixing two worthwhile issues as reckless, irresponsible. In debate on the House floor, he said: "I am somewhat distressed that legislation as vital as the Voting Rights Act has been obliterated by the Senate rider permitting entry into the franchise of 18-year-olds."[4]   Please, sir! What other germane legislative vehicle should an issue of their voting be attached?

In other instances, keeping his record of unequivocal opposition to all civil rights intact, he opposed a bill to establish an Equal Employment Opportunity Commission and another to extend the tenure of the Commission on Civil Rights for 4 years.

Bush Defeated in Race for U.S. Senate

Bush filed against incumbent Democratic Senator Ralph Yarborough in 1970. His major thrust was an attack on Yarborough's support of civil rights, including the 1964 Civil Rights Act which prohibited discrimination in places of public accommodations. Bush alleged the bill: "transcends civil rights and violated the constitutional rights of all people." Twenty-one of the 22 senators, Democrats and Republicans, from the eleven southern states voted against the bill. Yarborough was the only one to support the bill that banned racial segregation in places of public accommodation.

I was invited by the Texas State AFL-CIO to keynote its annual fund raising dinner. The prestigious affair attracted more than 2,000 of Texas' most important elected officials, labor leaders, and Democratic activists. My role was to counter Bush's intemperate attack on Yarborough's civil rights stance.

As a stranger to Texas politics, I was startled at the commotion of the enthusiastic crowd when a young black woman entered the hall and proceeded down the aisle toward the dais. The chairman of the state labor confederation rose, took the microphone and announced that the organization was throwing its support behind the creation of a black congressional district in Houston. The guests screamed wildly as he declared their candidate would be state senator Barbara Jordan.

I was wondering who in the hell is Barbara Jordan? Before long, I knew. She mounted the podium, took the microphone and with her booming voice, held the audience spellbound for five minutes. The rousing welcome, in my opinion, was justified.

In my presentation, I praised Yarborough as a leading advocate of justice for blacks and Hispanics and denounced his opponent [Bush] for equivocating on equality of opportunity at every instance.

Congressman Bush spent four years preparing to unseat Yarborough by building a case that the incumbent was too liberal and too aggressive in support of civil rights. In an odd turn of events, Yarborough lost the Democratic primary to a more conservative, but racially sensitive candidate, Lloyd Bentsen, Jr. Bush, unprepared to effectively switch gears of smut and smear campaigning, and unable to define Bentsen as a liberal, was defeated in the general election.

Vetoed Hatch Act Reform

Bush as President also had an addiction for vetoing progressive legislation. Among his many vetoes was legislation sponsored by me to reform the Hatch Act. The bill would allow Federal employees to attend political conventions, circulate nominating petitions, canvass precincts in off duty work hours, stuff envelopes, work telephone banks, place signs in the window at home, or bumper stickers on a private automobile. It passed the House 297 to 90 and the Senate by a large margin in 1991, but was vetoed by Bush. The House overrode the veto, but the Senate fell two votes short.

Vetoed Family and Medical Leave Act

The Family and Medical Leave Act (FMLA), also a bill I pushed through the House, mandated unpaid leave for working Americans to care for a newborn child or handle a medical emergency of parents or spouses. It afforded leave in times of family sickness or death. The overriding question was one of fairness. Should an individual's choice for leave be limited to the welfare of his/her family or his/her job?

The bill passed the House in 1990 by a vote of 237 to 187 which was 46 votes short of the two-thirds needed to override Bush's veto. The bill passed the Senate and Bush vetoed it.

Vetoed Unemployment Aid

Bush vetoed a $6.4 billion bill that would increase benefits from seven to 20 weeks of extra benefits to those who exhausted the basic 26 weeks of unemployment aid. There was a surplus in the trust fund established to address this kind of emergency.

More than 3 million workers had exhausted regular unemployment insurance benefits and an estimated 3.4 million were scheduled to do the same. The Senate fell two votes short of overriding the president's veto.

Vetoed Civil Rights Bill

Bush vetoed a major civil rights bill that would have expanded protection against employment discrimination for minorities and women. It also sought to overturn five Supreme Court decisions that substantially and negatively altered prevailing interpretations of Title VII of the 1964 Civil Rights Act.

The Business Roundtable, a consortium of 200 major U.S. corporations and the Civil Rights Leadership Conference met over a four month period to reach consensus on the legislation. As a compromise appeared imminent, Bush's White House intervened and applied pressure, persuading the business leaders to withdraw from negotiations. The bill passed without their support.

The president based his veto decision on the cynical advice of John Sununu, White House Chief of Staff, and Richard Thornburgh, the Attorney General who claimed the bill mandated racial and sexual quotas in hiring.

Condoned Racial Injustice in South Africa

Bush falsely declared that the oppressive, murderous government of South Africa complied with all conditions of the Anti-Apartheid Act which Congress had passed over the veto of Reagan. Violating two major legal requirements, provisions, namely the creation of free political activity and the release of all political prisoners, he shamelessly ordered the removal of sanctions. Ignoring legislative intent, his unconscionable fiat slowed the movement toward majority rule in a country violently resisting democratic reform.

Presidential Miscarriage of Justice

In 1992, before the legal process of the Iran contra criminal indictments were allowed to work its way to conclusion, the President abruptly brought the investigation to a halt. He pardoned six associates charged with, or convicted of, misleading Congress in the Iran-Contra fiasco. Included was Retired Admiral John Poindexter a former member of Reagan's national security team who was convicted on five counts of conspiracy, making false statements to a congressional committee and obstruction of Congress. He was sentenced to six months in jail.

Bush also pardoned former Secretary of Defense Caspar Weinberger. Without entering a courtroom and facing charges, Weinberger was exonerated of any and all previous wrongdoing prior to trial. Prosecutors predicted that a trial and his testimony would implicate Bush's personal involvement in the illegal activity.

This highly unusual activity of acquitting without trial was obvious. It prevented the guilty from establishing a possible link between them, President and the scheme to subvert the law.

Clarence Thomas: Bush's Legacy
Toward African Americans

Bush's contemptuous attitude and general disrespect for civil rights caused the chasm between whites and blacks to widen. Nominating Clarence Thomas to the Supreme Court, a person steeped in opposition to advancing the rights of his own people, was considered an abomination by a majority of African Americans.

In nominating Thomas, the President said: "He is the best person for this position. He is a delightful and warm, intelligent person who has a great empathy...who believes passionately in equal opportunity for all Americans."[5]

Describing an antagonist of affirmative action, an opponent

of the Voting Rights Act, and a critic of Brown v. the Board of Education as a 'believer in equal opportunity,' was an incredulous and cheap distortion of fact even for a life-time politician.

The nomination came as a shock but no surprise to black legislators who knew the President's proclivity for deception. The controversial choice, caused chaos and confusion within the ranks of liberals and moderates because of Thomas' demonstrated insensitivity for the plight of the poor, minorities and the aged. But ultra-conservatives were united, even euphoric that Thomas would be in position to tilt the court toward their ideological persuasion

Supporters of the nomination engaged in jaw-boning, manufactured instantaneous virtues of a make believe national hero. They heaped distinction on their straw man, obliterating facts in developing a fictitious character bigger-than-life. They waged an aggressive campaign to deflect debate surrounding his legal shortcomings, and to establish him as a victim of racial deprivation who overcame a background of poverty and deprivation. Neither, in or by itself, justifies or qualifies an individual for high office.

Julian Bond, former Georgia state senator and NAACP official bluntly stated: "If escape from poverty were the sole qualification for the Supreme Court. Thurgood Marshall might well be sitting there alone."[6]

To focus on Thomas' blackness and not his record was insulting to those who fought to create an atmosphere where minorities with qualifications could be considered for important positions. To paint him as rising from a life of destitution in Pin Point, Georgia was a fabrication designed to garner pity and sympathy. Thomas left the shambles of a house with an outdoor toilet and no running water at age 5, never to return. He went to Savannah, Georgia to live with his grandfather, a businessman, relatively removed from those wretched conditions.

No Basis for Comparison to Marshall

It was expected that Thomas' past record and prospective positions be compared to Thurgood Marshall, the black jurist he succeeded. Regrettably Bush, Republican partisans and the media went overboard in casting him a protector of women, minorities, the poor, and putting him in the same league of experience and competence with Justice Marshall.

Comparison of the two was not only juvenile and misleading, but disgraceful. What a tragic, demeaning tribute to the lifetime of sacrifice and suffering endured by the scholarly, crusading Marshall. Denying Thomas entry to a chintzy movie house in a hick town of Georgia and being called derogatory names by students in a Catholic school –was not the same as Marshall facing the tyranny of lynch mobs when representing black folk in court rooms across America. In dozens of towns similar to Pin Point Georgia, Marshall risked life and limb to bring justice to victims of discrimination. Thomas who never joined a picket line for jobs or demonstrated for the right to vote, may have been humiliated by "no colored" signs and "separate drinking fountains," but labeling him a courageous crusader for racial equality is akin to calling a termite an interior decorator.

Thomas himself said after joining the Court, "I will find it difficult to fill [Marshall's] shoes."[7] No truer words were ever spoken. Before becoming a judge, he never argued a case in federal court. Before confirmation, his experience on the bench was limited to 14 months and he only wrote 20 routine opinions during the period. His private legal background was equally as paltry, consisting of a minor stint as assistant attorney general in a Missouri state office.

Contrast that to Justice Marshall, a legal and judicial giant-respected, admired, emulated by his peers-envied by his adversaries. His experiences before appointment to the bench spanned more than three decades of fighting segregation, discrimination and other forms of injustice through the court system. He was an appellate court judge and a U.S. Solicitor General. He argued more cases before the Supreme Court than any lawyer in history (thirty-two, winning 29).

Support for Thomas Crystallized

Thomas' confirmation battle was a classic engagement between powerful individuals, organizations and institutions competing to promote or protect their causes. Forces lining up for and against him represented an awesome array of influences. On one side, President Bush and the colossal resources of the United States government were aided by politically powerful right-wing conservative groups.

Jerry Falwell, Phyllis Schlafy, Gary Bauer, the ultimate voices for extreme rightwing agitation and most vigorous opponents of minority rights, joined the campaign at the outset. But the most energetic of the right wing coalition was the Reverend Pat Robertson who raised more than 1 million dollars for the campaign. His prolific fundraising success proved that a poverty-stricken, anti-black, legally challenged Colored lad from the backwoods of Georgia was worth something to somebody in the political scheme of things.

As chairman of the Equal Employment Opportunity Commission, Thomas' rulings were disastrous. He changed the agency pursuit of class action suits against large employers that discriminated and insisted on the slow, unending, almost impossible procedures of proving discrimination on an individual case-by-case basis.

William Lucy, president of the Coalition of Black Trade Unionists testified before the Senate committee:

> *"His [Thomas'] statement opposing class action remedies strongly suggests that he believes that institutions should not be held accountable for their discriminatory behavior and should not be forced by government to change that behavior."*[8]

Thomas argued that statistical percentages showing lack of minorities on the payroll were not evidence of discrimination, contending that in many cases the absence was the result of a lack of education, training or experience. His position exonerated from prosecution large corporations, metropolitan police and fire departments that never hired minorities. It forestalled remedy in areas where black and Hispanics approximated 50% of the population and their presence in the workforce was nil.

Opposition to the nomination also came from powerful individuals and groups. Equally savvy operatives of organized labor, civil rights, black elected officials, women, and seniors launched a campaign to block it. The Congressional Black Caucus, except for Gary Franks, a Republican from Connecticut, lobbied against the nomination. Representatives Hawkins, Owens and I, who had more first-hand contact with Thomas than any member of the House or Senate, challenged the nomination. During his nine years in the Reagan and Bush Administrations, we interrogated him extensively in hearings. As chairman of EEOC, Thomas deliberately misled [i.e. lied] our committee about his failure to enforce civil rights laws more times than I care to recount.

The CBC testified that Thomas attacked Supreme Court decisions upholding voluntary affirmative action, ridiculed support for set-asides in licensing and contracting, and as the assistant secretary for civil rights, attempted to justify flagrant and intentional violations of a court order compelling timely processing of discrimination complaints.

Fourteen members of the House of Representatives, including 12 chairmen of committees having oversight responsibilities for the EEOC, in a letter to President Bush, raised, serious questions about Thomas' judgment, respect for the law and general suitability to serve as a member of the Federal judiciary.

Women opposed the nomination, fearing his confirmation would give a majority on the Court to those who consistently voted to deny their rights. The National Women's Law Center stated that Thomas posed a threat to Roe v. Wade which protected women's right to an abortion, and his confirmation might tip the scales in favor of overturning the decision.

The Women's Legal Rights group stated, "Thomas' articulated views and record are antithetical to the continued viability of the heightened scrutiny of protection against sex discrimination..."[9]

Organizations representing the elderly, testified that when Thomas was head of the EEOC, he initially testified before Congress that only 900 charges of age discrimination had expired because statutory limits had run out before his agency filed the cases. At the time, every top official of the EEOC, including Thomas, knew the statement was patently false. But, he proceeded to cover-up the flagrant and intentional violation of a court order compelling the timely processing of discrimination complaints.

Three months later, the truth was revealed–13,873 charges had expired prior to April 1988. In addition, the agency admitted that another 2,801 charges expired from April 1988 through June 1990. These were not merely numbers of disagreement in a report. The 16,000 plus were fathers, mothers, sisters, brothers, aunts, uncles of caring, concerned people who were denied their right to relief under the law. According to representatives of senior organizations, the oversight was deliberate. They accused Thomas of siding with businesses and employers against the interests of older workers.

Senator David Pryor (D-Ark.) politely summed up Thomas' lying to Congress, saying that he was dismayed to learn about several 'erroneous statements' made by Chairman Thomas.

NAACP Testifies Against Nomination

The politics of ethnicity and a strategy to garner sympathy for Thomas based on his race was evident from the time President Bush announced the nomination. It was obvious the administration and Thomas' supporters planned to use the NAACP and other African American groups as `attack dogs' in scaring off white liberal opposition, and drumming up support among minorities. Projecting race and the background of poverty would influence organizations as the NAACP, the Urban League and the Congressional Black Caucus from launching a vigorous campaign against him. The assumption was critically flawed.

Anyone slightly familiar with the long history of the NAACP challenging anti-black judicial nominees, and aware of the militant composition of the CBC, knew better. Predicting either organization would be silent, was arrogant, uninformed and wishful thinking that proved erroneous.

Despite the secret deal the White House allegedly made with several top officials of the NAACP in advance of the nomination, the group was neither intimidated nor blackmailed. Despite threats from large white donors, the organization refused to play "bogey man" in a scheme to frighten other groups.

NAACP Board chairman William F. Gibson said that the organization considered everything, including Thomas' membership, before taking a stance against his nomination. He stated that they concluded an all-white Supreme Court would be better than one with Clarence Thomas on it.

Benjamin L. Hooks, Executive Director of the NAACP and a well respected Republican who was appointed by several Republican presidents to high positions, in testifying before the Judiciary Committee dispelled the rumor that he had made a secret pact with President Bush to garner support for Thomas. He stated:

African Americans for 20 generations have cried vainly for the simple, decent entitlement of the most elemental civil rights, only to be denied...We must firmly resist [Thomas]. We did not come to this opposition lightly or recently. We opposed Judge Thomas' re-nomination to the EEOC, and when he became very hostile to our aspirations, we asked for his resignation...

[He] has rejected class-based relief as a major element of the solution to both past and present racial discrimination...Does everyone have to be a Rosa Parks and sit on the streetcar and be arrested? Do we have to have a million James Merediths applying to the University of Alabama or Ole Miss? Or should we have class action relief...based on the record, we must and we do oppose his confirmation.[10]

Rev. Brown, an Executive Board Member of the NAACP observed that Thomas did not understand the history of the black struggle. He said it was a misrepresentation to say that black organizations were only interested in civil rights. He cited the works of Benjamin Mays, James Weldon, W.E.B. Dubois and others who took initiatives and promoted self help but were not "so naive as to ignore" that institutionalized racism had to be attacked with all the resources available to the government.

CBC Takes Off the Gloves to "Prevent Destroying the Bridge Over Troubled Waters"

The CBC Foundation (CBCF) exposed the crux of a strategy employed by the President to garner support for a thoroughly incompetent candidate. Administration operatives and other advocates engaged in a jaw-boning campaign to manufacture virtues, inferring the candidate was a self-made, genuine hero. It was a game of smoke and mirrors to transform a selfish, self-centered egotist into a selfless crusader for righteousness. They attempted to deflect the debate by obliterating facts, and creating a fictitious character similar to Horatio Alger-bigger-than-life.

The CBC, the parent organization of the CBCF, testified to the Senate hearing committee acknowledging its previous opposition to other Supreme Court confirmations when they believed unusual circumstances justified it.

Because of the unique experiences of the CBC, it was pointed out that CBC members represented a larger number of black Americans than any other legislators or organizations and emphasized that "Along with state and local representatives, we are the only group of black Americans who have in no sense been self-selected to express the political, constitutional, economic and social views of black Americans."[11]

Twenty-six CBC members with 227 years of congressional service chaired five (5) full committees and thirteen (13) subcommittees in the House. They had documented a dossier on Thomas through legislative oversight of the agencies within their legislative authority.

Negative characteristics of his administrating programs made us cringe at the thought of him sitting on the Supreme Court. The extensive portfolio of his racial indiscretions, collected in our official capacity from interfacing with him, placed us in the best position to determine his fitness for the position.

We considered a lifetime appointment to the Supreme Court a matter of grave national importance that transcended the race of the nominee. Our constituents expected us be bold and colorblind in advocating equal justice.

The CBC took off the gloves, describing Thomas as an "opportunist, an ingrate and a traitor to the cause of black Americans."[12]

Twenty-five of the 26 CBC members issued a document enunciating reasons for opposing him. Republican Gary Franks was the lone exception.

Testifying before the Senate: John Conyers, John Lewis, Major Owens, Louis Stokes, Craig Washington expressed an obligation to "speak up because the reality of our experience" with this nominee compels us to oppose him. They cited his hostile, unresponsive performance in protecting the legal rights of people discriminated against. They introduced a 1988 audit report of the General Accounting Office (GAO) which showed a mounting backlog of EEOC discrimination cases, delays in their investigations and a decrease in the average amounts of settlements. Thomas' reply "was to cast doubts on the independence and integrity of the GAO, complaining that the report was a 'hatchet job' and adding "It's a shame Congress can use GAO as a lap dog to come up with anything it wants...[13]

In sharply worded testimony, Congressman Craig A. Washington of Texas told the Senate Judiciary Committee: Judge Thomas has a disturbingly paradigmatic disdain and disregard for legal precedent and stare decisis; has shown a previous, long-standing disrespect for the civil liberties of groups; has espoused, as a fulcrum of his legal thought, the concept of natural law, and has shown a lack of respect for the rule of law...the elevation of Thomas to the Supreme Court is dangerous for all Americans.[14]

Major Owens (D-N.Y.) said:

"Judge Clarence Thomas is a man who has clearly and consistently stood against those legal principles, philosophies and ideas which are vitally necessary for our [the black race] survival and continuing progress. The elevation of this man to the Supreme Court would be a gross insult, a cruel slap "in the face" of all African-Americans."[15]

Louis Stokes (D-Oh) testified:

"Our appearance here today, while borne in necessity, is also borne in pain... The difference between Judge Thomas and most black Americans who have achieved in spite of poverty, adversity and racism is that most of them have not forgotten from whence they have come...It is almost unheard of to see them utilize their educations and positions to impede the progress of those less fortunate than they."[16]

Congressman John Lewis, representing Thomas' state of Georgia, testified at the senate hearing that:

What you have is a nominee who wants to destroy the bridge that brought him over troubled waters! [emphasis added] He wants to pull down the ladder that he climbed up!

You have a nominee who has refused to answer your questions. A nominee who has defied the law. A nominee who has tried to stonewall this committee. A Nominee who changes his story to suit the audience. A nominee who is running from his record.[17]

Lewis was graphic in describing how he was targeted by some blacks in the Atlanta community for turning on a "brother" and a fellow Georgian. He said it was a "black thing." They accused him of betraying the race. But the Congressman stood his ground and strongly opposed the nomination of an individual who mocked the struggle of those "Who devoted and in many cases even sacrificed their lives for the principles it is now fashionable to dismiss."[18]

The congressman also testified, "I am the son of sharecroppers; I grew up poor; the house in which we lived had no indoor plumbing or electricity. But that does not make me qualified to sit on the highest court in the land."[19]

The following excerpts are taken from the document presented by the CBC:

The decision to oppose the Thomas nomination has come because the evidence is so overwhelming that the nomination of Clarence Thomas would be universally opposed in our community if he were white and had his present record.

He has attacked Supreme Court decisions upholding voluntary affirmative action plans against constitutional and statutory challenges. He has attacked Supreme Court support for set-asides in licensing and contracting...

While Assistant Secretary for Civil Rights in the Department of Education, he acknowledged and attempted to justify flagrant and intentional violations of a court order compelling timely processing of discrimination complaints.[20]

Senators Hatch and Danforth Criticize CBC

Senator Orrin Hatch (R-Ida.) Joined other senators, including John Danforth (R-Mo.) in assailing the CBC. Senator Danforth,

Republican of Missouri and the chief sponsor of Thomas' nomination, accused the Black Caucus of playing racial politics in seeking to generate opposition to Thomas. The senator said "The one thing that is totally intolerable to the caucus is [A] black who is a Republican and a conservative."

In response, I stated that Danforth supported Thomas, "not because of any worthy contributions made to his community or country...but he [Danforth] was so blind-sided by Thomas' color that he became oblivious to his offensive disregard for the feeling of his fellow black Americans."[21] I described Danforth's "blind support as a reflection of callous insensitivity toward Black Americans."[22]

Three years later the Senator admitted being so obsessed with getting Thomas approved that loyal members of his staff threatened to quit. In his 1994 book "Resurrection," he wrote: "I [Danforth] fought dirty." He said in an interview with the *Washington Post*, "People were just dumping stuff on Clarence. So I was trying to tarnish the reputation of his accuser by dumping stuff in the record where she (Anita Hill) didn't have any chance to cross-examine or confront."[23]

Danforth accused the Caucus of playing the "race card." Hatch said that the Caucus' position was simply a "knee-jerk liberal" reaction. Danforth, who recommended to President Bush the nomination of Thomas took exception to the CBC's opposition. He wrote to me:

> *Bill, I have been truly astounded by the reckless attacks that have been made on Clarence Thomas, which have been based on misstatements of fact. I was amazed that the Congressional Black Caucus rushed to judgment without bothering to find out what the facts are.*[24]

It took true grit for the Reverend Senator Danforth to write such a letter. His position was understandable because it was in sync with other white liberals who in their infallible wisdom, have "always known" exactly what black people needed the most.

I addressed his assault in a letter, stating it "was ludicrous to suggest the CBC in any way was guilty of racism. It reveals your own misconceptions about race in America. [Thomas] while serving in your employ as Missouri's Attorney General, brazenly displayed a Confederate flag on his desk at the state capitol office...I don't think you would have permitted any employee to display a swastika...You would never condone such an atrocious insult to the Jewish community. I only wish that you would have shown the same respect for the feelings of Black Americans."[25]

The CBC stated, "If some African Americans have seemed to approve of this nomination, it must also be noted that few members of the public have studied Clarence Thomas's record. Instead, they have been introduced for the first time to a black man and told his life story in order to deflect attention from his record..."[26]

Danforth accused us of playing the race card by opposing Thomas. My response was that the card had already been played by the "White House." The CBC was just trying to expose the "double standard" that people like Danforth embraced for judging black leadership.

In line with the same sentiment, other black leaders asserted similar concerns. Eleanor Norton Holmes, Delegate to the District of Columbia said that precisely because he was black, Thomas would seem to validate the far right wing claim that many blacks felt as he did. She stated they would believe that the renunciation of civil rights was an acceptable course even to blacks.

Division in the Ranks of the NAACP

After extended, time-consuming debate among the NAACP's Board of Directors, the organization went on record in opposition to Thomas' confirmation. Board Chairman William F. Gibson testified before the Judiciary Committee that the organization concluded: "An all-white Supreme Court would be better than one with Clarence Thomas on it." Benjamin Hooks, executive director of the organization, refuted Thomas' assertion that affirmative action only benefitted middle class, educated blacks.

Several NAACP branches in Georgia announced support of

Thomas. The East St. Louis Illinois chapter also disagreed with the national office and endorsed Thomas. The president of the local NAACP branch in Compton, California told the Associated Press:

> *"If we're not able to vote our conscience, we don't want to be part of the (NAACP)."*

But the most significant defection came from two of the nation's most prominent civil rights lawyers, Frankie Freeman and Margaret B. Wilson who joined the chorus of support for Thomas. Both from St. Louis and personal friends of the nominee, had first-hand knowledge of Thomas' thinking that differed from most civil rights leaders. Each offered favorable opinions attesting to his legal ability and personal integrity.

Wilson, former chairperson of the National NAACP Board, former president of the Missouri State NAACP, former president of the St. Louis Branch NAACP, testified before the Senate Judiciary Committee. Freeman, former member of the U.S. Civil Rights Commission, former national president of Delta Sigma Theta Sorority, wrote a letter to the committee endorsing Thomas.

[footnote]

Thomas even fooled Margaret Bush Wilson for a short period. But after his performances on the Supreme Court, she spoke of regret that she had testified in his behalf before the Senate Judiciary Committee. She later said, "That's not the same person who I spoke with for hours at my dinner table. I don't know where he is coming up with some of his reasoning."[27]

Frankie Freeman later recanted, stating she had no idea he would oppose class action suits.

An American Tragedy: Clarence Thomas Confirmed as Supreme Court Justice

The Senate Judiciary hearings considering the nomination began 10 September and ended 20 September. He was confirmed by a vote of 52 to 48 on the 15th of October.

That day was a blow to racial fairness that will hold a prominent place in the archives of horrendous acts perpetrated against African Americans. It was a day in infamy for millions who had fought, sacrificed, suffered to achieve personal, individual, and group respectability. They were appalled by the timidity of a Senate controlled by Democrats, cowardly succumbing to political pressure from right wing Republican zealots, and conniving media personalities.

The confirmation occurred because some Democrats joined a solid Republican bloc, to vote for a Negro Republican of dubious integrity and questionable legal ability. Two Republicans, Robert Packwood of Oregon and James Jeffords of Vermont, broke ranks with the President and voted against the nomination. Forty-one Republicans from the South, North, Midwest, and West were joined in confirming by eleven Democrats: Richard Shelby of Ala, Dennis DeConcini of Arizona, Wyche Fowler, Jr. and Sam Nunn of Georgia, Alan J. Dixon of Illinois, Bennett Johnson and John Breaux of Louisiana, Jim Exon of Nebraska, David Boren of Oklahoma, Charles Robb of Virginia, and Ernest Hollings of South Carolina.

Thomas' confirmation created a court majority inclined to cast judicial rulings consistent with that of the 1896 Plessy v. Ferguson decision which sanctioned the policy of separate but (un)equal, effectively ending Reconstruction and reestablishing a political and economic system merely a step above slavery.

Political Fallout of Votes

Three Democrats expected to oppose the nomination-Charles Robb of Virginia, Alan Dixon of Illinois and Wyche Fowler of Georgia, and one Republican, Arlen Specter of Pennsylvania-betrayed a substantial number of people who made their elections possible. They were not from marginal districts where angry white males held the balance of power but from areas where women and minorities constituted major, organized voting blocs — groups that overwhelmingly opposed the nomination.

In the election immediately following confirmation, forgiveness for the double-cross was not forthcoming. They paid an awesome price for reneging on the faith and trust placed in them by aroused African Americans and progressive women.

In the case of Dixon, a black woman, Carol Moseley-Braun,

shattered by his "wimpish" position, waged a vigorous campaign based primarily on his vote to confirm. She defeated him in the Democratic primary and went on to win the election.

Fowler claimed during the hearing that his black constituents demanded his support of Thomas, failed to win a clear majority in the primary and was forced into a run-off election with a Republican. In losing his senate seat, he was unable to rally enthusiastic support of his once loyal black voters. Apparently, he misread the sentiment of black constituents when he informed the CBC that a deluge of blacks implored him to support Thomas. Their euphoria must have evaporated as it never translated into a sea of votes in his losing campaign.

Republican Arlen Specter went through a bruising campaign for reelection. The major issue was his vote for Thomas which was considered 'anti-feminine' by many in his state. Democratic opponent, Lynn Yeakel, considered an underdog by all political analysts, lost by three percentage points (49% to 46%) with 2,358,125 to 2,224,966 votes. A third candidate receiving 219,319 votes was a major factor in her defeat.

Robb's support of Thomas disillusioned black Virginians. Once they secured their voting rights, Democrats like Robb benefitted from massive voter turnout in their precincts. His vote to confirm left them with a bitter taste. Fortunately for him, his campaign for reelection was not until 1994, three years later.

By then, factors other than Thomas were at hand. Yet, he barely won reelection. Black people who said any black conservative was better than any white on the Court must have had a Saul-like conversion. They cast the decisive vote for a white Robb over his more reactionary opponent, white Ollie North of Iran-Contra fame because they believed one less than perfect candidate can make a difference. Perhaps they surmised that one white man was indeed better than another.

Thomas a Threat to Minorities

Thomas on the Court shifted the balance to the far-right and advocates of limited government policy. His judicial elevation dampened but not stifled entirely African Americans in their drive for equal justice.

It took almost 200 years to get a black on the Supreme Court. It took Thomas two months to make clear that he would neither emulate Justice Marshall as spokesman for the causes of equal justice nor champion decent treatment of those unable to speak for themselves.

In Thomas' first two rulings, he joined the majority in diminishing voting rights of minorities, and limiting the right of union organizers to effectively communicate with members on the job. In another instance, he joined Justice Antonin Scalia defying all standards of common decency. The case involved a prisoner handcuffed by the wrists and shackled at the ankles that was taken from his cell by prison guards and severely beaten. The brutal act occurred in the presence of prisoners and guards. Seven members of the court agreed it was uncivilized, therefore, prohibited by the Constitution. Thomas and Scalia disagreed.

Eighteen months after confirmation, America's preference for a black Clarence Thomas on the Supreme Court dissipated. The public's endurance of his weird ideology as expressed in opinions gave way to deep resentment among former supporters, especially in the minority community.

Clarence Thomas had an ability to portray himself as sincerely concerned about suffering of his people and gave the impression that he was committed to working to alleviate the burden place on blacks through discrimination and segregation.

Courts Packed With Zealots

During the 10 years preceding Thomas' appointment, Reagan and Bush stacked the Federal District, Appellate and Supreme Courts with ideological conservative fanatics. They appointed almost 500, mostly right-winged, reactionary judges whose careers had been devoted to repealing laws and rescinding judicial opinions that protected the rights of minorities and women. Reagan, alone, appointed 360 lifetime justices and 3 supreme court jurists in 8 years.. In 12 years, he and Bush appointed 115 judges, mostly 'strict constructionists' to the U.S. Court of Appeals.

The nation's 60 year history of ignoring the legal expertise of black lawyers and the dearth of African American appointments to the judiciary must be placed in historical perceptive. Until President Truman placed William H. Hastie on the Third Circuit Court of Appeals, no black had served at that level of the judicial system. Johnson and Kennedy's naming of judges to the appellate level and Johnson's appointment of Marshall to the Supreme Court in 1967 were revolutionary moves toward a racially diversified court.

Bush and Reagan reverted back to the pre-Johnson era of shunning talented black lawyers. They named only three blacks in twelve years to the appellate court. That record pales in comparison to Carter's appointment of eight blacks in 4 years.

Bush and Reagan's appointment of reactionary judges redounded most harmful to Americans who had looked to the federal courts to right the years of wrong heaped upon the disadvantaged and denied.

Bush Defeated by William Jefferson Clinton

George Bush's bid for reelection in 1992 fizzled. He was defeated by Democratic candidate Bill Clinton who campaigned vigorously and independent candidate H. Ross Perot who diverted votes from Bush. Clinton received 44,909,889; Bush 39,104,545; Perot, 19,742,267. Large numbers of women and blacks voted against Bush. They saw both their civil rights and their economic well-being threatened by 4 more years of the Reagan-Bush philosophy.

Bush and Reagan Shame Of A Nation

The spectacle of shame that the country witnessed in the years of the Reagan and Bush Administrations revealed the depth to which the electorate is capable of sinking in accepting inequality for its minorities. Those years characterized in most frightening terms, the capacity of citizens to accept without protest the re-segregation of America.

In responding to an allegation leveled during the heat of Bush's campaign for reelection and mentioned earlier in this chapter, I declare, "Yes, Congresswoman Maxine Waters, you were correct. President W.H. Bush meets all the qualifications to merit the title of racist."

In closing, I assert that after 8 years of rule by Reagan and 4 years by Bush, the clock of civil rights progress indeed was shamefully turned back 100 years.

NOTES

1/Congressman William L. Clay, Sr., American Postal Workers Union, Washington, D.C., 1989.

2/Molly Ivins, "Whose Character?" *Washington Post*, 23 October 1992. A-21.

3/Bush Denies Saying Foe Got Big Contribution from Estes, *Dallas Morning News,* 28 October 1964, page 14.

4/*Congressional Record*, 91st Congress, 2d sess., 1970, page 20178.

5/President George H.W. Bush, *Washington Post* 2, July 1991, page A1.

6/*Washington Post:* My Case Against Clarence Thomas by Julian Bond, 8 September 1991, C7.

7/*Clarence Thomas, New York Times*, 13 September 1992.

8/William Lucy, testimony before Senate Judiciary Committee, September 17, 1981, Part 2 of 4 Parts J-102-40, Washington, D.C.

9/National Women's Law Center: Judge Clarence Thomas: A Record Lacking Support of Women's Legal Rights, 20 August 1991, pages 1 6.

10/Benjamin L. Hooks, testimony before the U.S. Senate Judiciary Committee on the nomination of Clarence Thomas, 20 September 1991.

11/Statement issues in testimony by the Congressional Black Caucus before the U.S. Senate Judiciary Committee on the Nomination of Judge Clarence Thomas, 19 September 1991.

12/Statement issues in testimony by the Congressional Black Caucus before the U.S. Senate Judiciary Committee on the Nomination of Judge Clarence Thomas, 19 September 1991.

13/Statement issues in testimony by the Congressional Black Caucus before the U.S. Senate Judiciary Committee on the Nomination of Judge Clarence Thomas, 19 September 1991.

14//Craig A. Washington, before the Senate Judiciary Committee on the Nomination of Judge Clarence Thomas, 19 September 1991, page 1.

15/Rep. Major Owens (D-N.Y.), Senate Judiciary Committee on the Nomination of Judge Clarence Thomas, 19 September 1991.

16/Stokes, Senate Judiciary Committee on the Nomination of Judge Clarence Thomas, 19 September 1991.

17/ John Lewis, Senate Judiciary Committee on the Nomination of Judge Clarence Thomas, 19 September 1991.

18/John Lewis, Senate Judiciary Committee on the Nomination of Judge Clarence Thomas, 19 September 1991.

19/John Lewis, Senate Judiciary Committee on the Nomination of Judge Clarence Thomas, 19 September 1991.

20/CBC document presented to Senate Judiciary Committee.

21/20/Letter from Congressman Clay to Senator John Danforth.

22/Letter from Senator John C. Danforth(R-Mo.) To Congressman William L. Clay, Sr. (D-Mo.), dated 17 July 1991.

23/Senator John Danforth's 1994 book *"Resurrection,"* interview with the *Washington Post*, February 2/2006, page C4.

24/Letter from Senator John Danforth of Missouri to Representative William L. Clay of Missouri, 17 July 1991.

25/Letter from Congressman Clay to Senator John Danforth.

26/Congressional Black Caucus document, 12 September 1991, "In Opposition to Clarence: Where We Must Stand and Why? Washington, D.C. , published at CBC HEADQUARTERS, Washington, D.C.

in order to deflect attention from his record..."?/

27 *St. Louis Argus*, August 13, 2009, page 3A.

14

"I believe in the brotherhood of man, not merely the broth-erhood of white men but the brotherhood of all men..."[1]

– Harry S. Truman

The election of William Jefferson Clinton was a breath of fresh air for those striving to protect human rights and to promote civil liberties. His demeanor and agenda signaled a kinder, gentler occupant in the White House. Insolence and indifference permeating policies of some chief executives since LBJ left office, gave way to promise of a much more genuine concern for ordinary people.

WILLIAM JEFFERSON CLINTON
A Voice for Justice and Tolerance

Clinton's presence in the Oval Office, for me, meant a reversal of the antagonistic policies toward minorities and the poor of the last five Presidents, starting with Nixon. Each, in varying degrees, stymied, retarded and frustrated progressive movement toward social equality and economic parity. The cumulative effect of unresponsive policy programs, severely crippled the drive initiated by President Johnson to root out poverty, religious bigotry, racism and sexism. Their budget decisions and legislative proposals failed to counter the human conditions of sickness, disease, unemployment and ignorance.

Clinton, former governor of Arkansas, restored the confidence of America's "have-nots" that had been badly damaged by another recent southern governor whom they had supported for president.

Clinton was cut from a different bolt of political cloth than that of other Arkansas politicians. He was unique in his refusal to be evasive on the issue of racial disparity traditionally characteristic of southern Democrats. Arkansas was and still is to a great degree reflective of the mentality displayed by Governor Orval Faubus who blocked the desegregation of public schools by force in Little Rock until President Eisenhower sent in the U.S. Army. Like Kentucky, both are southern states with large black populations stuck in an ante-bellum political time machine. Neither has every elected an African American to the United States Congress.

Clinton reversed the assault against the classes of powerless instituted in several previous administrations. Nixon's attack on social programs aiding the needy was intensified by Ford. Carters' ill-fated attempt to cut funding for life-support programs in the waning days of his administration, was a body-blow to minorities, the sick, and poor. Reagan continued the draconian, insensitive reduction of vital domestic programs, and went one step further, injecting into the equation an element of mistrust, suspicion, and hostile competition among ethnic groups vying for government funds. He stacked the Supreme Court with ideological demagogues that nullified many of the gains achieved in civil rights and civil liberties of the previous 40 years.

Clinton's Policy of Inclusion

Clinton's cabinet appointments indicated a drastic change in government concern and compassion had taken place. He named the most diverse cabinet and top government officials in history. In other administrations, blacks, Hispanics, and women engaged in internecine warfare to determine which one individual from their group would be appointed to the cabinet. The one eventually selected was hypocritically hailed as a sign of racial inclusion at the highest level of decision-making. But Clinton eliminated the destructive personality warfare by appointing 4 blacks, 4 women, and 2 Hispanics to his cabinet.

In the first year, he appointed 48 judges, including 14 blacks and 18 females. During his first term he nominated and the Senate confirmed 38 black judges compared to 7 by Reagan and 13 by Bush in their first term. In two years, Clinton appointed more blacks to the federal judiciary than all the presidents from George Washington through the administration of Gerald Ford.

I recommended three individuals to fill important positions: Floyd Kimbrough for U.S. Marshall, Eastern Missouri; two U.S. District Judges, Charles Shaw and Ronnie White. Kimbrough and Shaw were confirmed. White's confirmation was derailed by an underhanded political ploy of two Missouri Republican senators, Christopher Bond and John Ashcroft who distorted his qualifications and reneged on their publicly declared support of his candidacy.

The impression that Clinton walked on water and died on the cross for minority causes, is not the intent for my giving laudatory credit for his accomplishments. There were many confrontations between him, members of the CBC, civil rights leaders and me. But his overall record of positive accomplishments far outweighed any negative ones.

Several Issues of Serious Disagreement

We disagreed on capital punishment, the expansion of the North American Free Trade Agreement (NAFTA), handling of the nomination of his former law school classmate Lani Guinier, striker replacement legislation, and Welfare Reform. The latter which the Republican controlled House pushed and he supported, had horrendous negative impact on those most deprived in society.

Capital Punishment

During his election campaign, Clinton made a special trip back to Arkansas to witness an execution. It could not be described as anything other than a shameful act of political theater to garner votes of those who believe that murdering individuals in the name of the state is not as reprehensible as individuals murdering others in violation of state laws. I was appalled at candidate Clinton's gesture of appealing to advocates of this savage, revengeful practice. Despite voter popularity, the death penalty is a form of punishment that's immoral, counterproductive and uncivilized. All but a few nations have banned its use.

North American Free Trade Agreement (NAFTA)

I opposed the enactment of the North American Free Trade Agreement (NAFTA) initiated by President Bush and pushed through congress by Clinton. It proposed an extension of the U.S.–Canada Free Trade Pact and added Mexico as a component of the treaty.

The prospect of legislation allowing products produced in sweat shops of Mexico or by slave labor in third world countries, to compete with high-wage American workers, assured the lowering of living standards for millions in our country.

In opposing the measure, I predicted approval would increase downward pressures on wages of U.S. workers, nullify any movement toward greater labor-management cooperation, discourage efforts to improve the education and skills of low-wage workers, and exacerbate the inequitable distribution of income. Regrettably, my prophecy came true.

NAFTA was supported in large measure by mega corporations who saw unregulated trade as a means to transfer business enterprises below the border, manufacture low cost merchandise and ship the products back into the country at huge profits.

After passage of the trade bill, the number of exported factories increased one-hundred fold in Mexico and surrounding countries. Automobile parts that had been produced in moderation prior to enactment were now manufactured on a large scale. Workers in those plants doubled to more than one million. An extra 500,000 new jobs were traced directly to lost jobs in the United States.

Relocated businesses reaped excessive profits by exploiting cheap labor through the creation of "sweat shops" that paid subsistence wages. Downsizing jobs and income left a large pool of Americans unable to purchase expensive goods. Our favorable trade balance before the treaty became a trade deficit after its enactment.

Striker Replacement Legislation

I was disappointed after successfully passing a measure in

the House banning the permanent replacement of striking workers and President Clinton made no effort to break a filibuster that caused the bill to die in the Senate.

Firing of Lani Guinier

Joining many other black leaders, I opposed and resented the high-handed way in which Clinton abandoned Lanie Guinier, his nominee to the top position in the Justice Department's Civil Rights Division. Professor of law at the University of Pennsylvania and Clinton's longtime friend, she came under criticism from ultra-conservative media columnists, religious ideologues, and anti-quota zealots in the Jewish community. They labeled her an advocate of racial divisiveness and undemocratic ideas. Misquoted from her writings, citing false and pejorative statements never uttered, they accused her of favoring quotas.

Robert Bok, the rejected nominee to the Supreme Court, maliciously described her as a 'quota queen.'

In the furor, Clinton caved-in to the pressure and requested Guinier withdraw her name from consideration. She refused. Clinton, in withdrawing the nomination, surrendered to her critics without giving her an opportunity to defend herself before the Senate Judiciary Committee.

Welfare Reform

I was invited to the Blair House for a discussion on provisions of the welfare reform bill that President Clinton was negotiating with leadership of the majority Republican congress. At the session, I was permitted to state my position in opposition but it was apparent the die had already been cast.

Despite my position, the deck was stacked. The crowd at the session advocating workfare to replace welfare was in no mood to hear counter arguments that without adequate appropriations for job training and education, businesses would not hire uneducated, untrained individuals. They refused to admit that unless poverty is addressed, there can be no solution to the problems of those afflicted by it or of a society burdened with it.

The Clinton administration had already decided to place the bill on a fast track. Regardless of my concerns and that of other liberals, Clinton sided with those determined to radically diminish the amount of government assistance available to the poor and the Congress agreed.

More Agreement Then Disagreement

Despite these serious misunderstandings and disagreements about what policies best served the minority interests, blacks, including myself, were in agreement with Clinton more often than not on major considerations facing America: education reform, civil rights, affirmative action, reproductive rights, freedom of speech and a slew of other basic values. After witnessing administration after administration sabotage equal opportunity, and human rights, Clinton's strong stance in defense of these fundamental democratic principles was a change welcomed and I wholeheartedly supported his initiative to provide health care for the millions shut out of the health delivery system. But in the face of massive opposition from the American Medical Association, the pharmaceutical industry, health insurers, and right wing politicians, he and his wife Hillary were pilloried by congressional Democrats and Republicans who were guided by lobbyists and more wedded to their campaign contributions than constituents health needs. Thus, millions were wantonly denied adequate health care assistance.

Contrary to propaganda of special interests that our great health care system was the best in the world, the United States lagged behind 171 countries in critical areas. It ranked 151st in infant mortality and lagged behind most industrialized nations in other aspects, especially Europe that treats all its citizens free of cost. Despite having the highest health care costs of any nation, millions of Americans receive substandard care or worse, no care at all.

Bragging that patients in this country don't have to wait long periods in doctor's offices, or for surgery, is precisely that—bragging. Anyone wanting an appointment with a specialist knows the fallacy of such boasts. It would have been futile for more than 50 million Americans who did not have health insurance or money to pay to stand in line.

Golden Age of Progressive Legislation

My ringing endorsement of Clinton's eight years in office, reflects appreciation for his positive contributions to the advancement of decent consideration for those who government traditionally ignored or neglected.

I was impressed by his ability in getting Congress to pass major progressive legislation. Despite stern opposition from Republicans who controlled the House of Representatives six of his 8 years in office, he confronted problems of women, gays, minorities, workers, the poor and successfully addressed them through legislative reforms and administrative edicts. In a cooperative manner, the President advanced the programs and Democrats supported them.

Enacting legislation is a long, tedious, complicated process, rewarded when both Houses of Congress agree to the exact wording of a bill, and the President signs the final version. Countless hours of hearing testimony, conducting mark-ups of bills, managing floor debate and finally meeting in conference with the Senate to reconcile differences between the two chambers, paid dividends with the election of Clinton, a pro-worker, pro-consumer, pro-environment, pro-civil rights, pro-education advocate.

The "Real" Education President

Clinton aggressively worked to increase funding and improve standards for education. As the highest ranking Democrat on the House Education Committee, I led the fight in pushing his educational reforms which resulted in legislation to improve early reading programs, increase funding for school construction and technology.

I issued an annual report card on the state of education, and each year, he was given high grades. He earned an "A" for promoting world class schools for the 21st century. He challenged parents, teachers, and students to work for higher standards, and offered tools to assist.

Clinton supported the Elementary and Secondary Education Reauthorization Act which allowed for 100,000 new teachers to reduce class size in the early grades. In the House, I spearheaded his effort for Community Learning Centers to provide 250,000 students after-school opportunities, worked to increase Head Start funding, and pushed the School-to-Work Opportunities Act initiated by him. His programs made higher education more accessible and affordable for low and middle income families by lowering the interest rate on loans, and increasing the Pell Grant maximum from $3,000 to $3,125.

Major Clinton Policy Successes:

The President's legislative proposals led to increased funding for Women, Infants, Children (WIC), Child Care, Head Start, Child Poverty, Teen Pregnancy and Infant Mortality. He signed the Assault Weapons Ban outlawing automatic weapons, pushed through the Brady Bill to control the availability of handguns, and added 100,000 new police officers on the streets.

During his administration, the largest deficit-cutting plan in history passed, saving $1 trillion while reducing the deficit for three consecutive years and adding 7.7 million new jobs. His administration created nine Economic Empowerment Zones and 95 Enterprise Communities, made the Low-Income Housing Tax Credit and Mortgage Revenue Bond Program permanent. His economic policies held unemployment below 5 percent for 19 months in a row, the lowest since 1957.

During Clinton's presidency, I was a prime mover in enacting legislation of landmark significance. My Democratic colleagues and I, beneficiaries of a favorable climate in the White House, produced a rich harvest of people-oriented social legislation that had been stymied by Republican obstructionists in preceding Congresses, or by presidential vetoes of Ford, Reagan, and George H.W. Bush.

Family and Medical Leave Act

The first bill signed by Clinton-the Family and Medical Leave Act-was one I sponsored and promoted for 8 years. At the Rose Garden White House ceremony in February 1993, I said: "Finally, millions will have the basic right to take time off from their jobs to care for sick children or dependent parents without fear of losing their livelihoods."

The law mandated that companies with 50 or more employees offer 12 weeks of unpaid leave each year to care for a newborn, to care for a seriously-ill family member, or to recover from one's own serious illnesses. It prohibited the loss of employment due to exercising the right.

Signing of Hatch Act Reform

Seven months later, one of my proudest legislative days occurred when Clinton signed a second bill I sponsored: the Hatch Act Reform Bill. For 20 years I worked to give 3 million federal and postal employees the right to engage in politics on their own time, only to see the measure defeated in the senate or vetoed by two presidents.

In the East Room of the White House, 120 guests witnessed the signing. The President said: "The bill will permit federal employees to manage campaigns, raise funds and hold positions within political parties."

In my remarks, I said, "It will end an age of misguided and paternalistic treatment." The law permits government employees to endorse political candidates and organize fundraisers among other rights previously prohibited.

John Glenn the chief sponsor in the Senate, who worked on the bill for six years, said "I feel like a short-timer with Bill Clay here."

A Student Absent Without Leave (AWOL)

Several weeks after the bill signing, Michele, my youngest

daughter and my grandson Michael, attended a PTA meeting. In evaluating Michael's performance, the teacher revealed that he had a vivid imagination, citing the excuse he gave for being absent one day as an example. Laughing, the teacher whimsically said: "He claimed being at the White House, meeting with President Clinton, V.P. Gore and other dignitaries."

The next day, Michele who saw no humor in the comment, returned to the school with photos and articles from newspapers, to assure the teacher it was her lack of recognizing new realities about black children, not Michaels' vivid imagination that was at fault.

One news item, in particular, was from the *St. Louis Post Dispatch* which reported that after signing the bill, Clinton handed pens to Glenn and me, then: "walked across the room to shake hands with a 7-year-old boy in the audience who wore a "Mighty Ducks" cap. The boy was Clay's grandson."

Contract on America: Shame on a Nation

Six weeks before the 1994 mid-term elections, more than 175 Republican members met on the Capitol steps to sign a 'Contract With America.' It was divided into 10 sections emphasizing anti-crime measures, increased defense appropriations, term limits for elected officials, budgetary and tax reform, welfare changes, family oriented legislation and help for small businesses. It was an all-inclusive agenda designed to appeal to broad areas of interests to voters.

Republicans Win House of Representatives

The media asserted that "angry white men" tilted the balance in the election toward Republicans who won a majority in Congress. The alleged anger was a smoke screen that camouflaged the real motivation. The accusation lacked credibility and defied reality. White men, only 47% of the population owned 64 percent of the nation's businesses, held 95% of all senior corporate management slots, 73% of the lawyers, 84% of construction supervisors, 89% of U.S. Senators. They dictated government policy, owned the mass media, dominated religious institutions, influenced the judiciary, and controlled law enforcement apparatus.

In the 230 year history of the country, 42 persons served as President, all of them white men. Only 108 persons had been approved to serve on the U.S. Supreme Court. One hundred four of them white males. Every Majority Leader of the U.S. Senate and every Speaker of the U.S. House of Representatives had been white men.

What in Hell did white men have to be angry about? Unless they believed 100% of everything was fair, there must have been another reasons for supporting Republican candidates.

Who Supported the New Republican Majority?

Republicans won a slight majority in both houses of Congress in 1994. Many wondered who supported them and why. Large groups, traditionally aligned with the Democrat party, admitted voting for Republicans. Some menial task workers and day laborers who cast their votes for Republicans because they promised to authorize prayer in school, found an expected increase in the minimum wage was sacrificed on the Party's alter of insensitivity. Millions of blue-collar workers desperately in need of better plant safety protection, higher wages and more job security, found their new GOP representatives attempting to legislate less enforcement of occupational health and safety laws, new appointees to the National Labor Relations Board refusing to curtail abuses of businesses, and the lost of numerous jobs through steep cuts in the federal budget.

Housewives driven by the promise that a Republican majority would mean reduced inflation and lower prices, found no relief in grocery and utility prices. Skilled, highly paid union members who ridiculed their leaders for supporting civil rights issues, and programs to assist low-wage workers, found their own pensions and jobs in jeopardy. They experienced serious decreases in the benefits they were entitled to under Medicare and repeal of major protections for workers under labor laws.

[Foot note]

Nancy Pelosi (D-Ca) was elected the first female Speaker of the House in 2002. Barack Obama was elected the first black President of the United States in 2008.

Oh No! Why Bring Race Into It

In-depth polling indicated many who supported Republican candidates expressed no resentment of the way Democrats had protected their interests. Despite satisfaction with a thriving economic policy and delivery of essential government programs, substantial numbers of women, Catholics, construction workers, union members, consumers and environmentalist voted the Republican ticket.

What strange dichotomy! Intelligent people with no serious economic complaints don't usually cast protest votes in such large numbers.

This unusual pattern of voter rejection gives credibility to the contention that the media's heavy emphasis on the potential influence that black legislators would wield in a Congress controlled by Democrats played a significant role in their decisions.

For weeks, radio and television commentators, newspaper reporters, editors, political analysts, conservative prognosticators and Republican strategists hammered away at the powerful chairmanships that blacks would hold in a new Congress controlled by Democrats: John Conyers of Michigan, Chairman of Judiciary, Bill Clay of Missouri, Chairman of Education and Labor; Ron Dellums of California, Chairman of Armed Services, and Julian Dixon of California, Chairman of the District of Columbia. Additionally, Blacks would chair 16 subcommittees including key ones by Louis Stokes of Ohio on Appropriations, Charles Rangel of N.Y. on Ways and Means, and Donald Payne on Foreign Relations.

The possibility became so exhilarating and enticing that members of the Congressional Black Caucus, confident of retaining the majority, enthusiastically promoted it as an issue for their reelections.

CBS 60 Minutes ran a special program, emphasizing the influence of blacks and the powerful chairmanships they would inherit under a congress controlled by Democrats.

The prospect of black dominance in Congress shifted the traditional reasons for supporting candidates and awakened latent prejudices, causing an overwhelming number of white voters to desert the Democratic Party.

Contract with America Provisions Swept Aside

After taking control, the Republican majority walked in tall cotton, boisterously proclaiming its 'Contract on America.' Ignoring a major promise of the Contract to limit their own term of office, they moved with all deliberate speed to resurrect the most extreme anti-people, anti-poor, anti-middle class conservative issues.

Immediately, they rammed through controversial proposals without discussions or hearings. In March 1995, Republicans abruptly cut off debate on amendments in committee and pushed through provisions denying aid to many poor women and children. Democratic members of the Education Committee were denied the right to offer amendments that mattered deeply to the public, including the preservation of the school lunch and breakfast programs; the Women, Infant and Children (WIC) program; and access to safe child care. Major changes adopted by the Republican majority were rejected by the Senate or vetoed by President Clinton because they would impact adversely on major social programs and inflict harm on middle and low income citizens.

I was very disturbed by the new Republican attack on nutritional programs for children. Hunger and poor nutrition rob children of proper physical development and the ability to learn. They cause health problems for children and increase education and health care costs for federal, state and local government.

In the first 100 days of the Republican rule and their `contract on America,' school kids, college students, teen-age mothers, senior citizens, low-skilled workers and lower middle class families lost vitally needed benefits.

To accommodate 71% tax cuts for wealthy citizens, tax breaks giving the 12% of the Republican tax proposal to wealthiest Americans, to increase estate-tax shelters for the very rich, it was necessary to reduce spending in other areas of the budget.

And where did they cut? You guessed it right: school lunches for 2 million children, heating assistance for 2 million seniors, baby formula to tens of thousands of infants, increased cost of college education for 4 million students, and elimination of 100,000 college scholarships.

The public belatedly read fine print in the Contract, and Democrats eventually dared the majority to bring the most controversial features to a floor vote. Republicans resorted to taking credit for measures that passed despite opposition from a majority of them: an increase in the minimum wage was not in the Contract; the Safe Drinking Water Act which they opposed, was not in the Contract; the expansion of Medicare coverage which they opposed, was not in the Contract.

Republicans Shut Down Government

The Republican controlled Congress, unable to enact its radical, right wing agenda, in frustration, turned its venom toward killing progressive laws passed in prior congresses. They refused to pass appropriation bills to fund Medicare, Medicaid, education, Head Start, child nutrition, and the school lunch program. Railing at "large government", twice they failed to pass temporary funding to keep the government in operation. As a result, major parts of the government were shutdown twice in two months. All federal employees, except the few needed to avert crisis in health and crime were furloughed.

Each day the government was shutdown, thousands of elderly and working families were penalized. At least 600,000 risked losing "meal on wheels." Over 200,000 students were unable to get college aid forms processed and states lost $74 million in quarterly grants for child protection programs. The final act of defiance lasted 27 days and cost $1.4 billion.

Clinton's Initiative on Race

Clinton was the first of the six Presidents with whom I served who manifested a genuine concern for alleviating poverty, hunger, and discrimination. He provided critical support for those afflicted by Aids, exacted an administrative policy that protected gays from immediate and total expulsion from the military, and brought to a sudden halt the drive to repeal affirmative action.

Unafraid to challenge controversial issues, Clinton launched a major dialogue to study laws and policies dealing with race, confronted the issue head-on and insisted that all citizens have the chance to fulfill their citizenship potential.

He articulated the benefits of racial reconciliation and a just society, educated the populace about the facts surrounding the issue of race. He developed plans and implemented programs in the areas of education, economic opportunity, housing, health care, crime and the administration of justice.

Shortly after returning from a trip to Africa, Clinton expressed regrets about the nation's prior involvement of enslaving blacks. Conservatives immediately launched an attack on him for "pandering" to black voters.

Clinton and Republican Leaders

I praised Clinton for appointing a distinguished panel to study race relations, to evaluate existing government programs prohibiting equality and to advise the President how to arrest the cancerous growth of racial and religious intolerance toward minorities. Appointees to the seven member non-partisan Advisory Board were giants in the struggle to create one country, equal and indivisible for all. John Hope Franklin, retired Professor of Legal History at Duke University was named chairman. The list of distinguished panelists included William F. Winger, the former Democratic Governor of Mississippi where he fought to improve the education opportunities of minorities, Thomas H. Kean, former Republican Governor of New Jersey who served on the United States Delegation to Women's Rights Conference in Beijing; Linda Chavez Thompson, executive vice president of the AFL-CIO who was the first person of color to be elected to office at the AFL; Robert Thomas, CEO of Nissan Motor Corporation; Angela E. Oh, criminal attorney in Los Angeles; and Suzan D. Johnson Cook, Senior Pastor of the Bronx Christian Fellowship.

Negative Remarks Abound

Instead of supporting President Clinton in evaluating existing government programs designed to confront the accelerated growth of racial and religious intolerance, high ranking Republicans buttressed by reactionary elements in the conservative media, initiated a concerted counterattack.

As a political strategy, they attacked the apology as indecent and improper. Leading the criticism were such sterling Republican stalwarts as Senators Robert Dole and Phil Gramm.

The incomparable Speaker of the House, Newt Gingrich ridiculed the proposition as an "empty gesture" that would do nothing to improve the plight of children living in poverty. Then, in a true display of arrogance and ignorance, he suggested that the nation's race relation problems "can be solved by emulating the Chicago Bulls basketball team." The inimical Republican Majority Leader of the Senate, Trent Lott, made light of the nations' past horrendous racist behavior, stating: "I think we should be looking to the future, talking about the things we need to do to work together." The irascible, Ward Connerly, leader of the initiative petition Proposition 209 which eliminated affirmative action and equality of opportunity for minorities in California, stated it was absurd and unproductive. He said: "Apologizing for slavery is probably one of the dumbest things anyone could do."

Those well acquainted with Connerly's ignoble and ignorant track record in the field of race relations, hurried to verify his credentials as an expert witness on 'dumbness.' Many questioned the motives and integrity of this Negro 'Carpetbagger' with a financially profitable pre-occupation for challenging legitimate rights of his own people everywhere the issue of equality surfaces.

Why would Lott, Gingrich and Connerly oppose the expression of regrets for the country's atrocities in the slave trade? The answer may be found in a callous, insensitive leadership mentality proclaiming to live in a "colorblind" society while still giving sanctuary to racists and solace to racism.

In a press release I disagreed with Gingrich, Connerly, and

Lott because "the Cancer of racism cannot be eradicated from the body politic by ignoring its presence or past. A colorblind society cannot be produced if we are blind to color. President Clinton was morally right and politically courageous in bringing our collective attention to the destructive nature of racism and bigotry."

Gays in the Military: A Repeat of History

I also commended Clinton for ameliorating the policy of drumming gays out of the military. For years, I argued that denying gays opportunity to defend our country was based on ignorance, intolerance and misinformation about what characteristics are necessary to exhibit bravery in combat.

Opposition to gay's pursuing military careers was driven by the belief their presence, not their behavior, presented a threat to national security and jeopardized others in combat. The aforementioned argument contradicted the roles that homosexual and bi-sexual individuals have played in the history of warfare. Julius Caesar and Hannibal, two brilliant strategists and fearless warriors who conquered the known world, were also engaged in homosexual activity. It is reasonable to assume that gays in the military have been the recipients of the nation's highest honor—the Congressional Medal of Honor.

The same illogical assumptions of fitness were leveled when the subject of integrating blacks in the armed services was broached. Identical tirades, diatribes and denunciations were advanced by high-ranking military and civilian officials of the Military Establishment when President Harry S. Truman ordered racial integration of the armed services.

Four-star General Douglass MacArthur, Lieutenant General Willard Paul, director of military personnel, and Army Chief of Staff Omar Bradley, publicly disagreed with Truman's decision. But the President did not waver in effort to integrate the military branches of service. It was a huge success that opened new opportunities to blacks, benefitting the nation by making available for military service the courage, skills and talents of 12% of the country's population.

When a majority in Congress was poised to mandate the prohibition of gays serving in the military, and to automatically terminate their service, and the conservative media was saturating the public with propaganda about the threat that homosexuals posed to our national defense readiness, President Clinton in a stroke of 'political genius' offered the proposition of "Don't Ask, Don't Tell" to lessen the destructive unnecessary tension created.

The ploy, later becoming controversial because of over-zealous efforts to harass and ferret out gays, at the time, halted the stampede to drive them from the military. It slowed the push of Republicans seeking to preserve 19th century value standards, and it gave cover to timid Democrats who reluctantly sided with the President's compromise.

Clinton and Affirmative Action

Republicans across the board, their supporters on the extreme religious right, and their gang of conservative talk show hosts waged an extensive campaign to end federal programs that gave equal protection of law to women and minorities.

Repeal of affirmative action was the top agenda item of the new conservative majority. Clinton, determined to preserve the underlying principle of affirmative action, ordered a full scale review of its application. Acknowledging court approval of the procedure, if narrowly tailored, he said: "Although the court raised the hurdle, it is not insurmountable. Many are using the opinion even before the ink is dry to abandon the fight."

In defense of the compelling need to eliminate discrimination, the President issued a strong statement for continuing race-based solutions to inequities. He praised affirmative action for giving the country a whole generation of professionals in fields that used to be exclusive private clubs of privileged white males. In a speech delivered at the National Archives, Clinton concluded:

> *"The job of ending discrimination in this country is not done. We should reaffirm the principle of affirmative action and fix the practices. We should have a simple slogan: Mend it, but don't end it."*

Subsequently, he issued an executive order preserving affirmative action, insuring that all federal contracts meet the standards imposed by the Court order.

Republican leaders attacked his position in fiery partisan language. Pat Buchanan, ignoring the differences between legislative rights and actual rights, said: "affirmative action belongs in the same graveyard as Jim Crow." California Republican Governor Pete Wilson stirred the racial hate pot even more when describing Clinton's policies as "encouraging tribalism" in America. Senator Robert Dole accused the President of "complicat[ing] an uncomplicated issue with an avalanche of words and fine distinctions." Texas Senator Phil Gramm sarcastically observed the speech was fine. Republican Rep. Gary Franks vowed "to repeal all set-aside contracts" for minority companies.

House Speaker Newt Gingrich vowed to support legislation to end racial preferences. Ward Connerly of California said that race-based preferences was "a clash of values" and called those who wanted to dismantle affirmative action the "warriors of democracy."

The verbal assault starkly contradicted the position of Art Fletcher, a Republican and founder of government's affirmative action program. He was assistant secretary of labor in the Nixon administration, who designed and implemented the "Philadelphia Plan." It set a standard for government contractors, specifying a certain number of person-hours for minorities and women on each construction project. Fletcher, an outspoken opponent of employment discrimination, was offended by tactics used to oppose it, saying:

> *"Certain right-wing elements have succeeded beyond their wildest imaginings in making a case against civil rights advances and legitimate welfare legislation as a waste of tax-payers' dollars. How? By presenting their views in a way suggesting African-Americans don't pay taxes."*

I met with Fletcher on many issues and he never varied or vacillated on his belief that including African Americans in the country's economic mainstream was American as apple pie and grits and gravy.

Clinton Rescued Nation From
Ignorance, Intolerance and Stereotype

Assuming the mantle of leadership in the fight to save affirmative action, Clinton rescued the issue from the shenanigans of a histrionic and hysterical ideological cabal and placed it in a more dignified place for discussion-the public arena of political expression. His calm, rational dissertation on how best to eradicate racism, sexism and homophobia won support from a sizeable number of Americans. Promoting the values of equity, justice and fairness as universal rights resonated positively with the public.

Many came to realize their fears of race, sex and homosexuality were irrational wandering from accepted standards of morality. Apparently, Clinton convinced a sufficient number of legislators that affirmative action was a legitimate, effective, enlightened approach to minimizing the negative effects of unfounded biases and the effort to kill it as government policy was put on the back burner.

A Rare, Courageous Apology
(The Tuskegee Experiment)

The President's concern for rectifying history's maltreatment of blacks, defied conventional opinion, especially his admission that slavery and segregation stained the nation's character.

In 1997, responding to a request from the Congressional Black Caucus, he again recommended the nation apologize for the atrocities inflicted on blacks during its long and torturous barbaric history. Citing inhumane treatment at a government facility in Tuskegee, Alabama was one example, but by no means an isolated incident of the U.S. Government's role in brutal atrocities.

In the 1930s the federal government under the auspices of the U.S. Public Health Service carried out a scientific research project to study long-term effects of Syphilis. Four hundred black men unaware of their illness were used as guinea pigs in documenting its effect on the human body. The Tuskegee group participants were not told they had the disease nor were they medicated. Scientist merely recorded the advances of the disease in the individuals for long periods. The data was then compared to the health of blacks in another controlled group not suffering the affliction, or being medicated for it.

The study lasted almost forty years, long after penicillin was developed to treat it. The incident, in the category of grotesqueness, was equal to any medical experimentation being conducted simultaneously by Adolph Hitler's mad doctors. According to records haphazardly kept, more than 100 black men died of syphilis or related complications, 40 wives were infected and 19 children were born with the disease.

Sixty years after the fact, in a White House ceremony attended by five surviving victims of the inhumane assault, President Clinton stated, "We can stop turning our heads away, we can look at you, in the eye, and finally say, on behalf of the American people, what the United States government did was shameful, and I am sorry."

Because there was never a huge public outcry in the country against the horrors of the Tuskegee inhumane experimentation, there was also no regrets publicly expressed for a similar, massive disregard for the human rights of economically deprived, politically powerless Americans forced to be sterilized.

Another government sponsored program starting in the 1960s was responsible for sterilizing more than 65,000 people without their consent. The procedure surgically altered the ability of women to conceive and men to impregnate. The victims were mostly black, all were poor. The state of North Carolina admitted sterilizing 8,000. A number closer to the truth was 25,000.

The Virginia legislature expressed profound regret in 2001 for its role in officially sanctioning the sterilization of more than 7,000 state citizens in the name of "purifying the white race between 1924 and 1979."[2]

Within the parameters of our impeccable code of Christian morality, it was deemed permissible by state governments and sanctioned by the federal government to relieve society of its so-called burdens-the children of welfare recipients. The general public was not aware of these practices but it's impossible for most mayors, governors and presidents to plead innocent of authorizing or at least silently sanctioning the policy.

Sufficient evidence has been produced to prove the use of widespread involuntary castration in several other states. But with the general suppression of official documents, the real extent of sterilization, castration and other horrendous behavior may never be known.

Colorblind Society Blind to Color

People of moral conviction were appalled by the reaction of Republican leaders to the President's proposed dialogue on race and an apology for America's 200-year engagement in the morbid institutional vulgarity of slavery. Unfortunately, their voices were in the minority.

In a news release I asserted that Clinton's critics "never would have condemned the Chancellor of Germany" for apologizing to the descendants of 6 million Holocaust victims. Why are they so abrasive and so disrespectful to descendants of millions of slaves who died in the tortuous journey from Africa and the unconscionable existence experienced in this land?

The burning of protestant churches and the desecration of Jewish synagogues during the later years of the 20th century was a reminder that racial and religious hatred is still alive and kicking. Bigots of all stripes have succeeded in funneling their hatred safely underground. With the blessing of religious extremist leaders who are more committed to ideological doctrine than godly respect for morality, they continue to be a threat to "liberty and justice" for all.

Ken Starr Persecution

Shutting down the government or objecting to the President's apologizing for past inhumane treatment of its black citizens was not the only time the Republican-controlled congress looked petty, parochial, and power-crazed. The impeachment of Clinton was a classic example of its misguided, misdirected, contemptuous attitude toward the value of Constitutional precedents and protections.

Attorney Ken Starr was commissioned by a panel of partisan Republican judges to investigate alleged misconduct of the President and First Lady Hillary Clinton concerning a land deal that took place 14 years before he was elected President. After four years of rumors, leaks of possible misconduct, investigation of hearsay claims and the expenditure of $50 million in taxpayer's money, Starr produced a government document replete with salacious details of alleged sexual misconduct fit for reprint in a monthly pornographic magazine.

The Congress voted to release Starr's account with its ugly and unsubstantiated accusations. While Clinton was not allowed to review or refute the allegations, the media and its critics were given copies before the document was delivered to the White House. A few hours after Clinton received the politically charged statement, internet users were perusing the allegations online. Shortly thereafter, hurriedly printed copies from the internet were being sold on Capitol Hill for $3.00.

Denying the President review of the charges before public distribution was contrary to past policy of the House in similar cases. Others coming under investigation were given sufficient time to respond prior to public release.

President Nixon had two months to examine and respond to charges before the House began its preliminary impeachment inquiry. President Reagan and Lt. Col. Oliver North had five months to study charges in the Iran-Contra Affair before the public hearings. Speaker Newt Gingrich and other members of Congress were given 7 days to prepare responses to allegations brought by the House Ethics Committee before the public was given access to the charges of their ethical and criminal indiscretion.

In a more partisan attack, some in the Republican leadership called for public showing of the President's videotaped testimony before the grand jury. Embarrassing him may have served the political ends of political vultures, but public exposure would have been a disservice to the Office and to the nation.

Vote to Impeach

Attacks on Clinton were blatant political attempts to repudiate his 1996 election victory. The Republican controlled House put Clinton's accusation of sexual misconduct, a misdemeanor, in the same category with the felonious acts of Nixon. Where was the justification for the comparison?

Nixon faced charges: subversive of constitutional government, repeatedly engaging in conduct violating the constitutional rights of citizens, contravening laws governing agencies of the executive branch, obtaining confidential information in income tax returns, misusing the FBI, and maintaining a secret investigations unit within the office of the president.

Charges against Nixon spoke for themselves. None of Clinton's charges met the required Constitutional standard for impeachment-treason, bribery, or other high crimes and misdemeanors. The House equated sexual misconduct with the Founding Father's constitutional grounds enacted for impeachment. The official charges had no relationship to Clinton's official duties. None involved a breach of the public's trust or a failure to properly perform official duties. He was charged with two counts of perjury, obstruction of justice and abuse of power.

The American system of justice is predicated on the principle of due process dictating that the accused has the right to confront the accuser. The rule of law, not public opinion, must be the determinant factor in considering impeachment. But the House, based primarily on demand of conservative ideologues and a frenzied hatred of Clinton by partisan politicians, pushed ahead and impeached the President. The Senate refused to convict him.

In a show of distrust and contempt toward extreme elements of the Republican House majority to force Clinton from office, seventy-percent of Americans polled believed Clinton was satisfactorily performing his job. Sixty-three percent supported him, and considered the Republicans' call for impeachment ludicrous. They gave the president credit for the healthy economic condition that rebounded during his administration.

Clinton's exciting, productive eight years in office came to an end in January 2001. He was succeeded by George W. Bush who was declared winner over Al Gore in a disputed election where the U.S. Supreme Court arbitrarily cancelled the counting of votes in Florida and named Bush the winner.

NOTES

1/Harry S. Truman, June 15, 1940, Sedalia, Missouri

2/*USA TODAY,* 2 February 2007, Wendy Koch, "State Of Virginia Moving to Issue an Apology for Slavery.", page 3A.

15

"On some issues cowardice asks the question is it safe? And vanity asks is it popular? And expediency asks is it political? But conscience asks is it right?[1]

– A Methodist Minister in England
Name and date unknown

My Share of Disappointments

No matter how successful individuals are in government service, elected officials experience the same regrets, rejections and disappointments common to other professionals..

During 42 years in political office, I interacted with persons of legendary proportion, enjoyed the highest respect among my colleagues, and achieved legislative milestones. Yet, like most members of Congress I suffered my share of disappointments and setbacks considered the hazards of the job.

At the beginning of my legislative endeavors, like so many newcomers, minor defeats were more of a personal nature, because I believed, egotistically that my proposed resolution of problems was far superior to ones recommended by colleagues. In my first term, President Nixon vetoed the $9,500,000 manpower training bill that as a member of the Education and Labor Committee, I was instrumental in drafting protective language for retraining those who lost their jobs in the resent economic downturn.

The President in his veto message cited the cost as too great. I was livid. In my opinion, it was another example of the underprivileged, poverty-stricken, educationally deprived made to sacrifice more than the well-to-do. I thought the critical need to retrain the group losing jobs in the economic crisis outweighed everything else.

On another occasion, I expressed great displeasure with Democrats who supported a crippling amendment to a labor bill that I managed on the House floor. In disgust, I later wrote to Speaker O'Neil, stating:

> *The vote on Thursday of a crippling amendment offered by Mr. Bartlett of Texas and supported by fifty- six Democrats, convinces me that our Party has serious problems with representing workers who keep us in the majority.*

Many of us hoping to maintain Party unity, voted to support cotton, peanut, tobacco and dairy subsidies which are of minimum political concern to our inner-city residents, in anticipating that reciprocal consideration would be given when legislation affecting urban areas came before this Body.

Several other actions, however compared to these petty rebuffs, were equally annoying and much more offensive: among them (1) failure to establish an African American Museum on the Mall near the Capitol, (2) a prestigious black education association proposal to honor Senator Strom Thurmond at the same time and on the same program with Congressman Stokes and me, (3) the Congressional Black Caucus cuddling in its midst a reactionary, anti-civil rights Negro member, (4) Republicans capturing control of the House of Representatives, and (5) the U.S. Senate rejecting the nomination of Ronnie White for the federal judiciary.

Requiem for the African American Museum
(First Major Disappointment)

Failure to create an African American Museum hurt me in a very personal way because I devoted much time in an effort to make it a reality. Witnessing months of hard work and long hours undermined by members of the CBC, who struck the lethal blow, was a bitter pill to swallow

The bill was originally introduced by George "Mickey" Leland of Texas. After his death in an airplane crash, it was championed by Rep. John Lewis of Georgia. In the Senate, Paul Simon of

Illinois was its primary sponsor.

As chairman of the subcommittee with jurisdiction, I conducted comprehensive hearings, interviewed numerous experts of African American history, met with influential officials of the Smithsonian Institute in negotiating an agreement for financing the endeavor, and assisting in selection of professional staff to oversee start-up of the facility.

After three years of inquiries, meetings, investigations, and hearings conducted by the Subcommittee on Libraries and Memorials, a bill was unanimously approved in committee to create a museum on the National Mall alongside other facilities administered by the Smithsonian Institute.

The advisory committee of twenty-one black scholars, cultural administrators, and private citizens recommended housing the museum in the Smithsonian's Arts and Industries Building that once served as the temporary home of the National Air and Space Museum, and for the National Museum of American History during the years they were assembling artifacts.

The advisory committee included the most knowledgeable, respected authorities on black art and history—Lerone Bennett, Jr., senior editor of *Ebony* Magazine, and renown historian John Hope Franklin of Duke University.

Bennett testified that the facility was "needed on the Mall and under the supervision of the Smithsonian." The committee issued a report in 1991, stating:

> *There is not a single institution devoted to African Americans which collects, analyzes, researches and organizes exhibitions and [which maintains a continuous, day-by-day watch over function from an authoritative level of power on a scale and definition comparable to those of the major museums devoted to other aspects of American life.*

In the closing days of the 102nd Congress (1991), the senate passed Simon's bill while its chief antagonist, Senator Jesse Helms (R-N.C.) was hospitalized. Helms, a powerful, vindictive member, had sworn to block its enactment in retaliation to Senator Carol Moseley-Braun of Illinois who successfully forced reversal of a measure that granted a congressional design patent to an insignia of the

United Daughters of the Confederacy. The design prominently displayed an emblem of the original flag of the rebellious Southerners who bolted from the union.

Upon the measure's arrival in the House, the Parliamentarian referred it jointly to a subcommittee on Public Works and to my subcommittee. The public works subcommittee, chaired by Rep. Gus Savage, a member of the CBC had responsibility for construction or renovation of Smithsonian buildings but Savage was never involved in developing the legislation and had never held a hearing on its merit.

In a hurriedly convened 45 minute session, Savage orchestrated a drastic revision of the measure, proposing: construction of a new $100 million building on a sight remote from the National Mall, rejecting involvement of the Smithsonian Institution, and mandating that a black majority constitute the board to oversee operations.

The revision was identical to recommendations offered in testimony before our subcommittee by spokesmen for an ad hoc committee of African Americans representing the National Council for Education and Economic Development. They opposed the Smithsonian financing and administering the project, and argued that blacks should raise the funds and manage the project. But in eight years of solicitation, their efforts produced only seven thousand dollars ($7,000) for its construction.

The unrealistic list of conditions offered by Savage was nothing more than 'black power' rhetorical folly. Any neophyte student of congressional procedure realized it automatically doomed the legislation. Outspoken enemies of the museum, Helms included, could not have devised a better strategy to derail the project.

Black Members Killed Museum Bill

I was astounded when a majority of CBC members voted to support Savage's quixotic and impractical appeal to racial fantasy that assured defeat of the measure.

First, the CBC was fighting to keep food stamps, low income housing, Pell Grants, and neighborhood health clinics from budget cuts. Envisioning an appropriation of $100 million for the African

American museum was unrealistic and irresponsible. This estimate was not based on any architectural study, but rather on the amount spent for the Holocaust Museum and the National Museum of the American Indian. The government gave the land for the Indian Museum after substantial private sums were raised for the project. Private corporate interests donated funds to erect the Holocaust Building and the government provided the land.

Second, funding for the project was not included in the current budget which meant it would automatically be eliminated on a point-of-order raised by any member of the Appropriation Committee.

Third, acquiring a new site and constructing a building would take an estimated ten years while risking the lost of irreplaceable art treasures. A collection of more than one-million objects had been amassed for the American Indian Museum before its building was erected.

Fourth, to build on a remote site in the inner city, would limit attendance to a relatively small number of scholars and historians. Millions annually visiting Congress and nearby museums on the Mall would not have easy access to learn of African American contributions.

Savage's refusal to sign-off on the legislation meant the bill developed by my subcommittee (identical to Simon's) could not be voted on by the House. The Speaker of the House refused to inject himself into the controversy caused by the two different proposals. Instead, he referred the decision to the Congressional Black Caucus for its recommendation. By a two vote margin, the group supported Savage's proposal and the inevitable occurred—the issue was doomed to rest in peace.

A Dream Deferred

The parliamentary situation was dictated by House rules which provided that any change in the bill passed by the Senate, no matter how insignificant-a comma, a period, a word, or a paragraph—required reconciliation of the two measures in a conference committee between the two bodies of Congress. If conferees were able to iron out their differences in the several days remaining before the session ended, the bill would be sent back to each chamber for final approval. Complicating the matter of returning it to the Senate, Helms was out of the hospital and back at work.

Acceptance of Lewis' version which was identical to the senate bill would have sent it directly to the White House. President George H.W. Bush had agreed to sign the bill into law. The CBC's action, assured the death of the African American Museum.

At the time, I stated: "Savage's demands are counterproductive and could cause the project to linger unresolved for another twenty years."

Apparently, my projection was accurate. The measure died in the waning days of that Congress, and in the next Congress, Helms blocked the Senate from voting on the matter.

Twenty years later (2011), the African American Museum has not become a reality. But the determination of Rep. Lewis did finally pay off. In 2003, he teamed with Senator Sam Brownback (R-Ks), and the two successfully led a bipartisan coalition to establish a National Museum of African American History and Culture (NMAAHC) within the Smithsonian. President George W. Bush signed the bill into law on December 19, 2003, which provided that one-half of the funding to be provided by Congress and one-half by the private sector.

Terms of legislation enacted are almost identical to those sabotaged by the CBC.

Lonnie G. Bunch was named the first director of the Museum in 2005. In 2006, the Smithsonian Board of Regents selected a five acre site on the National Mall for the Museum.

The NMAAHC will be located adjacent to the Washington Monument, between 14th and 15th Streets and Constitution Avenue. The architectural firm of Freelon Adjaye Bond was selected from a pool of national and international architects to design the Museum, which is expected to open to the public in 2015 if $250 million can be raised from private donations.

Republicans Win Control of U.S. House
(Second Major Disappointment)

Another major disappointment was the 1994 election which propelled Republicans into the House majority for the first time in forty-three uninterrupted years. Losing control elevated Newt Gingrich to Speaker, jolted Democratic hopes of further enacting President Clinton's agenda, and destroyed my chance of chairing the Education and Labor Committee.

Gingrich and a few overly optimistic party loyalists predicted the upset. Veteran political analysts dismissed the rosy forecast as campaign hyperbole and ridiculed it as partisan daydreaming.

Defeating more than fifty Democrats to take control, gave Republicans the right to name committee chairmen, appoint key staff, and to determine the legislative agenda. As ranking member of the Education and Labor Committee, based on 27 years seniority, rules dictated that in a Democratic majority, I would have become chairman, succeeding Congressman William Ford who did not seek reelection.

Failure of Democrats to set the legislative priorities was a staggering blow to the millions who looked to the Congress for protection of civil liberties, civil rights, women's rights and programs enacted to protect the poor.

Bigot with Better Civil Rights Credentials
(Third Major Disappointment)

One disagreement of less world shaking import was a prestigious African American organization misreading my unwavering opposition to an historical revision concerning achievements of our race.

Some groups cannot resist showering honors on people who have earned reputations of bigotry and racism. It's not hard to discern the underlying, illogical motivation of singling out unrepentant racist for special recognition. Many believe that conferring plaques and citations on powerful persons will entice generous financial responses in return. Although the naïve practice flies in the face of past reality, it's incredible that otherwise intelligent people still suc-cumb to the scam.

The National Association for Equal Opportunity In Higher Education (NAFEO), a well respected lobbying group for black col-leges and black educators, offered to honor Rep. Stokes and me at their annual banquet luncheon. We were appreciative that the group decided to celebrate our widely known contributions to the advance-ment of black educational institutions.

But, as often happens inside the Washington beltway, a fly was in the ointment. Without informing us, the group also decided to present Senator Strom Thurmond (R-S.C.) the same award, at the same time. Needless to state, Stokes and I were flabbergast by the affront.

Thurmond, elected to the U.S. Senate in 1954, was the epit-ome of provocative, anti-civil rights leaders who fostered their po-litical careers by engendering racial hatred that encouraged physical brutality to deny citizenship rights to minorities. For more than 50 years, he was among the foremost nemesis in blocking the progress of black people.

Unfortunately, in the 1980s, historical revision was perva-sive, and Thurmond benefitted from a wave of insanity sweeping the country that expected black people to "forget the past. Concentrate on the future." The fairyland atmosphere was created to exonerate unrepentant goblins who had devoted entire lives using their magi-cal charms to dehumanize the black race.

Acknowledging Thurmond as a "reformed segregation" was part of the decadent deceit engulfing America in its attempt to white-wash the miserable racist acts of the past.

My outrage was evident in the sarcasm of a letter written to the organization's president:

"I received your invitation to accept your prestigious Congressional Award to be presented during your 21st national conference. However, I am com-pelled by integrity and principle to reject your kind offer. I would not want my presence to diminish the significance of the award you bestow on Senator Strom Thurmond that great crusader for civil rights, racial justice, economic parity and equal educational opportunity. His lifetime of dedicated struggle to the advancement of these causes stands him head and shoulders above all others. Championing the cause of the disadvantaged, dispossessed and the

▶

persecuted, uniquely qualifies him for this "singular" honor.

In my opinion, this distinguished award should not be shared by individuals of lesser commitment."

The response from the organization was hilarious. It could have been drafted by the Wizard of Oz. The organization leaders insisted that the Senator had atoned for a lifetime of racist behavior and cited his vote for the Martin Luther King Holiday bill as proof.

In a second letter more caustic than the first, I challenged the erroneous assertion of his conversion. Hoping to jolt little Dorothy back to the rolling plains of Kansas, I wrote:

"To embrace the fantasy of Thurmond's vote for the King Holiday bill as evidence of fundamental change, contradicts fact. After years of conniving to delay passage of the measure, and of offering gutting amendments to undermine the bill, to now give him hero status for his vote is part of the charade that leads our adversaries to question our seriousness about attaining civil rights.

Thurmond's vote came when it was already determined the bill would pass by a two-to-one margin and his vote was unnecessary. The vote he cast was non-controversial. No committee hearings were held, and under the rules, no amendments were permitted to be offered. Passage was pro forma."

Strom's Record after the King Holiday Bill

Apologists for the senator's 75 year legacy of unabashed hostility toward equal rights maintained that the holiday vote proved his moral transfiguration. I am always amazed at how easy it is in our community for lifelong advocates of white supremacy to become instant civil rights heroes without changing their habits or atoning for their crimes.

The alleged transformation of Thurmond through his miraculous vote for the Martin L. King Holiday is an example.

In deference to my black compatriots, I informed them it was my pleasure to accept that date as a point of departure in re-evaluating his alleged glorifying transfiguration and nomination for the Civil Rights Hall of Fame.

I reminded them that when Republicans won control of the

senate, Thurmond became chairman of the powerful Judiciary Committee which had jurisdiction over all civil rights legislation, and the responsibility to confirm all federal judges.

Upon his ascension to the position, he immediately announced his first priority was to repeal the Voting Rights Act of 1965. For several years, he doggedly but unsuccessfully pursued that mission.

In addition, he willingly and vigorously supported President Reagan's ultra conservative appointees to the U.S. Civil Rights Commission and the Federal District Courts despite many of them publicly admitting their determination to frustrate efforts to extend rights for minorities and women. Acquiescing to these sinister ploys to undermine civil rights law occurred after his MLK vote.

I brought to the attention of black educators the list of negative public positions their "newly reformed but still addicted racist awardee" took after his MLK holiday vote:

1. In 1984, opposed an amendment to overturn the Supreme Court decision in Grove City College v. Bell which narrowed the reach of Title IX, the law was designed to ban sex discrimination in educational institutions receiving federal aid.

2. In 1985, supported the racist apartheid policies of South Africa, voting against the imposition of sanctions.

3. In 1986, voted to bar federal courts from ordering school busing to achieve racial desegregation.

4. In 1986, voted to reduce Pell Grants by $1.5 billion (a   program that is an educational lifeline for poor students and the largest, single financial contributor to black colleges).

5. In 1986, he supported President Reagan's veto of a bill that would have imposed economic sanctions against apartheid South Africa.

6. In 1988, he offered an amendment specifying that only a particular department of an institution found guilty of discrimination should be barred from receiving federal aid, not the entire institution.

7. In 1988, voted against the Civil Rights Restoration Act which would restore broad coverage of four civil rights laws, and supported Reagan's veto of the measure.

8. In 1988, voted against a bill that would delay the imposition of the death penalty while a defendant facing capital punishment presents evidence to a court demonstrating that the death penalty had been imposed in a racially discriminatory manner.

9. In 1989, supported an amendment to prohibit the executive branch from implementing policies that permit officials to use evidence that race was a

statistically significant factor in the decision to seek the death penalty.
10. In 1990, he voted against stopping debate of a filibuster that was delaying the vote on the Civil Rights Act of 1990.
11. In 1990, voted against passage of the Civil Rights Act of 1990.

The record of the Senator from South Carolina was non-am-biqorous. There was no compromise in his fight to keep minorities as second-class citizens. His actions clearly adversely impacted the welfare of blacks, while on several occasions he bragged, "I have done more for black people than any other person in the nation, North or South."

Rep. Bennie G. Thompson (D-Miss.), a plaintiff in the higher education desegregation case, Ayers v. Fordice, expressed his outrage at the organization honoring Strom Thurmond. He called it appalling that NAFEO can give an award to "an individual who is a symbol of times past...I hope your members sleep well knowing that they are betraying those who died fighting for their rights to have equal educational opportunities."

Failure to Expel an Enemy from the CBC
(Fourth Major Disappointment)

The Congressional Black Caucus' refusal to expel Gary Franks, a reactionary black Republican from Connecticut, turned into a comedy of errors. In my opinion, it directly contradicted the philosophical justification of the organization's reason for existing, namely: to protect and promote the permanent interests of black constituents in their pursuit of equal citizenship and to enjoy the same rights and privileges as all others.

Elected from a district approximately fifty-five percent Republican, only 5% African American, Franks assumed his majority white voters expected him to rail against policies granting equality to blacks. He traversed the nation parroting anti-black conservative propaganda, and ridiculing black leaders for advocating programs to eliminate racial discrimination. Appearing before white audiences in southern communities, he trashed the Congressional Black Caucus for supporting the concept of majority-minority race based legislative districts. In northern communities, before white conservative groups, he railed against affirmative action and heaped insult on welfare recipients. During his nomadic wanderings, he praised Supreme Court decisions that diminished the effectiveness of the Voting Rights Act. Seemly, he relished in his 15 minutes of fame in the national media spotlight.

He was more than an irritant or a free spirit seeking a difference in approach to solving problems. His aggressive legislative activity aimed at undermining civil rights, was humiliating to a majority of blacks, and offensive to whites fighting for racial equality. In a six page letter circulated on Capitol Hill, I branded Franks a pariah who gleefully assisted in suicidal conduct to destroy his own race.

The Caucus acquiescing to Franks' bizarre notions justifying racial inequality became an issue among its membership. Without divorcing itself from Frank's weird ideological heresy, in a sense, constituted gross dereliction of responsibility.

CBC members Earl Hilliard and Mel Reynolds felt compelled to rid the Caucus of its malignant tumor. But a majority, following the misguided advice of its chairman, rather than facing the issue head-on, resorted to questionable subterfuge. At one point, it adopted a rule that resolved the group into something called the Democratic Black Caucus, and meeting immediately following its weekly luncheons, asking Republican Franks to leave the room.

The not-to-well thought out scheme was comical, juvenile and naïve. It was destined to backfire. Franks appeared on radio programs of conservative commentators Patrick Buchanan and Rush Limbaugh, blasting the group for its `audacious gall.' The deluge of media criticism made the CBC look like idiots. Widespread criticism from right wing organizations forced them to meekly rescind the preposterous dodge.

Gimmicks were not necessary. The plausible or legal reason for ejecting his membership was on the sound basis that his behavior was inimical to the best interests of black folk. The cause was clear, unambiguous and in sync with sensible rules long established to preserve the integrity of private, non-tax supported organizations.

The CBC chairman however disagreed, stating in a press

conference that "the Caucus would accommodate diversity and plurality at any cost. The ideological arms of the Caucus are large enough to embrace all trends of political thought." Again, a majority of CBC members followed his unintelligent, incoherent counsel.

The matter rested in limbo until Franks' majority white constituency saved the CBC from itself, and voted him out of office in the next election.

Betrayal of Judge Ronald (Ronnie) White
(Fifth Major Disappointment)

On October 5, 1999, the U. S. Senate voted strictly along party lines to reject the nomination of Ronnie White to the Federal District Court. As the one who recommended him to President Clinton, I was outraged by treatment afforded an extremely qualified, well respected black jurist. His defeat was the result of a despicable campaign to assassinate his character.

Two Missouri Republican senators made untrue accusations against the legal scholar, a former member of the Missouri legislature, and a sitting member of the Missouri Supreme Court. His confirmation was sabotaged by senators Christopher Bond and John Ashcroft of Missouri who orchestrated the smear campaign. There was no public debate of his qualifications, only a back room deal made in the Republican caucus where the two senators blatantly maligned his character by falsifying his judicial positions.

Republicans who controlled the Senate distorted Judge White's record, describing it as "pro-criminal" with a tendency to "condone criminal activity." This complete fabrication was the basis used by Ashcroft, Bond and 50 other Republicans in derailing his confirmation.

Ironically, Bond earlier while in the midst of a close campaign for re-election testified before the Senate Judicial Committee in support of White's confirmation, heaping praise on the nominee.

Congresswoman Maxine Waters (D-Ca.), a friend of White and a former St. Louisan spoke out against the tactics employed by the two senators.

On 22 October, Ashcroft stated in a press release that Congresswoman Waters and I chose to attack his character, claiming our accusations were "unrelenting, severe, and an attack on his family."

We responded that once again the senator exhibited his inability to understand the meaning of veracity. We did not attack his family. We did not attack his character but rather his lack of character.

Ashcroft declared in his press release that he was not a racist. History seems to repeat itself. He sounded exactly like another Republican declaring "Your President is not a crook." Well, he was a crook and the world found it out.

NOTES

1/A Methodist Minister in England, name and date unknown

16

"Well done, thou good and faithful servant."[1]
– The Holy Bible

I always behaved as a leader–exerting authority, never waiting for pollsters to ascertain its interpretation of the politically popular mood. Often I took positions opposed by a majority and explained successfully to the public why the, consensus view, attractive and appealing was not necessarily best for the country or for the people who elected me.

Retirement from Public Life

In April 1999, *Roll Call*, a Capitol Hill newspaper ran a story with the headline "Clay Contemplating Retirement." The subtitle read "Friends Say They'll Lobby Veteran Democrat to Stay." One month later was the red-letter day concerning this issue in my life. After four decades in public service, I finally reached that decision to pass the torch "to a younger generation."

A group of St. Louisans led by Michael Newmark visited my Washington office to encourage my seeking reelection. With deepest respect, I listened to their concerns, than pointed to a photograph on the wall. It was members of the St. Louis Board of Aldermen taken forty years earlier, my first year in an elective position. I noted that only four of the 29 members were still alive.

My long-time friend, Barbara Newmark, corrected me, stating that Harold Elbert, one of the four died the previous week. I said, "You are making my point. Like it or not, one way or another, each of us is subject to term limits. I am only seeking a few days to peacefully reflect on the meaning of it all without the pressures associated with public life. Please do not expect me to forsake that dream."

Some retirements are sad occasions, especially for the retiree and his immediate family. The final culmination of an active career is often looked upon as bittersweet. Remembering the glorious deeds of the past, while lamenting roads not taken, conjure up mixed emotions of sad and happy experiences.

I had the rare privilege of representing my country at its highest level of government. Only a few have or will ever participate in so rewarding an experience. Improving the quality of life and raising the standard of living for millions of people, by itself, is sufficient compensation for the toil and sacrifice devoted to fulfilling the responsibilities required of public servants.

In alliance with others, I fought the good fight, overcame great obstacles, helped change many government programs for the better. I take comfort knowing that our nation and its people live easier, more enjoyable, more productive lives because our efforts assisted them in achieving lifelong desired goals.

Knowing my announcement would set off a political firestorm of activity to fill the vacated position, I decided to give potential candidates ample time in preparing their campaigns.

A surprise announcement close to election would have generated the charge from my adversaries that it was timed to benefit chances of my son winning the seat. But that was one less accusation he would have to face in the campaign. So confident of the Clay family's reputation for public and community service, I announced the decision 18 months in advance of election without fear of the charismatic, effective, consummate public official Lacy Clay, Jr. losing if he chose to run.

Friends and Enemies Assessed My Career

The *St. Louis American* wrote that "While many area politicians and civic leaders were not always in agreement with U.S. Rep.

William "Bill" Clay, he set a standard for African-American public service for decades."

A veteran political analyst reported in reference to my announced decision that he did not remember as much printer's ink devoted to the retirement of a Missouri political figure since President Harry S. Truman's departure.

Compliments and criticisms defining the affect of my service and long tenure in office appeared in hundreds of articles, in scores of local and national journals, in numerous radio and television programs. The decision to step down was covered extensively in news items and editorials throughout the state. St. Louis City weeklies, the St. Louis suburban journals, the Kansas City daily, out-state newspapers, especially the several hundred black weeklies reported aspects of major and minor details involving my 32 years in congress, and its impact on state politics. Surrounding states of Illinois, Kansas and Arkansas ran similar accounts.

Typical of various and differing opinions were reported extensively in the local media. A labor lobbyist praised my staunch defense of labor's interests, but said, "Clay does not pay enough attention to issues." A former White House lobbyist under President Carter remembers "Clay as an arrogant congressman who was difficult to work with." A lobbyist with an opposite view, Jim Brown, St. Louis City's point man in D.C., stressed my persistence in securing funds for the Metro Link despite President Reagan's hold on new rail starts. He said, "Clay simply hound-dogged the Department of Transportation (a particular assistant secretary) until they finally dropped the prohibition." Scott Fleming of the Department of Education said, "I have enjoyed every chance to work with you." Under Secretary of Agriculture Shirley R. Watkins wrote, "Millions of families and children across the country can thank you for the compassion and caring you have shown them."

Louis G. Hutt, attorney, author and C.P.A. wrote, "Clay opened doors of opportunity for African Americans during the height of the civil rights movement."

Sam Slade of the *St. Louis Sentinel* wrote "In the 40-years that Clay has made his mark on politics in this country, he has been the master craftsman in creating trickery that has manifested into victories for minorities. Many non-Blacks have crossed the line in support of Cong. Clay and banned together in major political races and legislation that have benefited both Black and white citizens."

Among the hundreds of letters I received was one from the postmaster of Springfield, Missouri, Robert W. Roberts. He wrote, "I wish to thank you for your efforts on behalf of postal employees nationwide." Another person described by the *Post Dispatch* as a liberal leaning voter, stated "Frankly I don't think he [Clay] cares much about representing the whites in the district." Kenneth A. Brown of Auburn, New Hampshire noted my "extreme dislike for President Richard Nixon" and advised that I "could not see over his (Nixon's) shoe strings or carry his books." Another from New Hampshire had his say, "I wish to thank you for understanding that bigotry is not the sole and exclusive domain of any race, creed, color or religion. In fact, you wear your bigotry, ignorance and hatred right up front for the world to witness." And Ruth Brown agreed with his feelings, "I don't think he cares much about representing the whites in the district." Wow! What a send-off for a lifelong confirmed integrationist like myself.

Harry Doepke, a county resident said, "He [Clay] was too much for himself...I don't think he did anything for the district." A 48 year old North Side woman said, "I am glad he is retiring. Maybe he was effective in the beginning, but if you're in Congress that long, your district should look better than it does." A nearby neighbor in Walnut Park said he had never known politics without the Clays, "All these years, even when I was a kid, I never hear of any reason that he shouldn't be the one in office." A constituent living south of Fairground Park reflected, "The government saw him as a good guy. He was for labor and the little man, and I'm one of them." A neighborhood auxiliary volunteer of the Penrose police district mused that "Clay really inspired us to do what was right." Jo Ann Decker of Clayton, Missouri said, "I am glad to have a liberal Democrat representing us. He is a good politician with the right instincts." Rose White wrote "I will always remember you as our greatest congressman in my lifetime."

Dr. James Billington, director of the Library of Congress

wrote, "You have really been one of the forces that has helped shape and reshape this institution." Willis Drake, chairman of the St. Louis Club in Washington, D.C. stated, "We thank you for making a positive difference in the world." Billy and Marilyn Davis of the Fifth Dimension sent thanks for a career of "effectively dealing with this government to insure adequate representation for all." Karla Williams Wallace of Bowie, Maryland said, "I look forward to telling my grandchildren about you."

St. Louis businessman Joe Edwards said, "(Clay) was a tough, savvy politician, a steadfast champion for human rights. Henry H. Brown, Vice President of Anheuser Busch said, "Your exemplary service to our nation has been and continues to be an inspiration to me and so many of my professional associates." Attorney Larry Carp stated, "Heartiest congratulations on your outstanding, meaningful, productive career."

Gail Weiss, staff director of the Post Office and Civil Service Committee and a friend of more than 30 years wrote, "Who could have dreamt that a young New York girl would meet a vibrant, firebrand mid-west congressman and get to have the experience of a lifetime." Pearlie Evans, a civil rights activists, grassroots advisers to many candidates for public office, and my long time employee said, "In his district, Bill Clay is a political legend…On his watch as alderman, committeeman, and congressman he soundly rejected the politics of accommodation and appeasement and embraced the politics of inclusion and coalition." Roscoe Dellums of Washington, D.C. wrote, "You have set a very high standard, one that should be emulated." Kenneth Seeney of Missouri wrote, "Your years of public service is a testament to your dedication and commitment to the citizens of the state and the nation."

Indicative of the contempt the business community held for my agenda promoting the basic interests of workers and the poor, was William Maritz' statement to the press. In a curt remark, the former head of Civic Progress, representing the 20 largest companies in the area, stated, "I have had no relationship at all with Clay." So much for the city's most influential business leader's inability to interact with "all elements in a thriving, progressive community." His sentiment was countered by others who knew I was not cowered or intimidated by the anti-racial, anti-worker cartel that he represented.

The *Post Dispatch* editorialized, "Mr. Clay, who announced his retirement Monday, was one of those rare politicians who was able to seize and hold power without playing by the rules. In fact, Clay gained power because he violated the rules."

The description, in my opinion, accurately assessed the situation. Acknowledging and endorsing my unorthodox but effective style of leadership was a great compliment. The rules referred to, in many instances, were developed by a racially insensitive white 'power structure' like Mr. Maritz' Civic Progress to keep black folk in their place. Beneficiaries of my insolent behavior were proud that I boldly challenged and intentionally ignored rules that demanded polite, meek acceptance of deep-seated, hate-filled imperfections in society. Thank God that Rosa Parks and Dr. King "violated the rules."

The *St. Louis Argus* a newspaper that closely followed my years in Congress from the first day, wrote, "Clay's stepping down will signal the end of an era." The *St. Louis Sentinel* editorialized:

"Throughout his brilliant career, Congressman Clay has been outspoken. First against labor, on how it has treated poor and Black people. Then, Clay for 30 years, has become one of the best friends of the LABOR MOVEMENT. However, he brought to St. Louis politics, a style that will not be forgotten, for a very long time. He was the type of individual who would not take back seat to anybody, including those with money."

At a reception honoring me during the AFL-CIO Federation's Executive Council meeting in New Orleans, President John Sweeney announcing a scholarship endowment in my name at the National Labor College in Maryland said, "I can't think of a member of Congress who's made a greater impact on worker's rights and civil rights than Clay." He said in fact, "there was no legislation affecting working families in the past 30 years that Clay hasn't help shape, including health insurance and the right to organize."

Hugh McVey, president of the Missouri AFL-CIO said, "Clay has been a champion for us. The workers of America—organized and unorganized—owe him a debt of gratitude." International President Andrew L. Stern of the Service Employees International Union (SEIU) said "You have been a tireless champion of the most essential legislation for working people." Patricia A. Ford, International Executive Vice President of the same union wrote, "From your days as an Alderman, union staffer, and firebrand civil rights activists in the 1960's, through your 32 years in Congress, you have been a champion on the issues that matter to working people."

Dan Pollitt, labor lawyer at the School of Law, University of North Carolina at Chapel Hill said, "Your retirement will be a big loss to the nation."

Politicians Responded to Leaving

Former Lt. Governor Harriet Woods said, "I always respected his [Clay's] intelligence, his record and his courage. He effectively created a coalition with the white liberals in his district's urban suburbs." Representative Quincy Troupe said, "Clay was the only one who really had the presence to mold black elected officials into the force that we really are."

Frederick N. Weathers, dean of black politics in St. Louis, once said, "He's been a maverick ever since I've known him. But I admire him. He's one man that I have enough confidence in to go to sleep at night and know he'll take care of the interests of blacks and the poor."

St. Louis Mayor Clarence Harmon said that although the area has several congressmen, "If you say in this community `The Congressman', everyone knows you're talking about Bill Clay."

Mickey McTague, political activist, author and contributor to many news outlets wrote, "Bill Clay has left a legacy of wonderment in liberal thought and deed. If J.F.K. had lived, you [Clay] would have been in his new edition of "Profiles in Courage."

Congressman Stokes (D-Oh) said, "Bill Clay's Life story is an important chapter in black history in America. His brand of politics, always controversial, always outspoken, and always dedicated to the progress of black people, is a lesson in leadership and old school politics by a master.

The adulation, adoration, exhalation among elected officials was a mixed bag, ranging from Vincent Schoemehl, former mayor of St. Louis labeling me the "Nelson Mandela of Missouri, to the censure and condemnation of others.

One writer stated, "Admirers call Clay courageous and committed for advancing civil rights and protecting the poor. Adversaries call him cunning and calculating, accusing him of caring mainly about his own advancement." Another reporter wrote, "His [Clay's] friends view him as capable and independent. His foes assail him as arrogant and combative." A nationally circulated newspaper printed, "A committee staff aide who worked with Clay for years, described him as a "lightweight."

Tim O'Neil, a former investigative reporter of the defunct *Globe Democrat*, working for the *Post Dispatch* commented in an article:

> *Many blacks, especially those old enough to remember Clay's role in the civil rights days regard him almost with reverence. Labor leaders admire his reliable advocacy. Liberals like his votes on the hot-button issues, like abortion.*
>
> *Conversely, many conservatives can't stand him. Many of his white constituents, even some who like him overall, think he spends too much time representing only the blacks in his district. Some younger blacks think he has hung on too long."*

Former Alderman Steve Roberts asserted, "Clay's leadership was invaluable in passing numerous school and tax issues." Alderwoman Sharon Tyus expressed regret of my resignation, stating, "Clay told me this would be his last term and I hoped he would change his mind." Wayman Smith, former alderman and President of the St. Louis Police Board commented, "If you want to be on the right side of an issue, all you have to do is align yourself with Bill Clay."

St. Louis County Council Chairman Charles Dooley stated "His [Clay's} leadership and his contributions will not be forgotten. As an African American elected official, I want to personally thank him for his pioneering efforts to tear down the walls that divided this community racially."

Willie Brown, former Speaker of the California Assembly and former Mayor of San Francisco wrote, Clay "has been so great."

Educators Appreciated Clay's Leadership

Educator Doris Moore said, "Clay has a way of motivating people. In fact, I got involved in community issues because of him." Reverend Earl Nance, Jr. member St. Louis Board of Education referred to me as "Not the kind of politician who licks his finger and sees what way the wind is blowing." Barbara Howard of California School Employees Association said, "The U.S. Congress will be losing an important statesman upon your retirement."

Blanche Touhill, Chancellor Emeritus, University of Missouri-St. Louis, said, "Bill Clay was the embodiment of the civil rights movement in Missouri on behalf of African Americans in the 1950s-1970s. He was the right man for the right times. Without a doubt, he has made a difference in the American struggle for decency, justice, and equity." Dr. Marshall C. Grigsby, former president of Benedict College echoed Touhill's sentiments, "Bill Clay has consistently been an undisputed champion for the dispossessed. He has been a clear voice for the voiceless and an unabashed leader who has been a thorn in the side of the powerful elite in America." Educator Danny Kohl said, "with gratitude for all you have done over the years." Dr. June Harris, specialists in education with the U.S. House of Representatives for more than 25 years, referred to me as a "legislative icon." Ida Woolfolk, Assistant Superintendent for Community Outreach wrote "You, through legislation, have worked many miracles for the students and staff in the St. Louis Public Schools."

The National Alliance of Black School Educators in a tribute participated in by many members of congress stated "It is with great pride that we pause to salute a consummate public servant."

Robert R. Archibald, Ph.D., President of the Missouri Historical Society wrote, "Bill Clay's…four decades in public life could be nothing less than passionate, personal, and courageously, sometimes brazenly, outspoken, for that is his voice, heard and heeded by his own African American community in St. Louis and eventually by the broader population of our region and of the nation."

Dr. Henry Givens, president of Harris-Stowe State University said, "Clay has devoted almost his entire career in Congress to promoting educational endeavors at all levels."

Dr. Andrew Billingsley, president of Morgan State University, an author and leading scholar of the African American experience said, "We appreciate your leadership and especially your writings."

Rev. Wyatt T. Walker who served as Chief of Staff to Martin Luther King, Jr. wrote, "You [Clay] have been a great public servant." National President of the Urban League Hugh Price said we cite you for "stellar leadership in Congress on behalf of our nation and in particular, our people for over 32 years."

Kenneth Warren, Professor of Political Science at St. Louis University wrote, "Clay has not been just a stellar U.S. Congressman, but a man of principle and integrity who has had a positive and significant impact on civil rights, civil liberties, and labor in St. Louis and America. St. Louisans and Americans owe him many thanks!"

Sister Mary Mangan, Department of History, Politics and Law at Webster University wrote, "You have been one outstanding legislator. As you retire, please know your work does not go without congratulations for a job well done."

Richard B. Teitelman, Vice President of the Missouri Bar wrote, No one as ever served my district better than you."

Attorney Margaret Bush Wilson, former National Chairperson of the National Association for the Advancement of Colored People, a legend in the civil rights movement paid me the highest compliment in telling her Soror Congresswoman Juanita Millender-McDonald that she regretted my retirement because "He [Clay] has not only been a personal friend but a legend in my world."

William H. Gray, the former Majority Whip of the House of Representatives stated, "Having the chance to serve with you has been one of the great privileges of my life."

Media Comment on Retirement

Media coverage reflected the same heated pro and con opinions in evaluating the effect of my retirement as those prevalent during my tenure. Analyzing my years of "confrontational politics" and assessing what my departure would mean ran the gamut. Debate speculating how the impact of my career would be viewed in the future, continued loudly and at a vigorous pace.

Radio, television and newspaper personalities joined in the expression of editorial opinions. Commentators, in praise and condemnation, took advantage of liberal `political speech' to characterize my achievements and faults in assessing my career. Hyperbole in some cases was `wonderfully' appreciated, even if over the top, as in an article by Chris Hayden of 'Take Five.' He wrote in the June 1999 monthly, "Let all pretenders to his [Clay's] throne beware: You are taking over as head coach of Green Bay after Lombardi; you are taking over U.C.L.A. basketball after John Wooden; you are assuming the heavyweight crown after Muhammad Ali."

Jo Mannies and Mark Schlinkmann of the *Post Dispatch* in a lengthy article captured various and conflicting opinions about the quality of my leadership. They wrote "In Washington, his reputation is that of an unwavering advocate for civil rights, liberal Democratic causes and organized labor. Locally, he's best known for his deep involvement in state and local politics and policies."

They interviewed many residents of the congressional district—the powerful and ordinary citizens. Their reactions were mixed. Former mayor Vincent Sdhoemehl said "Bill Clay is the single most powerful politician in the state." President of the St. Louis Labor Council Kelley added that "Clay could deliver the votes."

But their views are not universally shared. Z. Dwight Billingsley, an unsuccessful perennial candidate for office, charged [Clay is] "One of a dying breed of black politicians who sucks the life out of the black community and gives nothing back."

Most were not as vitriolic in evaluating my government service. President of the Board of Alderman, James Shrewsbury, called me a "political institution." State Senator Wayne Goode observed, "Clay's personal strength was unmatched at the polls."

Philip M. Dine of the *Post Dispatch* said, "Bill Clay, was a great Congressman and a friend of working people."

One columnist quoted, Gerald M. Boyd of the St. Louis *Post Dispatch* from an earlier period wrote, "...the most powerful black politician in the state–William L. Clay has been a lightning rod for controversy in St. Louis."

Another, in an Op-ed article about the same time cited Dr. Ernest Patterson, professor of Political Science, University of Colorado who wrote, "The courage and leadership that he [Clay] displayed during the Jefferson Bank affair well established him as a fighter against racism."

The Metro Sentinel Journal wrote, "When it came to deal making or agreeing to disagree, you had no better politician that ever lived, his name is Congressman William Clay, Sr."

Greg Freeman of the *Post Dispatch* remembered how he campaigned for Clay as a 12 year old kid. He recalled a person showing up at the polling place where he was handing out leaflets and people began leaving their posts and surrounding him. I knew he was someone important. Then someone said, "That's Bill Clay. I could see how he had been elected to Congress, very easygoing, very charismatic, Clay looked like a leader. He did more than just look like a leader. He acted like one."

The accolades and acrimonies were numerous and from varied sources. The Congressional Black Caucus Foundation News reflected on the occasion of my retirement in an article titled, "[Clay] a Statesman, Politician Extraordinaire, Announces Final Chapter of Distinguished Career." Jo Mannies of the St. Louis *Post Dispatch* wrote:

> *"Declaring an intention to retire will set off a political earthquake like St. Louis hasn't seen in decades. Nobody–not even House Minority Leader Richard A. Gephardt, D-St. Louis County–personally wields more local political influence than [William L.] Clay."*

George L. Miles, Jr., President of WQED in Pittsburgh said, "After a long and distinguished career...The time has come to sleep that extra hour in the morning!" Lionel Fultz author of "A Look Behind the Tip of the Iceberg" wrote, "Clay paid [his] dues and many have benefitted from his efforts."

Earl G. Graves, publisher and CEO of *Black Enterprise Magazine* assessed my career as, "continuing leadership on behalf of so many who could not speak for themselves."

Connie F. Gibson author of *"The Black Man's Guide to Parenting"* wrote, "Appreciate all your efforts to make life better for all Americans."

A *St. Louis American* editorial compared my involvement on the political scene with that of a former great political leader. It wrote, "For nearly four decades William L. Clay, Sr. had reined almost unchallenged, as first the dominant, and later the most influential political leader in the St. Louis black community. Not since the legendary Jordan Chambers has any individual wielded as much political clout in our community. Congressman Clay has had a truly remarkable political tenure by any measure."

Columnist Sam Slade said, "Clay had it all, money, power, education and connections. But, most of all instilled FEAR in most of his opponents."

Chris Hayden of "Take Five" expressed a different viewpoint. He wrote, "I guess the thing that I felt most ill-at-ease with the congressman was the way in which anyone who challenged him was so utterly destroyed. It offended my idealism; seemed out of place in a democracy."

The *St. Louis Riverfront Times* in May 1999 wrote, "His [Clay's] comments made him come off as an unapologetic old school liberal, a trail-blazing African American politician and a backroom power broker. St. Louis has grown to love or endure [him] since he was first elected in 1968."

Steve Hartman, a design artist, said, "In the end, Clay, using his tremendous vote-getting apparatus, became one of Missouri's most powerful political voices in controlling election-year issues and determining the success of candidates' campaigns in both citywide and statewide elections.

Sister Claudette Marie Muhammad, Chief of Protocol for Minister Louis Farrakhan wrote, "Thanks for all that you have done."

Ofield Dukes, one time public relations assistant to Vice

President Hubert H. Humphrey stated, "Clay stood toe-to-toe, eye-ball-to-eyeball fighting the enemies of civil rights."

A very proud and sentimental moment for me was a letter received from a former official of the UAW offering congratulation and with a copy of an article he wrote about me almost 20 years prior. He quoted from a speech I made to the labor union at its conference in Black Lake, Michigan. He said my retirement brought back happy memories of earlier days and he felt compelled to share his thoughts about the speech. In writing about it many moons ago, he titled the editorial appearing in the union newspaper "Rocked Our Socks Off", saying......every once in a while there will come a speaker you think you can just sit back and relax to. Such was the case when Congressman William L. Clay from Missouri took the podium. That image did not last long. From the calm manner of one who knows his material, the tempo of his speech started to rattle the rafters. He cajoled, chastised, humored, demanded, dared, and preached. The note takers stopped taking notes, the camera bugs stopped taking pictures, the apathetic woke up, the cynical smiled, the pacifiers became defiant and they all listened to the politician, no let's say statesman, from St. Louis. When he had finished, he took a drink of water and sat down. There was an ovation. A standing ovation that was well deserved, gave rise to a new feeling in the conference hall. To sum up the reaction of the audience, a question was addressed to him, "Why didn't you run for president"? The experienced politician of 25 years answered with a smile. There came another standing ovation for the man from St. Louis.

Post Dispatch Writes Life Story
(Portrait of Representative Bill Clay)

In addition to several editorials, and lengthy news articles, the *Post Dispatch* assigned its Washington, D.C. correspondent, Tim Poor, to write an in-depth story of my growing up "as a skinny kid in the ghetto when Carol [my wife] met me" tracing life through 16 terms in Congress. The biography titled "Tailoring His Legacy" was a series of eight articles, included 39 photos among the full pages of type. It was a comprehensive, panoramic examination of my life from birth to the day of retirement. Mr. Poor, in a front page Sunday article announcing the coming of the featured series, stated, "In a public career spanning nearly 40 years, U.S. Rep. Bill Clay has been a commanding figure in the history of St. Louis. He got his start as a noisy leader of the civil rights movement...His strong ties to organized labor and his streetwise mastery of urban politics made him a figure to be reckoned with, both in Washington and Missouri. The rich robust story of Bill Clay isn't just the tale of a politician. In many ways, it's the story of all of us."

Poor's coverage of my political odyssey was elaborated in sections, laced with exciting subtitles like: "Raising Hell on an army post shortly after graduation from college"; "Alderman Clay passing the city's first laws forbidding discrimination in jobs"; "Congressman Clay railed at Nixon, opposed the war in Vietnam and still gave fiery speeches"; "Kingmaker traveled through much of the 1970s under investigation"; "*The Globe Democrat* sent reporters out to nail him"; "The Anatomy of an Economic Murder"; and "Bill Clay on "Meet the Press.""

Tim Poor talked of Nixon putting me on the "enemies list", "The Justice Department (sniffing) around" and the *"Wall Street Journal"* accusing me of padding my travel account, causing the government to sue me for $189,000. But he told how it ended with the government [embarrassingly] reimbursing me $2500.00 for trips I had never claimed.

Reporter Poor's story of my life's achievements, and the many features by other newspapers–the accolades, even the criticisms were of great comfort to a person like me who coming from humble beginnings, learned the meaning of power and most of all, through trial and error, used it properly for good.

Appreciation to a Crusading Press

The achievements, celebrations, brouhahas, trophies, victories would have been impossible without the support of thousands of loyal friends and constituents who were instrumental in persuading others to cast votes in election after election. Nor would it have lasted so long without the unshakable faith and contributions of members of the press: the *St. Louis American,* the *St. Louis Argus,* the *St. Louis Crusader,* the *People's Guide,* and the *St. Louis Sentinel.* Their editors and staff waged constant battle against unprincipled reporters in the larger media, and dishonest political opponents who attempted to silence my speaking out in behalf of justice and equality for every citizen. In addition, three reporters of the *St. Louis Post Dispatch,* Bob Adams, Robert Joiner and Lawrence Taylor performed yeomen's jobs in uncovering plots against me by seven (7) federal agencies attempting to illegally indict and convict me of criminal conduct.

Retirement of the Clay Team

My major successes would not have been possible without Carol Ann and our three children. During the journey, they were there every step of the way. Carol stood next to me in this noble endeavor for the entire stretch. Her charming and understanding attitude was a pillar of strength behind our excursion into the uncharted waters of confrontational politics. She partnered with me for over 40 years in raising a family, creating a home and working to improve the quality of life for people everywhere.

Those involved in my career from its very beginning, are aware that she was a real source of inspiration and stability in the family-the driving force behind many of our political initiatives. She was a caring, devoted mother, grandmother, a homemaker who raised our three children, Vickie, Lacy and Michelle–managing to do it with style and grace.

Upon retirement, Carol received many compliments and congratulations. The CBC Spouses presented a grand reception in her honor at Washington, D.C.'s Museum of Women in the Arts. The premiere salute billed as a 'Celebration of Leadership Gala,' recognized her who along with Alma Rangel, Jay Stokes and Roscoe Dellums founded the tax-exempt Congressional Black Caucus Foundation (CBCF), an organization to support the agenda of black congressmen. They established the CBCF Spouses Education

Scholarship Fund, and also the Internship and Fellows Program. From 1988 until our retirement, she and her colleagues raised millions of dollars for college scholarships.

Mrs. Rangel and our granddaughter Angie Clay treated those in attendance to an overview of Carol's role in the life of the Capitol.

Private Dinner at the Library of Congress

Carol and I were given a private dinner at the Library of Congress hosted by director James H. Billington and his wife. In attendance were the top executive staff and major contributors to the Library. It was a casual, intimate occasion, to thank me for protecting the institution from political intrusion and for assisting in the advancement of the Library to fulfill its mission. Billington said in his remarks, "You have been a main force in helping to shape and reshape this institution."

Congressional Black Caucus Pays Tribute

I was honored in a special ceremony by the CBC, at the National Democratic Club. Rep. Eva Clayton (D-N.C.) who presided, recalled my "blunt" approach to making law and shelling out advice to friend and foe alike. She said that sometimes I directed my ire toward "our own party and particularly the Black Caucus." She stated that "Stokes and I would double-team on issues: "Louis would come in a sweet-talk you way, and Bill would come and knock you out."

Tributes were offered by Congresspersons Eddie Bernice Johnson, Maxine Waters and Louis Stokes. Wayman Smith, Board Chairman of Howard University, and Ramona Edelin, executive director of the CBC Foundation presented me with a rare copy of Emmett J. Scott's *"Official History of the American Negro in the World War."*

CBC Foundation Tribute

In a special ceremony, the Congressional Black Caucus

Foundation cited my accomplishments in its January 2001 publication, writing:

> *"The tally sheet for Rep. Clay's career reads like that of a heavyweight boxer surveying the end of a long and successful career. Clay had a long reach–having sponsored or cosponsored 295 bills that were enacted into law. He has been an influential leadership force, a voice of courage and conscience, and an insightful author-historian."*

Missouri Progressive Vote Coalition

Pro Vote, a coalition of statewide community activists, presented me with its first Achievement Award for a lifetime of commitment to progressive issues including worker's rights, the environment, reproductive rights, and quality public education.

Other Awards

The Executive Committee of the AFL-CIO at a conference in New Orleans established a scholarship in my name to train labor organizers at the National Labor College (formerly the George Meany Institute Center).

Service Employees International Union at its annual Political Action Conference held in the nation's Capital, presented me with its Lifetime Achievement Award for protecting the rights of workers.

National Alliance of Black School Educators (NABSE) presented "An Evening With a Champion-the Honorable William L. Clay, Sr. The dinner was held at the Hyatt Regency Capital Hill Hotel in D.C. Ten outstanding leaders gave tributes. Among them were Congressmen Stokes, Dellums, Bill Gray and James Clyburn.

The Jesuit Society recognized me for work in behalf of higher education. I received the Appreciation Award from the Association of Jesuit Colleges and Universities (AJCU) and for legislative service to educational institutions.

Magnet Schools Award

I received the Magnet Schools of America's National Award. The organization represents over 4,000 K thru 12th grade magnet schools.

Awards for Public Service

The National Urban League, the organization presented my son Lacy and me with the "Legends and Leaders for the Future Award" for my effort in preparing the next generation to continue the commitment, dedication and quality leadership needed to move our people forward.

World Federalist Association presented its "Golden Statesman Award"

Leonard Slatkin, Internationally famous conductor, devoted a "Bill Clay" night at the symphony. The program was held at Powell Symphony Hall in St. Louis to say thanks for my support of the arts and humanities.

The Black Repertoire, an actor's guild in St. Louis, gave me its prestigious Woody Award for leadership in preventing efforts to abolish federal financial aid to the preservation and expansion of the arts.

Walk of Fame, Three separate municipal jurisdictions inducted me into their sidewalks of fame: St. Louis City's Gateway Classics Walk of Fame; University City, Missouri Blueberry Hill Walk of Fame; and Atlanta, Georgia's International Civil Rights Walk of Fame.

U.S. Post Office Building in North County St. Louis, named by Congress.

Science and Technology Center at Harris-Stowe University established by (NASA) to provide mathematics and science programs

William L. Clay, Sr. Leisure Living Community a 78 unit housing complex for the elderly and persons with disabilities

William L. Clay, Sr. Molecular Science Building on the campus of Missouri University @ St. Louis to enhance molecular electronic research.

William L. Clay Early Children/Parenting Building on the campus Harris-Stowe State University, devoted to a state-of-art early childhood development center

William L. Clay Park and Street in West St. Louis

Awards, Citations, Benefits

To commemorate years of service, public places were named in my honor: a city street, a sculpture park, an adult/child day care center, a special room providing information on space technology at a second college, a computer room for students on a third college campus, and a post office with private mail boxes for students at a fourth, the room where the St. Louis Board of Education holds its meetings..

St. Louis Gateway Classic

In announcing William L. Clay 1996 St. Louis Gateway Classic's "Honoree of the Year," Earl Wilson, Jr., president and executive director said, "We proudly give a testimonial award dinner in honor of Bill Clay, Sr. for his lifetime achievement in educational, civic and community services. We salute him as a man of integrity and honesty who has been a role model for youth and an inspiration to adults."

Harris Stowe University Honors the Clays

One of the numerous activities that touched Carol and I greatly was sponsored by Dr. Henry Givens, President of Harris-Stowe University. He honored us with the Distinguished Martin Luther King, Jr. "Legacy Award." Carol and I also received the Anheuser Busch's coveted sculptured Eagles for outstanding public service. Presentation of the awards was a first class affair held in the school's auditorium.

Dr. Givens sponsored a fabulous retirement ceremony that

was attended by an overflow crowd of friends and supporters. A month before the gala, he dispatched Sheila Banks, the school's director of communication to our home in Silver Spring, Maryland, to interview us for the occasion. She taped a 15 minute video which reflected highlights of our lives, going back to the first years of marriage, our continuing involvement in civil rights, and recapping many of our political endeavors.

The emotionally-laden account brought back memories to family and friends in the audience who traveled the journey with us.

Dr. Givens remarked, "The number and caliber in attendance speaks volumes about who and what the Clays represent." Acknowledging our service to the young, old, poor, middle class, affluent, black and white, he said, "We thank Carol and Bill for a job well done."

Thanking Dr. Givens, I responded, "I have a year and a half remaining in my present term and I promise to continue speaking loud and boisterously about the inequities in society." As I struggled to thank friends and allies, my remarks were interrupted repeatedly with applause. Continuing, I said:

> *I want all to know how proud I am to have represented the citizens of this district...to have served as your trustee in the people's House of Representatives long enough to become third in seniority. Words are not capable of expressing thanks to you who labored, sacrificed and achieved with me in these 32 years. But there is much more to a career than longevity. There must also be vision. I had a vision of what America should be and could be, and I pursued a course that attempted to make it so.*

In closing, I stated:

> *"They say that the happiest time in the life of a politician is the day of his first victory. The saddest day is when he suffers a final defeat or decides to call it quits. This is a sad day. Thanks for traveling this historic journey with me and my family."*

Congressional Colleagues Pay Tribute

The singular most striking honor paid an individual is one by his peers, acknowledging his outstanding accomplishments. President Bill Clinton said:

> *"You [Clay] have been a staunch champion of working families, and your legislative achievements have strengthened vital education programs like Head Start, improved health and safety benefits for workers, and opened the doors of higher education for all our people."*

Congressman Charles Rangel (D-N.Y.) said, "Clay has been able to cut through the rhetoric. One of his biggest assets is he's a no nonsense type of fellow and that is respected within the cause."

Democratic leader Congressman Dick Gephardt stated, "Clay has been a constant and unfailing ally in getting things done for our region on a day-to-day basis." Former Congressman Ronald A. Sarasin wrote, "Your place in the history of Congress and our nation's government is assured." Another retired member, Mervyn M. Dymally expressed "surprise and disappointment" in the ending of "such a distinguished career." Former Congresswoman Yvonne Brathwaite Burke wrote, "I can't imagine a Congress without you." Congressman Vernon J. Ehlers of Michigan wrote, "I assure you that you will be sorely missed."

William Goodling, my Republican counterpart on the Education Committee with whom I collaborated to revise virtually every statute of importance to education, including the Individuals with Disabilities Education Act, the Carl D. Perkins Vocational and Technical Education Act, the Elementary and Secondary Education Act and the Higher Education Act said during a congressional hearing, "Despite our differing philosophies, we've been able to work together on a variety of bills...He's a hard worker and a gentleman."

Karen McCarthy (D-Mo.) said "I will miss your wisdom and guidance." William J. Jefferson (D-La.) stated "You have truly been a special treasure to the CBC and the CBCF, indeed an irreplaceable one." Sonny Callahan (R-Ala.) wrote "Thanks for your years of dedication and commitment."

Former Senator Thomas f. Eagleton wrote, "You [Clay] have been a forceful and fearless representative of your district. You never bent to the 'power structure.' You espoused your ideals with consistency and fervor." Carolyn McCarthy of New York stated,

"Your accomplishments and your commitment are a tribute to the true meaning of public service."

Congressman James E. Clyburn, chairman of the CBC said, "This august body will lose one of its most productive and Congress and I consider it a high point of my service to be able to say that I served with him." Former Congresswoman Patricia Schroeder wrote, "There is life after! Have a great finale." James W. Symington elected the same day as I, penned a note: "Congrats on a fabulous Congressional career."

The endorsement that meant the most came from the heartfelt, poignant words uttered by my son Lacy who said, "Although I am not my father, I am my father's son, in that we share the same values and commitment to principles, such as fairness and justice."

Congressman Charles A. Gonzales of Texas said, "It is indeed an honor to have served with you." Rep. Eva Clayton of North Carolina said, "Making government work is a tough task that really requires the best, the brightest, the most honorable, the most dedicated among us. During your time in Congress, you have met and exceeded all of these qualities, and your departure must surely be a loss to our Nation."

Nancy Pelosi wrote, "I am very pleased to have had the good fortune to serve with you in the House." Dennis Kucinich of Ohio said, "I commend your service to your constituents and our Nation."

Unique Session in House of Representatives

October 27, 2000, Donna Christensen, delegate of the Virgin Islands, rose to declare that members had gathered on the House floor to pay special tribute to Congressman Clay. She yielded time to the first speaker, Eva Clayton (D-N.C.) who said, "Mr. Speaker, next year this Congress will be without the wit, the wisdom, insight, the genius of one who has become a fixture and fact of life. The loss [of Clay] is irreplaceable." She further stated, "Clay is passionate when he speaks, because he is compassionate in his heart. This son of Missouri has lived his life in sacrifice that millions could live theirs in pride. He has been both the first and the last line of defense for the voiceless and voteless."

The praise and salutations continued. Maxine Waters, after acknowledging our family relationship by marriage and my congressional district as her birthplace, spoke of my involvement in civil rights and politics: "Clay was a young man who had a mission and put his life on the line for his mission." She said, "He is one of the best historians this House has ever known. He has sponsored successfully 295 pieces of legislation." Following her in the well of the House chamber was Richard Gephardt, Minority Leader, who spoke of my "....deep and intimate involvement in education, health care, labor and human rights." Eddie Bernice Johnson of Texas said, "Clay was a hero for justice before he came to Congress. His record is amazing. Virtually every piece of legislation he touches has a direct and decisive impact on Americans." Juanita Millender McDonald of California said, "There are three words that epitomize Bill Clay. Those are determined, dedicated, and distinguished." Ruben Hinojosa of Texas observed, "Clay has proven himself to be a national leader on civil rights and human rights who truly cares about people." Major Owens of New York remarked, "Mr. Speaker, when Clay arrived during the age of the Afro hair style, he already had a chest full of invisible medals from the civil rights movement. He helped to guide the years of maximum Congressional Black Caucus solidarity." Jim Talent of Missouri stated, "I've always respected him [Clay] as a political leader."

Nine other members–Danny Davis and Bobby Rush of Illinois, John Conyers of Michigan, Julian Dixon and Lynn Woolsey of California, Sanford Bishop of Georgia, Ed Towns of New York, Bobby Scott of Virginia, Shelia Jackson Lee of Texas and Harold Ford Jr. of Tennessee–spoke. Each cited some aspect of my congressional career. Bishop stated "His service has earned him widespread recognition as one of America's great voices for justice and opportunity." Ed Towns said, "...in spite of the many victories we had won during the Civil Rights Struggle, you knew we still had a long way to go." Davis said, "The fact that he [Clay] could cause the ordinary person to feel empowered is the true mark of a genius." Rush said, "It is one of the most pleasurably experiences having looked at a hero, at a role model, at someone you idolize and then to have God's blessing of serving with him [Clay]." Dixon said,

"The House is losing one of its most extraordinary members." Alcee Hastings of Florida said, "Bill Clay has given so much of himself to improving public education for our children."

Other members wanted to speak but Mr. Nick Smith of Michigan made a point of order that "the time of the gentlewoman from the Virgin Islands had expired." Under House rules, the Speaker had no choice but to suspend the session.

Smith's rude, impolite gesture denied colleagues an opportunity to share their experiences. His discourteous, intemperate act even kept me from thanking those who made such generous and flattering remarks. A few colleagues who were denied, later that evening and the next day inserted written statements into the record. They described the meaning of my departure, speculating that a void would be created among their ranks. Several referred to me as a strong voice for women and minorities, a persistent advocate for workers and the poor, a friend of educators and students.

Stokes said, "Bill does not mince words. You always know where he stands, he always stands up for what he believes in, and wherever it is, he speaks his piece." Congressman Xavier Becerra of California said, "I respect deeply Clay's tenacity and heartfelt commitment to progressive causes." John Lewis of Georgia said, "He [Clay] has been our historian. He will be the last of a breed in the Caucus, and when we need to draw upon institutional memory and history, we will be lacking."

I can honestly say that my colleagues honoring me in such glowing terms on the floor of Congress was a moving, emotional, memorable event that I will cherish until my final breath.

Highlights of a Roller Coaster Adventure

Following my colleague's tribute, despite the euphoria experienced by the sincere expressions of my fellow congresspersons, I drove home feeling a bit down in the doldrums. Ending a way of life that totally consumed me for 42 years left a feeling of numbness, of emptiness.

Although overwhelmed by the hundreds of congratulatory letters, plaques, citations and receptions, and especially impressed by the session on the House floor, giving up a life's vocation, as my mother would say, "It must have been a hard pill to swallow."

Driving home, slowly maneuvering in and out of D.C.'s all day rush hour traffic I began to nostalgically retrace the path of a whirlwind life. I experienced flash backs on the pathway of life in the fast lane. Recapturing events of spectacular happenings was mind-boggling. In rapid succession and no particular sequence, I remembered the highlights of my life from boyhood to the present.

Growing Up

Episodes emanating from my memory bank quickly pulled-up wonderful times like my oldest sister Hazel taking me to the movies every Monday night from age 8 until I reached 11, my becoming an altar boy at age 11, and the next year with cousin Earl Wilson and friend Tilmon Bell, we started our own Boy Scout troop. I remembered the overnight hikes at Osage Hills with Earl and friends Tillman, Levi and Bobby. Then there was the graduation from St. Nicholas Elementary School. Oh! What memories. I still think of Dr. Henry Hampton bringing to our 8th grade class the famous bandleader Jimmy Lunceford who told us that "with hard work, determination and education" we could overcome all barriers.

Other pleasantries crept into the recesses of my mind: marriage to the wonderful Carol Ann Johnson, the birth of our three children, driving 2,200 miles on route 66 to Los Angeles. Our trip with Vicki, Lacy and Michelle took eight days, stopping at every site to marvel at the natural wonders of the most beautiful country on earth. It was an adventure none of us will ever forget–the Grand Canyon, the Painted Desert, Yosemite, and of course Disneyland, Knots Farm and the Hollywood movie sets.

Struggling With Segregation

Looking back, I remember growing up a notch above the poorest of the poor. But, we did not know the meaning of poverty because everybody else around us were in the same precarious financial boat. We were more fortunate than most in the neighborhood because my dad had a steady job and it was not necessary for my six siblings and me to go on government assistance.

We came from a large family. Dad had eight siblings. Mom had seven brothers and sisters and each of their siblings had large families. The sheer numbers (of the tribe) provided protection against neighborhood bullies who might prey on the Clay children. So, we went about enjoying the normal activities of childhood without "thugs" harassing us, a common occurrence in the ghetto.

The area I grew up in was thoroughly integrated, yet rigidly segregated. We lived in the same block with Irish, Italian, Polish people, but were isolated to tenement houses reserved for Negroes. Although making friends with the others, we were yet stung by difference in treatment. The playground across the street from our house was divided into two sections: one for whites and one for blacks. There were two sets of swings, two softball diamonds, two volleyball courts, two swimming pools–one 4 feet deep for whites, the other a wading pool, 2 feet deep for blacks.

Our tenements had no central heat, no hot running water, no indoor plumbing. The others had them all. Even though we played with those of the other races after closing time of the playground, we could not go to public schools or the two Catholic schools in our neighborhood with them. They went to movie houses that prohibited us from entering. My brothers and sisters walked past an all-white public school one block away to attend an all-black school four blocks away. When I enrolled in Catholic School, I passed a Catholic School two blocks away to walk thirteen blocks to one for black children.

Recollecting this phase of life was a defining moment for many of us who were psychologically scarred by the injustices of the traumatic experiences.

Adjusting to Manhood

Now my adrenalin was really charged. Memories of yesterday came in hurried flashes: the first job at age 12 as a custodian in a downtown clothing store during the 2nd World War, tending bar in the private Musician's Club while working toward a college degree, two years in the military during the Korean War, driving a public service bus and motoring Senator Estes Kefauver and his vice-presidential campaign staff and reporters through the streets of St. Louis in the 1956 election for the White House.

I dwelled on my years as manager of a national insurance company, opening a fancy cocktail lounge of my own and watching baseball superstar Curt Flood paint pictures of cocktail scenes on the ceiling.

Induction into the Civil Rights Movement

Thoughts of what determined the life I was to live, rapidly cascaded through my mind. I distinctly pinpointed the exact time and place that I decided to take a stand against racism and racist. It was at Fort McClellan Alabama, just prior to the Supreme Court ruling in Brown v. Board of Education, outlawing segregated public schools. Black soldiers were being treated as second-class citizens on military property in violation of two Presidential Executive Orders. Carol and I led protests against the illegal infractions. I organized black soldiers to boycott the barbershops until we were permitted to get haircuts like the others. We picketed at an all-white dinning room and NCO club. Carol and I took children from our off-post neighborhood to the all-white swimming pool and jumped in.

I was threatened with court marshal, but on second thought the commander transferred me to another post.

I also recalled my first arrest in St. Louis after being discharged. It was at a Howard Johnson Restaurant that refused service to blacks. The demonstrations lasted six months before we succeeded in changing the policy. Then of course there was the arrest at the Jefferson Bank, the 4 year protest and my 118 days in jail before we ended the policy of not hiring blacks in clerical and managerial jobs in the banking industry. After arriving in the Capital, I joined other members of Congress, being arrested for demonstrating at the South African Embassy against the country's apartheid policy.

Election and Seeing the World

The joy of campaigning and election victories crept into my mind: defeating a 12 year incumbent to win my first political office, the Board of Aldermen, at age 27. Ten years later after much water passed under the bridge, being sworn into the U.S. Congress at a very young age.

My mind was now swirling. It seemed the euphoric reminiscence would never end. Recalling the many great personalities and world renown talents that I rubbed shoulders with-if only for a casual moment-riding with Lyndon Baines Johnson in his convertible Cadillac around his 2,700 acre Texas ranch, listening to him brag about the 400 head of registered Hereford cattle. Then came recollections of attending two White House State Dinners, touring Hitler's old summer retreat at the Eagle's Nest in Burgess Garden, Germany, spending two nights in the summer cottage of Albert Spears the architect for the Third Reich, breakfast with Cab Calloway in St. Louis' Mayfair Hotel. I conversed with another musical legend, Duke Ellington in the lobby of a Tokyo hotel. Befriending Muhammad Ali, Billy Eckstine, Nancy Wilson and other great entertainers. Just knowing Hubert H. Humphrey, Robert Kennedy, Malcolm X, and James Farmer was worth the ride.

I relived the emotional scene on the campus of Jackson State University, investigating the senseless murder of 4 students by local police; going to Chicago to assure that the states' attorney responsible for planning and plotting the race-motivated assassinations of Black Panther leaders did not escape justice.

Thoughts of mingling with the rich and the famous meandered through the shadows of my memory: introducing Ossie Davis, keynoter at the first Congressional Black Caucus dinner, joining Congressman Charles Diggs and Augustus Hawkins on Meet the Press to explain the newly formed CBC being on the cutting edge of a new politics, speaking on the same program with Dr. Martin Luther King, Jr. at a Baptist Church in St. Louis, sitting with Bill Cosby eating hot-links at Ben's Chili Bowl in D.C., the guest of St. Louis Cardinal baseball owner August Busch in his private box, as

Lou Brock threw out the ball opening the first game of the World Series. I could see Minnie Minosa signing an autograph for my son at the Toronto All-Star game. Taking my granddaughter Angie to see Yul Brynner's last performance in the King and I on Broadway just before he died of lung cancer. Hearing him recount his life and death struggle with nicotine addiction, was a touching event.

The Grim Reaper Strikes Often

In scanning the past without much success, I tried not to dwell to long on depressing happenings. My life had it share of downs. Politics and public service are rich in challenges and rewards but there is a high cost in terms of personal and family sacrifice. I recalled sometimes missing birthdays, anniversaries and weddings, but Carol and I were always there for the funerals.

In the midst of the glorious and glitzy lifestyle, there were times of sadness and sorrow–death knocked on our door often. During. the first six years after election, I lost two sisters, a brother-in-law, a nephew, three aunts, two uncles and my father. Carol lost a brother-in-law, nephew and grandmother.

I remember one very sad occasion in Kansas City. Along with Barbara Jordan, Louis Stokes, Detroit Mayor Coleman Young and the Rev. Ralph Abernathy, I was there to celebrate with our friend Bruce Watkins, a mover and shaker in the city's political community. Shortly before presenting remarks, I received word that my father was dying.

An aide and I drove 6 hours to St. Louis, arriving at 4:30 a.m.. My father was still conscious when I walked into the hospital room. His eyes lit up and a smile appeared on his face, as if recognizing my presence. My eyes filled with tears to see this once strong man unbelievably reduced to a vegetable by lung cancer. Three hours later, he was gone.

Regaining composure, my mind drifted to my mother who was married to dad for 58 years. It was now five years since I was in Jamaica and the call came that she had died suddenly from a heart attack. My sister assured me that mom did not suffer. At 95 years, she had lived a long and good life, seeing the dreams for her seven children fulfilled. She and dad set two goals for us: finish high school and if you marry, it's for life. All of us finished high school and none divorced.

It was several years before I knew the reason for emphasizing graduation from high school. I came across a bit of history that said in the 1930s, only 11 percent of blacks finished high school.

Remembering the demise of mom and dad left me momentarily shaken.

Reappearance of Happier Times

After a period of solace and sorrow, flashbacks of better days reappeared: Lacy and I attending the baseball All-Star game in St. Louis, refreshed my memory of uncle Bill Hyatt who took me to my first major league game. I was ten years old. It too was an all-star contest played at the old Sportsman Park in St. Louis. We caught a trolley car at 6:30 a.m. for the 2:00 p.m. game, waiting in line for the ticket window to open at 9:00 a.m., and spent the rest of the day in the bleachers with fans who knew Uncle Bill.

They knew him because he was a regular supporter of the Cardinals. As I remembered, he didn't care much for the other major league team, the Browns.

Was it an exciting day! Eating hot dogs and popcorn! Learning to keep score on a big card! My first game and I got to see the greats who eventually ended up in the Hall-of-Fame: Ted Williams, Hank Greenberg, Jimmy Foxx, Carl Hubbell, Bucky Walters, Joe DiMaggio, all of the American League that my uncle dreaded. Then, there were Leo Durocher, Joe Medwick, Mel Ott and other greats from his beloved National League.

The National League won 4 to 0 on a three run homer by Max West of the Boston Braves. I became an avid baseball fan afterward. Using the 'Knot Hole' free pass, I seldom missed a game at the old stadium. I even paid to see the Black Baseball Association teams when they came to town. At one game, I saw the great Reece 'Goose' Tatum and also witnessed Jesse Owens winner of four gold medals in track at the 1936 Olympic, run against a race horse and win.

My travels through time continued: I was present when my friend, air force General Daniel "Chappie" James received his fourth star, thinking of him personally escorting Carol and I through the NORAD Strategic Defense Command our defensive shield against world-wide attack. How could I not remember conferring with President Bill Clinton on Air Force One. What a cruise down memory lane with ordinary people, great personalities and super-stars: meeting kings, queens, diplomats, heads of state, Peace Corps volunteers. Yet, there was more-visiting with Anwar Sadat, Fidel Castro, Margaret Thatcher, Menachin Begin, Pope Paul VI, and Nelson Mandela. It's hard to put into words what it means to be in the company of renowned leaders and to hear their views on world situations.

Then there was the time that the gracious, charming Hillary Clinton spent an hour in my office discussing the President's proposal for national health insurance and another hour outside the door shaking hands, talking and snapping photos with the hundreds who had gathered after hearing we were meeting.

I thought of the wonderful afternoon shooting pool in my rec room with one of my heroes, the charismatic Carl Stokes, Mayor of Cleveland. How could I not remember the good times with Morty LaPayover and Johnny Miller, two army buddies with whom I have talked on the telephone every Christmas day for more than 46 years.

How about our annual trips to Spain visiting our friends Perry and Ursula Jones, and annual treks to Jamaica to be with Jamie and Camille Delgado. Then the April vacations at Hilton Head and the last two weeks of August at Martha's Vineyard. Recalling Carol and I seeing the snow capped Alps in Switzerland, war torn Bosnia, changing of the guard at Buckingham Palace, ruins of the Coliseum in Rome, gondolas in Venice, the pagodas in Thailand, Pyramids in Egypt, Hitler's hideaway at the Eagle's Nest, and the splendor of Monaco. Cobblestone streets in Holland, sidewalk cafes of Paris and Barcelona, 14th century castles–we saw the wonders of this awesome world.

How Great It Was!

It dawned on me that as a member of the U.S.. Congress, I was a representative of the American people on the Board of Directors of the greatest and richest corporation in the history of mankind. I ranked high among the decision-makers–the ones who influenced change and enacted laws. I was third in total seniority in the House; had passed nearly 300 bills that became law, many landmark and had been the floor manager of hundreds more.

I was proud of the role played in organizing the Congressional Black Caucus that many alluded to as the conscience of the Congress. I agreed with the assumption and for 32 years I attempted to be its "Guardian Angel," forever reminding my colleagues of the purpose for our existing as a group.

Saying goodbye to Congress was one of the most painful days of my life. I spent a third of a century walking its historic halls and speaking in its grand chamber. Always trying to give voice to the concerns of many unable to speak for themselves; always intent on envisioning their suffering and empathizing with it.

Unlike the old soldier who just fades away, I believe my good friend, Congressman Harold L. Washington was correct when he said, "Men of ambitious character don't just die, they live on as inspiration to instill men with the desire to better themselves."

The last Two Miles

About two miles from home, I was overtaken with sorrow and happiness. It was a crisp fall afternoon, the leaves turning slightly golden brown and falling. I noticed the soccer game in the elementary school yard and further down the road a group of seniors playing softball. Closer to home, kids were engaged in a spirited basketball game. My eyes blurred as I remembered passing familiar sights that I had observed on the same route for more than three decades. There was the middle school that my 3 children attended, the church where my youngest daughter was married, the nursery where I bought plants, shrubs and the four-feet evergreens that had grown to 15 feet and provided shade for the rear of the house.

But I didn't really see these things clearly because the tears were welling-up in my eyes. Yet, I was able to recognize the brilliance of the setting sun partially hidden by a few dusty clouds.

It was one of the saddest days in an otherwise sunny, happy-go-lucky, illustrious life. As that "lucky ole sun" set on my 32 years in the United States Congress, I predicted my legacy would not disappear immediately into the horizon. Proudly and confidently, I declared, "There will be joy in the morning when the sun rises and my replacement is sworn-in because the person elected to take my place, will be an admirable, effective, talented legislator–an individual of character and integrity, William Lacy Clay, Jr., my son. *

In thanking voters for his victory on election night at campaign headquarters Lacy said, "I'll never be able to and never want to lose that connection that people make between Dad and me."

As the journey continued, remembering the connection between my dad and his always telling us to follow our dreams, I cleared my throat and stated in a loud assertive voice that I imaged the whole world heard, "I did follow my dreams and while making waves, I made a difference. The cruise was worth it."

Minutes later, the sentimental journey into the past disappeared as I parked in the driveway of my home in Silver Spring, Maryland. Carol Ann, my wife of 48 years, met me at the door with a hug and a kiss.

---

*My prediction came to be as Clarence Lang wrote, "…a measure of the extraordinary influence he [Clay Sr.] had amassed during his incumbency, voters elected his son, William Lacy Clay, Jr., to fill his seat. The younger Clay was part of a new generation of black politicians that had matured after the civil rights—Black Power period…"[2]

NOTES

1/The *Holy Bible*, Matthew 25-23
2/*Grassroots at the Gateway, Class Politics & Black Freedom
   Struggle in St. Louis*, 1936-75, Clarence Lang, University of
   Michigan Press, Ann Arbor, 2009, page 240.